The Bodily Self

The Bodily Self

Selected Essays on Self-Consciousness

José Luis Bermúdez

The MIT Press
Cambridge, Massachusetts
London, England

This book was set in ITC Stone Sans Std and ITC Stone Serif Std by Toppan Best-set Premedia Limited.

Library of Congress Cataloging-in-Publication Data

Names: Bermúdez, José Luis, author.
Title: The bodily self : selected essays / José Luis Bermúdez.
Description: Cambridge, MA : MIT Press, 2018. | Includes bibliographical references and index.
Identifiers: LCCN 2017026383 | ISBN 9780262037501 (hardcover : alk. paper) ISBN 9780262551083 (paperback)
Subjects: LCSH: Self (Philosophy) | Self-consciousness (Awareness) | Mind and body.
Classification: LCC BD438.5 .B465 2018 | DDC 128/.6--dc23 LC record available at https://lccn.loc.gov/2017026383

Contents

Preface and Acknowledgments

I have encountered many collections of previously published essays where authors report in the preface that they have successfully resisted the temptation to revise and update the work of their earlier selves. I admire their fortitude, but sadly have been unable to emulate it. Almost all of the essays that follow have been edited and reworked, some extensively so.

I have made stylistic changes throughout, both to improve readability and to standardize punctuation and spelling to the US model. I have also added cross-referencing notes and, where appropriate, updated references, particularly to the scientific literature. Some expository sections have been rewritten to avoid duplication and overlap. And in a few places, which I will not identify, weak arguments have been replaced with stronger ones (or so I hope).

Two essays have received a much more drastic treatment. Chapter 7 ("Bodily Ownership, Bodily Awareness, and Knowledge without Observation") was originally published in *Analysis*, a journal that adheres to enviable standards of concision. On rereading the essay, however, I realized that there is a fine line between being concise and being cryptic. Accordingly, I substantially expanded this essay, which has nearly doubled in length. Chapter 10 ("The Thinking Self, Commonsense Psychology, and the Springs of Action") appears here for the first time. Or more accurately, the title is here making its first appearance. The essay itself combines and develops material from two previously published papers, one of which ("The Domain of Folk Psychology," 2003) was published in a volume of lectures delivered at the Royal Institute of Philosophy, while the other ("Arguing for Eliminativism," 2005) appeared in a festschrift for Paul Churchland. Neither essay quite made the grade on its own, but the amalgam does, I hope, add value to this collection.

Each of the essays contains its own acknowledgments and thanks, all of which of course still stand. In addition, I would particularly like to record my debt to Philip Laughlin at the MIT Press for initially supporting this project and then for being a model editor. Thanks also to Judy Feldmann for copyediting and steering the book through the production process. It has been a pleasure to work again with the MIT Press, nearly twenty-five years after my first project with them.

Sources

1. "Nonconceptual Self-Consciousness and Cognitive Science" was originally published in *Synthese* 129, no. 1 (2001): 129–149. It is reprinted here with some changes.
2. "Ecological Perception and the Notion of a Nonconceptual Point of View" was originally published in *The Body and the Self*, ed. J. L. Bermúdez, A. J. Marcel, and N. Eilan (Cambridge MA: MIT Press, 1995), 153–173. It is reprinted here with some changes.
3. "The Sources of Self-Consciousness" was originally published in *Proceedings of the Aristotelian Society* 102, no. 1 (2002): 87–107. It is reprinted here with some changes.
4. "The Elusiveness Thesis, Immunity to Error through Misidentification, and Privileged Access" was originally published in *Self-Knowledge and Privileged Access*, ed. B. Gertler (Aldershot: Ashgate, 2003), 213–231. It is reprinted here with some changes.
5. "The Phenomenology of Bodily Awareness" was originally published in *Phenomenology and Philosophy of Mind*, ed. D. W. Smith and A. L. Thomasson (New York: Oxford University Press, 2005), 295–316. It is reprinted here with some changes.
6. "Bodily Awareness and Self-Consciousness" was originally published in *Oxford Handbook of the Self*, ed. S. Gallagher (Oxford: Oxford University Press, 2011), 157–179. It is reprinted here with some changes.
7. "Bodily Ownership, Bodily Awareness, and Knowledge without Observation" is a significantly expanded version of a paper of the same title that first appeared in *Analysis* 75, no. 1 (2015): 37–45.
8. "Ownership and the Space of the Body" was originally published in *Minding the Body*, ed. A. Alsmith and F. de Vignemont (Cambridge, MA: MIT Press, 2017), 117–144. It is reprinted here with some changes.

9. "Bodily Ownership, Psychological Ownership, and Psychopathology" is forthcoming in the *Review of Philosophy and Psychology.*

10. "The Bodily Self, Commonsense Explanation, and the Springs of Action" is newly written for this volume, with antecedents in "The Domain of Folk Psychology," *Royal Institute of Philosophy Supplement,* ed. A. O'Hear (Cambridge: Cambridge University Press, 2003), 25–48; and "Arguing for Eliminativism," in *Paul Churchland,* ed. B. L. Keeley (Cambridge: Cambridge University Press, 2005), 32–65.

Introduction: Understanding the Bodily Self

We, like many animals, are conscious of our environment, both physical and social. We think about and experience the objects and people that the world contains. But at the same time, those very thoughts and experiences can themselves become the objects of conscious thought and experience, so that we can think critically about them. When this happens, we are often thinking about ourselves—holding ourselves to account by evaluating our own reasoning, for example. According to a long philosophical tradition, rationality and self-consciousness go hand in hand. A rational thinker is one who constantly monitors her own thoughts and updates her beliefs in the light of changing evidence in order to ensure consistency and to increase the likelihood that they will track the truth.

Moreover, it is because we are aware of ourselves as temporally extended beings with a past and a future that we are able to develop a narrative understanding of our lives. The narrative we tell of ourselves can incorporate an interpretation of our personal history. This personal history, in turn, can inform a forward-looking sense of the kind of person we strive to be. That forward-looking sense of how we want to turn out sets the agenda for our plans and projects. It also sets the agenda for how we navigate the social world, for how we engage with other people and with institutions.

The fundamental source for these (and many other) abilities and achievements is our capacity for self-consciousness, or self-awareness. This capacity is at the heart of much of what is typically taken to be distinctively human. Some aspects of self-consciousness have been studied extensively. Every student of philosophy will be familiar, for example, with Descartes's *cogito ergo sum*. Most will have encountered Kant's guiding idea, in the *Critique of Pure Reason*, that self-consciousness and consciousness of the physical world are inextricably linked.

For Descartes, Kant, and many other philosophers, self-consciousness is a phenomenon closely tied to language. Kant famously wrote of "the 'I think' that accompanies all my representations." To be self-conscious for Kant (and again, for many others) is to be capable of thinking about oneself in a special way. He took that special way of thinking of oneself to be coeval with the ability to refer to oneself using the first person pronoun "I" (or its equivalent in other languages). And this is not surprising. The ability to think about oneself and the ability to refer to oneself seem inextricably linked. After all, how can one think about oneself without referring to oneself in thought? And, many have thought, referring to oneself in thought is really just an internalized form of how one refers to oneself in public language. It is no accident that self-conscious thoughts are often referred to as "I"-thoughts.

The close connections between self-conscious thought and linguistic self-reference raise many fascinating and important questions. I explore some of them in my recent book *Understanding "I": Language and Thought* (Bermúdez 2017). However, they are not the focus of the essays in this volume. In one form or another, all of the essays collected here explore different dimensions of a single basic idea. This guiding idea is that the rich and sophisticated forms of self-consciousness with which we are most familiar (not just as philosophers or psychologists, but also as ordinary, reflective individuals) rest on a complex underpinning that has largely been invisible to students of the self and of self-consciousness.

Full-fledged linguistic self-consciousness emerges from multiple layers of more primitive forms of self-consciousness, and, even when linguistic self-consciousness is fully operational, these more primitive forms of self-consciousness persist in ways that structure and frame self-conscious language and thought. Moreover, and unlike linguistic self-consciousness, these primitive forms of self-consciousness extend widely throughout the animal kingdom. Some are present in human infants from the earliest moments outside the womb.

The essays in this volume focus on three primitive forms of self-consciousness in particular:

• modes of awareness of one's spatial orientation and trajectory built into outward-directed perception,
• modes of awareness of how one's body is disposed that are derived from awareness of our own bodies, and

• the complex spatial self-awareness implicated in navigating through the environment.

The object of these forms of self-awareness is primarily the embodied self. Hence the title of this volume: *The Bodily Self.*

The distinction between conceptual and nonconceptual content offers a way of understanding some of the significant differences between full-fledged linguistic self-consciousness, on the one hand, and these primitive forms of self-consciousness, on the other. The issue of content is important because the three primitive forms of self-consciousness all yield representations of the bodily self (in the context, usually, of representations of the physical/social environment). Whereas the content of linguistic self-consciousness is conceptual, that of primitive self-consciousness is nonconceptual. Precisely characterizing the differences between conceptual and nonconceptual content is a complicated undertaking (see Bermúdez and Cahen 2015 for an overview of relevant debates), but a rough characterization will be adequate here.

A representational state has conceptual content just if it can only be truly attributed to a thinker who possesses the concepts required to specify the relevant content. So, for example, my belief that Bishkek is the capital of Kyrgyzstan has conceptual content because my ability to entertain it requires me to possess all the relevant concepts (*Bishkek, Kyrghyzstan,* and —— *is the capital of* ——). Someone lacking even one of those concepts would not be able to have a belief with that content. Representational states have nonconceptual content, on the other hand, when that requirement of concept possession does not hold. So, to be in a state with nonconceptual content is to be in a state that one need not be in a position to conceptualize or articulate—because one lacks some or all of the relevant concepts. In fact, as I understand the notion of nonconceptual content, it is perfectly possible for a creature possessing no concepts whatsoever to be in states that have nonconceptual content.[1]

---

1. A brief moment of intellectual autobiography. My first publication in a peer-reviewed journal (Bermúdez 1994) was an article taking issue with Christopher Peacocke's denial that nonconceptual content could be autonomous (i.e., could be completely independent of possession of any concepts). Peacocke was gracious enough to write a response (Peacocke 1994), and then, even more graciously, he published a short note some years later (Peacocke 2002) repudiating his earlier rejection of the autonomy thesis.

The essays that follow explore three different, but of course interrelated, dimensions of these forms of nonconceptual self-consciousness.

• First, I make the case that it is indeed correct to describe them as forms of self-consciousness. My principal strategy for doing this is to argue that they share certain structural and epistemological features with full-fledged linguistic self-consciousness. Several of the essays discuss, for example, how forms of nonconceptual self-consciousness give rise to judgments that have the important property of being *immune to error through misidentification relative to the first-person pronoun.*

• Second, I try to give accounts of the content of certain important classes of states of nonconceptual self-consciousness that elucidate how they represent the self. In this context I focus primarily on the self-specifying dimension of visual perception and on the content of bodily awareness.

• Third, I explore the role of nonconceptual self-consciousness more generally in our cognitive and affective lives. One topic here is the role nonconceptual self-consciousness plays in epistemically grounding fully conceptual first-person judgments. A theme that recurs in several essays is the relation between nonconceptual awareness of our bodies and what many theorists call our "sense of ownership" for our own bodies.

The remainder of this introduction explains how these themes are developed in the individual essays.

1   *The Paradox of Self-Consciousness*

The intellectual framework for these essays is set in part by my first book *The Paradox of Self-Consciousness* (Bermúdez 1998). The paradox referenced in the title comes from taking self-consciousness and self-reference to be interdependent. It is natural (and common) to think of self-conscious thoughts as thoughts that are typically expressed through the first-person pronoun "I." What is distinctive about self-conscious thought is often expressed by contrasting how one might talk about oneself using a linguistic device of intentional self-reference, such as "I," as opposed to a third-person linguistic device, such as one's name. Philosophers such as Héctor-Neri Castañeda and John Perry have emphasized that third-person self-reference always leaves open the possibility of errors of self-identification. It seems to be a defining feature of self-conscious thought that it knowingly and intentionally be about oneself. And yet, one might not realize that one is in fact referring to oneself when one uses a device other than the first-person pronoun or its equivalent—a dramatic example being an amnesiac who has forgotten his own name. So it is natural to think that the capacity for self-conscious thought depends on the capacity for self-reference using "I."

At the same time, however, as Elizabeth Anscombe observed in her famous article "The First Person" (Anscombe 1975), it seems impossible to characterize the reference rule for the first person without building into it the requirement that the self-referrer be self-consciously thinking of herself. After all, it is not enough to say that "I" is the pronoun that a speaker uses to refer to herself, because that leaves open the possibility of an error of self-identification (not knowing that one is actually referring to oneself). To rule out the possibility of an error of misidentification, "I" must be used knowingly and intentionally as a device of self-reference. But to intend to use the pronoun "I" to refer to oneself is of course itself a form of self-conscious thought.

In *The Paradox of Self-Consciousness*, I suggested that this interdependence between self-conscious thought and self-reference creates two forms of circularity. The first type (*explanatory circularity*) arises because neither capacity can be explained in terms of the other. The second type of circularity (*capacity circularity*) arises because this explanatory circularity seems to rule out the possibility of explaining how either the capacity for self-conscious thought or linguistic mastery of the first-person pronoun arises in the normal course of human development. It does not seem possible to meet the following constraint:

The Acquisition Constraint   If a given psychological capacity is psychologically real, then there must be an explanation of how it is possible for an individual in the normal course of human development to acquire that capacity.

Neither self-conscious thought nor linguistic mastery of the first-person pronoun is innate, and yet each presupposes the other in a way that seems to imply that neither can be acquired unless the other capacity is already in place. I termed these two types of circularity collectively the *paradox of self-consciousness*.

The resolution I proposed to the paradox of self-consciousness is sketched out in chapter 1, "Nonconceptual Self-Consciousness and Cognitive Science," originally published in 2001 in the journal *Synthese*. Chapter 1 summarizes the overall argument of *The Paradox of Self-Consciousness* and identifies key points of contact with research programs in scientific psychology and cognitive science. As it makes clear, the basic strategy for defusing both the explanatory and capacity circularities is to show how full-fledged linguistic self-consciousness is grounded in forms of nonconceptual self-consciousness that do not presuppose linguistic mastery of the first-person pronoun.

Full-fledged self-consciousness is conceptual. It presupposes mastery of the first-person pronoun and, correlatively, of the first-person concept. But neither is presupposed by the nonconceptual forms of self-consciousness. That is the key to escaping the paradox of self-consciousness.

These forms of nonconceptual self-consciousness are more primitive than linguistic self-consciousness in three ways—theoretically, ontogenetically, and phylogenetically. The first of these opens up the possibility of analyzing linguistic self-consciousness in terms of the various forms of nonconceptual self-consciousness. The second and third open up the possibility of explaining the emergence of linguistic self-consciousness out of nonconceptual self-consciousness, both (ontogenetically) in the normal course of human development and (phylogenetically) in evolutionary development.

In addition to the three forms of nonconceptual self-consciousness identified earlier, *The Paradox of Self-Consciousness* discussed the psychological self-awareness that emerges from joint attention and other primitive forms of interpersonal interaction. As outlined in chapter 1, this psychological self-awareness is important in explaining mastery of the first-person pronoun. Circularity is averted, I claim, because the communicative intentions that make it the case that "I" is used knowingly and intentionally as a device of self-reference implicate nonconceptual psychological self-awareness, rather than any form of conceptual self-awareness. The remaining essays in this volume do not develop this analysis further, focusing instead on forms of self-awareness implicated in visual proprioception, self–world dualism, and bodily awareness.

2 Nonconceptual Self-Consciousness in Visual Perception

The starting point for chapters 2 through 4 is the ecological theory of perception proposed by the psychologist J. J. Gibson, particularly in his two books *The Senses Considered as Perceptual Systems* (Gibson 1966) and *The Ecological Approach to Visual Perception* (Gibson 1979). Gibson's ecological approach to visual perception is almost completely unknown to philosophers, and has had less influence than I believe it deserves within scientific psychology and cognitive science. Yet, as I illustrate in these three essays, Gibson's work points to one of the most basic forms of nonconceptual self-consciousness.

Part of the reason for Gibson's relative neglect is that he very polemically set himself against the dominant information-processing paradigm at the heart of contemporary cognitive science (preferring instead to speak of perceptual systems "resonating" to the environment and picking up information directly). This aspect of his thinking, however, is in many ways orthogonal to his insights into the nature of visual perception (and indeed the other sensory modalities). In particular, it seems independent of the aspect of his thinking that is most important for thinking about self-consciousness, namely, his insight that all forms of perception contain both *propriospecific* information about the self and *exterospecific* information about the environment.

For Gibson, the starting point for thinking about visual perception (which was the modality on which he primarily focused) is the flow of movement in the ambient optic array—what he termed *optic flow*. The basic constituents of the ambient optic array are visual solid angles—angles with their apex at the eye and their base at a perceived surface. Optic flow is, in essence, the changing patterns of visual solid angles, as surfaces move relative to each other, occlude each other, and so forth. The optic flow contains both variant and invariant features, and is constantly changing as the perceiver moves through the environment (which can itself be moving). Because of this, as Gibson himself puts it, "information about the self accompanies information about the environment, and the two are inseparable" (Gibson 1979, 116).

Gibson identifies three principal categories of propriospecific (or: self-specifying) information in the optic flow. These include:

Self-specifying structural invariants

These are features of the bodily self that directly structure the optical array (such as the nose, which has the highest value of motion parallax of all directly perceived objects) as well as bodily extremities that have distinctive visual properties (such as subtending visual solid angles that cannot be reduced below a certain minimum).

Visual kinesthesis

This refers to information about the perceiver's relative motion that is available in the optic array. The flow of the ambient array originates from the aiming point of locomotion, for example.

Affordances

According to the ecological approach, the perception of objects is not neutral. Instead, the optical array carries information about the possibilities that surfaces and objects afford the organism. A surface might be seen as affording support, for example, or an object as being manipulable or edible. Affordances carry information about the behavioral possibilities open to an organism.

In these respects, then, Gibson's concept of ecological perception reveals a basic awareness of the bodily self that can serve as the core of a comprehensive account of full-fledged self-consciousness in thought and action. On the ecological understanding of perception, sensitivity to self-specifying information is built into the very structure of perception in such a way that, as Gibson famously put it, all perception involves coperception of the (bodily) self and the environment. Nonetheless, his suggestive analysis opens up (at least) two obvious questions. How do we scale up from this type of self-perception (or rather, these types of self-specifying information) to full-fledged self-consciousness? What role, or roles, do they play in conceptual thought about ourselves and about the world? The first of these questions is addressed in chapter 2, and the second in chapters 3 and 4.

Chapter 2, "Ecological Perception and the Notion of a Nonconceptual Point of View," was first published in 1995 in *The Body and the Self*, which I coedited with Anthony J. Marcel and Naomi Eilan. This essay offers a way of bridging the gap between the ecological coperception of self and environment, on the one hand, and full-fledged self-consciousness, on the other. The link between the two follows from the notion of a point of view on the world, an idea initially developed by Peter Strawson in *The Bounds of Sense* (Strawson 1975), his commentary on Kant's *Critique of Pure Reason*. One of the guiding ideas of Kant's *Critique* is that self-consciousness and consciousness of an external world are inextricably linked. Strawson's distinctive gloss on Kant's interdependence thesis depends crucially on the notion of a point of view, which he sees as a necessary (but not sufficient) element in full-fledged self-consciousness. For Strawson, a creature can count as a subject of experiences only if it can draw certain basic distinctions—most fundamentally, a distinction between its experiences and what those experiences are of. A genuine subject of experience must, moreover, be able to draw this distinction not just at a time, but also over time. Being able to do this is, in Strawson's phrase, possessing a point of view on the world.

For Strawson and Kant, having a point of view is a highly sophisticated cognitive achievement, requiring the ability to ascribe experiences to oneself as well as the ability to conceptualize the basic spatiotemporal and causal structure of the world. Chapter 2 develops a more pared down notion of a nonconceptual point of view. Key here is the idea that an awareness of the distinction between self and nonself can emerge from the ability to engage in spatial reasoning. In particular, spatial reasoning depends on the interplay of two cognitive capacities, one self-directed and one outward-directed. The self-directed capacity is the awareness of one's own agency—of one's ability to bring about changes in the world. The outward-directed capacity is the ability to recognize and reidentify places over time. Both of these capacities can exist in a nonconceptual form, I argue, and possessing both of them yields a nonconceptual point of view on the world.

The general theme of the relation between nonconceptual self-consciousness and full-fledged linguistic self-consciousness is pursued further in chapter 3, "Sources of Self-Consciousness," first published in the *Proceedings of the Aristotelian Society* in 2002. The starting point for this essay is that we can think about the sources of linguistic self-consciousness in two different ways. On the one hand, we can take a *genetic* perspective. That is, we can think about the origins of the capacity for thinking and articulating self-conscious thoughts—about how this capacity emerges in normal human development, or how it emerged in the course of human evolution. Alternatively, we can take an *epistemic* perspective on the sources of self-consciousness. To take an epistemic perspective is to ask not where those judgments come from, but rather what the warrant for them is, or how they are justified.

Within philosophy, these two types of question are typically kept completely separate, with only questions of the second, epistemic variety held to count as genuinely philosophical, on pain of committing some version of the genetic fallacy, or fallacy of origins. A key claim of chapter 3 (and, in fact, of my work more generally) is that this approach can be, and often is, a mistake. In that spirit, the essay explores the role that the genetic dimension of self-consciousness plays in understanding the epistemology of self-consciousness. I take the representation of the bodily self in "ordinary" visual perception as a paradigm example of a genetic source of (full-fledged) self-consciousness, since it seems to be primitive and foundational from the perspective both of ontogeny and of phylogeny. I claim that these primitive foundations from which self-consciousness emerges in the course of cognitive development are also the foundation for the epistemic status of full-fledged self-conscious thoughts.

My foil in the essay is Christopher Peacocke's account, in his book *Being Known* (Peacocke 1999), of the epistemic dimension of a particular type of self-conscious judgment. Peacocke distinguishes two types of self-conscious judgment—those that are, in his terminology, *representation dependent* and those that are *representation independent*. A representation-dependent judgment is one that involves taking a first-person content at face value. Perceptual states can have first-person contents. I might see that I am in front of the football stadium, for example. If I take that visual content at face value and on that basis judge that I am in front of the football stadium, then my judgment would count as representation dependent. For self-conscious judgments that are representation independent, however, there are no such corresponding first-person contents.

The distinction is a subtle one. To go back to the original example, I might see that I am in front of the football stadium and, by taking that content at face value, judge that I am in front of the football stadium. The corresponding first-person content is my seeing that I am in front of the football stadium. Here we have a case of representation-dependence. At the same time, though, I might judge that I am seeing the football stadium. Here the basis for my judgment is the same—namely, my knowing that I am in front of the football stadium and looking at it. But the judgment does not count as representation dependent, because it does not involve taking my visual state at face value. The fact that I am in front of the stadium is part of what I see, which is why it counts as a first-person content. But the fact that I am *seeing* the football stadium is not part of what I see, and so is not available to be taken at face value.

Clearly, an important question here is what "taking at face value" means. At one extreme, if a perceptual belief takes a perceptual content at face value, then that requires the content of the belief to be exactly the same as the content of the perception. Since belief contents are standardly taken to be conceptual, perceptual states would also have to be conceptual.[2] Peacocke himself is neutral on this question.[3] But (as one of the principal theorists of nonconceptual content) he certainly wants to leave open the possibility that first-person judgments can involve taking nonconceptual first-person contents at face value. Chapter 3 develops this possibility, arguing that properly understanding both the first-person content and the content of perception requires a nonconceptual model of how the self is represented in perception. The self cannot be represented conceptually in perception because the first-person concept lacks the perspectival dimension built into perceptual self-representation. Instead, I argue, a broadly Gibsonian account of how the bodily self is represented in visual perception better captures the epistemic dimension of representation-dependent first-person judgments.

Both representation-dependent and representation-independent judgments can have the important property of being immune to error through misidentification relative to the first-person pronoun (henceforth: the IEM property). A judgment "I am F" has the IEM property just in case it is not possible to be mistaken about whom it is one is judging to be F. To continue with the earlier example, if I judge that I am in front of the football stadium because I see the football stadium in front of me, then I cannot be mistaken about whom it is that I am taking to be in front of the football stadium. I can of course be mistaken about every other aspect of the judgment. I might be behind the football stadium, not in front of it, for example, or it

2. One reason for thinking this would be if one held that relations of justification and warrant can only hold between conceptual states. For influential statements of this view see Davidson 1986 and McDowell 1994.

3. See the passage quoted at p. 81 below.

might not even be a football stadium at all. But it would make no sense for me to ask: "Someone is in front of the football stadium, but is it me?"

Judgments either have or lack the IEM property relative to the grounds on which they are made. My judgment about being in front of the football stadium could well lack the IEM property if it were made on different grounds. Suppose, for example, that I am trying to locate myself on a GPS map. I see a blue dot in front of the football stadium and mistakenly think that it corresponds to my GPS tracker, while actually it is someone else's tracker and mine is malfunctioning. Then I have misidentified the person who is in front of the football stadium. The grounds on which I made my judgment do not confer the IEM property upon it.

So, can we say anything specific about the types of ground that do confer the IEM property upon self-conscious judgments? One thing is clear. A judgment with the IEM property cannot involve any identification of the self. So, it must be derived from sources of information that can only provide information about the self (so that no identification is required). In other words, judgments with the IEM property must ultimately be based on what might be termed *identification-free self-awareness*. The forms of nonconceptual self-consciousness that we have been discussing all fit this description.[4] Self-specifying information in visual perception can only be about the perceiving self. Likewise for bodily self-awareness and the self-awareness implicated in spatial reasoning.

The relations between nonconceptual self-consciousness and the immunity property are the focus of chapter 4, "The Elusiveness Thesis, Immunity to Error through Misidentification, and Privileged Access," originally published in 2003 in a volume entitled *Privileged Access: Philosophical Accounts of Self-Knowledge* edited by Brie Gertler. The essay explores two ideas that have played a prominent role in philosophical discussions of self-knowledge. The first is the idea that we enjoy *introspective* ways of finding out about ourselves that are fundamentally different from our ways of finding out about ordinary physical objects and other psychological subjects. These ways of finding out about ourselves yield a certain type of privileged access to our own properties and states that we do not have to the properties and states

4. As, of course, does introspection, which is a paradigmatically conceptual form of self-consciousness. Autobiographical memory is another paradigmatically conceptual source of judgments with the IEM property. I discuss it extensively in *Understanding "I."*

of other people (and nor do they have it to our own properties and states). The second is an idea most often associated with David Hume. According to the so-called *elusiveness thesis*, when we find out about our own properties through introspection we are not acquainted with any object whose properties they are. It is natural to think that these two ideas are related—and, in particular, that it is (at least partly) because we do not encounter the self as an object in introspection that the knowledge of the self gained through introspection is epistemically privileged. In other words, the elusiveness thesis explains the IEM property. This idea has been emphasized by Sydney Shoemaker, who bears primary responsibility for bringing the IEM property to the center of philosophical discussions of self-awareness (see the essays reprinted in Shoemaker 1996).

The forms of nonconceptual self-consciousness that we have been considering, however, show the limitations of the elusiveness thesis as an explanation of identification-free self-awareness. Simply put, the bodily self just is directly encountered in nonconceptual self-consciousness. This means that we need to provide an alternative account of the warrant for self-conscious judgments with the IEM. This account will have two components. First, we need an explanation of how and why these self-conscious judgments are identification free (and hence of why they have the IEM property). At the same time, though, we also need to explain how the thinker is justified in trading on identification-free information sources. Where φ is some property whose presence is revealed by a form of nonconceptual self-consciousness, what justifies the immediate transition from one's awareness of φ to the self-conscious judgment that one is oneself φ? Chapter 4 offers an answer to that question for two forms of nonconceptual self-consciousness—bodily awareness, and the self-specifying dimension of ordinary visual perception.

3   Nonconceptual Self-Consciousness in Bodily Awareness

Whereas chapters 2–4 focus primarily on nonconceptual self-consciousness in visual perception, chapters 5–9 turn to the complex phenomenon of bodily awareness.

In a sense, of course, visual proprioception is a form of bodily awareness, since it incorporates awareness of the bodily self. The principal emphasis in these chapters, however, is on what is often termed awareness of one's body "from the inside." This awareness of the body from the inside comes from multiple information sources. Some of these information sources are nonconscious. Others are conscious. Of the conscious varieties, some are conceptual and others nonconceptual. Figure 6.2 (reproduced here) offers an overview of the typology of bodily awareness. Bodily awareness from the inside corresponds to the branch labeled "First-person."

It is hard, and not particularly profitable, to try to disentangle the philosophical study of bodily awareness from the scientific study in psychology and physiology of how the mechanisms of bodily awareness function, or from neuropsychological inquiries into what happens in disorders of bodily awareness. In part, this is because bodily awareness is a somewhat concealed phenomenon. We depend on it constantly, but rarely attend to it. In part, it is because (unlike vision, touch, hearing, taste, and smell) it does not derive from a single dedicated sensory modality. And, in part, it is because bodily awareness plays an important role structuring and framing

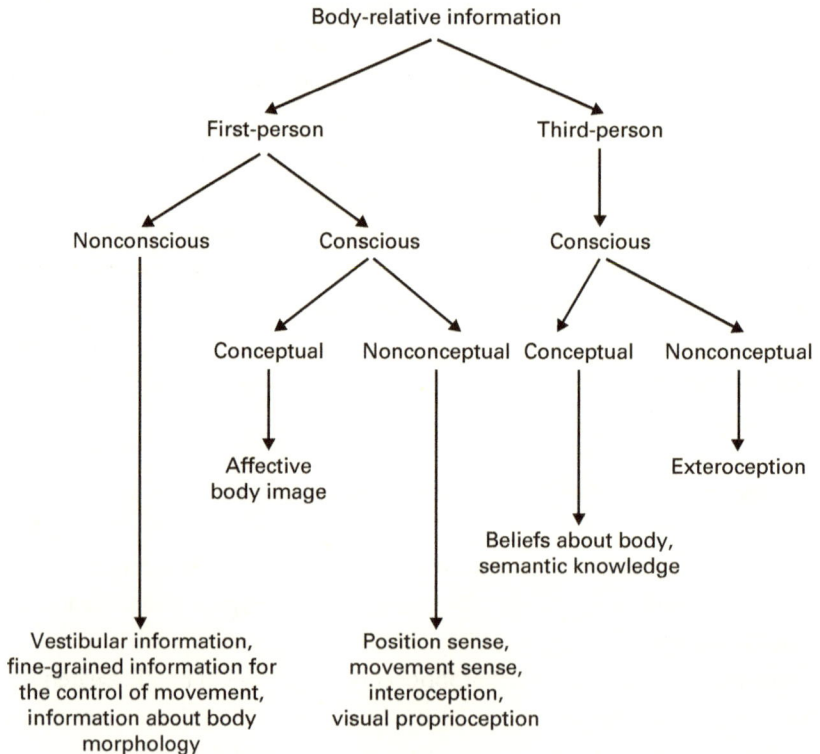

Body-relative information

First-person   Third-person

Nonconscious   Conscious   Conscious

Conceptual   Nonconceptual Conceptual   Nonconceptual

Affective   Exteroception
body image

Beliefs about body,
semantic knowledge

Vestibular information,   Position sense,
fine-grained information for   movement sense,
the control of movement,   interoception,
information about body   visual proprioception
morphology

our general perceptual experience of the world (and of ourselves) so that it is not always easy to identify which elements in our multimodal experience of the world are contributed by bodily awareness.

Both the significance of bodily awareness and the importance of studying it in an empirically informed and multidisciplinary way were recognized in the phenomenological tradition long before philosophers in the analytic tradition started to take notice. Maurice Merleau-Ponty's *The Phenomenology of Perception*, originally published in French in 1945 but not translated into English for another two decades (Merleau-Ponty 1962), is undoubtedly the most important work here. Chapter 5, "The Phenomenology of Bodily Awareness," first published in a volume entitled *Phenomenology and the Cognitive Sciences* edited by Daviod Woodruff Smith and Amie L. Thomasson, is framed by Merleau-Ponty's discussion, exploring how phenomenological insights into bodily awareness and its role in agency can be developed and illuminated by research into somatic proprioception and motor control.

From my perspective (as a sympathetic reader from a very different philosophical tradition, rather than as a Merleau-Ponty scholar), Merleau-Ponty's guiding aim was to elucidate the distinctiveness of the experience of embodiment—the distinctiveness of how we find out about, and act through, our physical bodies. In doing this, he was deeply informed by the scientific study of the body. At the same time, though, he drew a sharp distinction between how we experience the body from a first-person perspective (as something that structures and gives meaning to our engagements with the physical world) and how we study the body from a third-person perspective as one physical object among others, as a complex organization of muscles, bones, and nerves. He formulated this distinction through the contrast between the *for-itself* and the *in-itself*, terminology that goes back at least as far as Hegel but may be unfamiliar to many contemporary philosophers and cognitive scientists. Still, the basic distinction he draws between these two ways of thinking about and studying the body seems incontrovertible.

However, Merleau-Ponty seems (at least to this reader) to draw significant, though ultimately untenable, metaphysical conclusions from his basic starting point. He distinguishes, for example, between objective space and what he terms "the natural system of one's body." He makes the evocative remark that "the frontier of my body is a line that ordinary spatial relations do not cross" (Merleau-Ponty 1962, 68) and draws a sharp distinction between the phenomenal body and the objective body (as a special case of his more general distinction between the phenomenal world and the objective world). It is not always easy to see how exactly these remarks are supposed to be read, but if one takes them at face value they appear significantly to constrain the explanatory power of the scientific study of the body.

So, is there a way to do justice to the phenomenological distinctiveness of our experience of our own bodies that Merleau-Ponty so eloquently characterizes, while still treating the body (from an ontological perspective) as one object among others? Chapter 5 sets out to do this, proposing a way to understand the phenomenological distinctiveness of somatic experience at the level of sense, not at the level of reference (to borrow Frege's terminology). The strategy is to emphasize distinctive features of how the space of the body is represented within bodily experience, contrasting it with how extrabodily space is experienced.

It is standardly assumed within scientific psychology and cognitive science that extrabodily space is represented in multiple frames of reference. Some of these frames of reference are allocentric (centered on a nonbodily object). Others are egocentric (centered on the subject's body). The egocentric frames of reference differ according to which body part they take as their origin, which in turn can depend on the relevant sensory modality. So, for example, visual information is standardly represented in retina-centered coordinates (coordinates centered on the retina), while information from smell and hearing is coded in head-centered coordinates and tactile information in hand-centered coordinates.

Despite these differences, all of these frames of reference are in essence Cartesian. That is, they allow spatial locations to be identified relative to axes centered on an origin. The experienced space of the body, however, seems fundamentally non-Cartesian. The simple reason for this is that there is no single part of the body that can serve as the origin of a Cartesian frame of reference, in the way that the eye (for example) is the obvious origin for a visual frame of reference. Whereas it makes perfect sense to ask, of any two visual perceived objects, whether they are in the same direction from the perceiver, or which is further way, neither question makes sense for bodily events apprehended through bodily awareness. These questions about direction and distance incorporate an implicit self-reference (further away *from me*, for example) and there is no privileged part of the body that can count as *me* for this purpose.

To accommodate these facts about the phenomenology of bodily experience, I proposed in *The Paradox of Self-Consciousness* an alternative model of how we experience the space of the body. The model starts from a distinction between two ways of thinking about bodily location. We can think about the location of a bodily event without taking into account the body as a whole. This would be to identify a bodily location relative to an abstract and relatively unchanging bodily map. Alternatively, we can think about the bodily event in a way that takes into account what the rest of the body is doing. I term these A-location and B-location, respectively.

Developing these ideas further exploits the fact that the human body can be viewed as a relatively immoveable torso to which are connected moveable limbs, each of which is further articulated into multiple, independently moving body parts connected by joints. The basic idea is that A-location specifies a bodily event within a particular body-part, while B-location fixes the location of that body part in terms of the angles of the joints that lie between it and the immoveable torso. So, the B-location of the pain in the ball of my foot is its A-location within my foot, supplemented by specifying the angles of the foot relative to the lower leg, and the lower leg relative to the upper leg.

Chapter 5 suggests that this fundamentally non-Cartesian model of how we experience the space of the body offers a metaphysically neutral way of doing justice to Merleau-Ponty's insights about the distinctiveness of our experience of our own bodies. To illustrate how the model can be integrated with the scientific study of the body, I also show how it is consistent with important work in motor control and action planning.

Chapter 6, "Bodily Awareness and Self-Consciousness," originally published in the *Oxford Handbook of the Self* edited by Shaun Gallagher, gives an overview of how bodily awareness functions as a form of self-consciousness. Emphasizing the multiple and complex sources of bodily awareness, the essay addresses why bodily awareness counts as a (nonconceptual) form of self-consciousness. This involves exploring topics continuous with those discussed in the context of visual proprioception, such as the significance of the IEM property for self-consciousness, as well as considering (and rejecting) some of the objections raised in the literature to characterizing bodily awareness as a form of self-consciousness.

Chapter 6 also introduces the topic of ownership, which is the focus of chapters 7 through 9. It has become common both in philosophy and in the cognitive sciences to talk about the sense of ownership that subjects have for parts of their body and, indeed, for their bodies as a whole. An important part of how each of us experiences our own body in a distinctive way is that we each experience our body and our limbs as our own. This seems to be a ground-level fact about bodily experience, which is often described by saying that we each have a sense of ownership for our own bodies and body parts. This raises a number of questions about how exactly we should understand that sense of ownership and how it is grounded. This is the problem of bodily ownership.

The concept of ownership seems to mean different things to different people, and, in an attempt to clarify the structure of ongoing debates, I make a distinction in chapter 6 between inflationary and deflationary conceptions of the sense of ownership. According to the inflationary conception, our awareness of our own bodies incorporates a specific feeling of "mineness" or "myness," and it is because we have this feeling that we experience our bodies and body parts as our own. For the inflationary theorist, therefore, the sense of ownership is grounded in what might be termed a phenomenologically salient *quale* of ownership. According to deflationary theorists, on the other hand, the sense of ownership is grounded in other, more fundamental, aspects of bodily experience—with different theorists looking to different aspects of bodily experience as potential grounds. To be clear, both deflationary and inflationary theorists hold that the sense of ownership is phenomenologically salient, where that means that we experience our bodies and body parts as our own.[5] Theorists differ on how they explicate that phenomenological salience.

Chapter 6 offers an argument against the inflationary conception of ownership (an argument that is developed further in chapter 7). The argument adapts and develops some important themes from Elizabeth Anscombe's discussion of knowledge without observation in her classic paper "Sensations of Position" (Anscombe 1962) and in her book *Intention* (Anscombe 1957). In brief, Anscombe poses a dilemma for the thesis that our knowledge of how are limbs are disposed is derived from bodily

5. This point was not sufficiently clear in the original version of chapter 6, and so this is one respect in which the essay has been rewritten.

sensations. The dilemma emerges when we ask about the content of bodily sensations and how that content is supposed to ground our knowledge. On the one hand, we can think of the content of sensations purely internally (in terms of feelings of pressure, for example, or strain in muscles, or inchoate tinglings). On the other hand, we can think of their content externally (in what we would now call representational terms).

According to Anscombe, neither way will allow sensations to serve as a source of knowledge. When construed internally, the content of sensations is too vague and general to ground fine-grained knowledge of how limbs are distributed. But when construed externally, the content of the sensations is effectively the same as the content of the knowledge it is supposed to be grounding, and hence incapable of providing independent support for it. It is straightforward to extend this argument to the putative quale of ownership postulated by inflationary theorists, who typically fall foul of the external horn of the dilemma. The "feeling of myness" is invariably presented as precisely that—namely, as a feeling whose (external) content is that the body part within which the feeling is located is mine. So, they are susceptible to the charge that the feeling of ownership simply recapitulates what it is supposed to be independently justifying.

One of the targets of my argument in chapter 6 was Frédérique de Vignemont, who subsequently published an essay in the journal *Analysis* objecting to my argument and offering a new line of argument appealing to the rubber hand illusion in support of the inflationary conception. Chapter 7, "Bodily Ownership, Bodily Awareness, and Knowledge without Observation," a much-expanded version of an article first published in *Analysis*, continues the discussion. I remain unconvinced by her arguments and objections, but welcome the opportunity to clarify further my own thinking about ownership and bodily awareness.

In particular, chapter 7 addresses an important contrast between the content of visual perception and the content of bodily awareness that emerges from the discussion of Anscombe's argument and the rubber hand illusion. Visual perception stands in justificatory relations to perceptual judgments. This was explored in chapter 4 in the context of a very specific class of first-person judgments, but of course it holds more generally. Visual perception is a paradigm example of knowledge through observation and hence that to which bodily sensations and the sense of ownership are being contrasted.

At the same time, though, it would be reasonable to ask why the content of visual perception does not fall foul of Anscombe's dilemma—which surely would be a reductio both of her argument and of my use of it.

We know from the demise of sense datum theory that there is no prospect of characterizing the content of perception in purely sensational terms (at least, not if one wants perception to justify belief). But if we think about the content of visual perception externally or representationally, then in what sense is it sufficiently independent to ground beliefs and judgments that are based on it? And, if it is sufficiently independent, then why can the same not be said for the content of bodily awareness?

This challenge raises subtle questions that go back to the discussion in chapter 3 of what it is to take a perception at face value. The answer to the challenge that I propose in chapter 7 is, in brief, that the nonconceptual content of perception can be specified in ways that are completely independent of any of the concepts featuring in those perceptual judgments that they might be called on to justify. The theory of scenario content developed by Christopher Peacocke is a good example of how this might be done, and in fact Peacocke has used his model of scenario content to elucidate how perceptual states with nonconceptual content can justify belief states with conceptual content (see particularly Peacocke 1992). The same cannot be said, however, for the putative "feeling of ownership." The type of feeling proposed by the inflationary theorist cannot be specified in the type of "ownership-neutral" manner that would be required to escape an Anscombe-type argument. This is because the feeling of ownership itself counts as a bodily sensation and hence will have the same general properties as any other bodily sensation. One such general property is that facts about ownership are an integral part of the content of bodily sensations (and other forms of bodily awareness). So, as a bodily sensation, the feeling of ownership proposed by the inflationary theorist is insufficiently independent of the phenomenon that it is being called on to explain.

This basic point about bodily sensation and bodily awareness in general is developed in much more detail in chapter 8, "Ownership and the Space of the Body," published in a volume entitled *The Subject's Matter* edited by Frédérique de Vignemont and Adrian Alsmith. In that essay, I take the following two principles as starting points for discussing the content of bodily awareness and how it supports the phenomenology of ownership.

Boundedness

Bodily events are experienced within the experienced body (a circumscribed body-shaped volume whose boundaries define the limits of the self).

Connectedness

The spatial location of a bodily event is experienced relative to the disposition of the body as a whole.

Chapter 8 does not directly discuss the inflationary view of ownership, but it offers a natural way of extending the line of argument from chapter 7, since a *quale* of ownership that satisfies Boundedness and Connectedness will plainly fail Anscombe's independence constraint.

The main focus of chapter 8 is providing a deflationary account of ownership—that is to say, an account that grounds the phenomenology of ownership in other, more fundamental aspects of bodily experience. My proposal is that judgments of ownership are ultimately grounded in the distinctive way we experience the space of the body. To develop this idea, chapter 8 extends the model of A-location and B-location proposed in chapter 5 (and earlier in *The Paradox of Self-Consciousness*). The A-location of a bodily event is its location in a specific body part relative to an abstract map of the body. A-location does not take into account the current position of the body. That is the main difference from B-location, which is a bodily event's location relative to the current disposition of body parts. In *The Paradox of Self-Consciousness* and chapter 5, I discuss A-location and B-location very generally, in terms of a model of the body as an articulated structure in which a relatively immoveable torso connected by joints to moveable body parts, each of which is further articulated into smaller body parts and joints. Chapter 8 develops this general picture further in light of two very different (but complementary) approaches to modeling the body.

The first approach is most prominent in kinesiology and robotics, where the body is typically modeled as a system of rigid links connected by mechanical joints. This way of modeling the body typically represents both bodily position at a time and movement over time in terms of the angles of the relevant joints. The second derives from the well-known model of object recognition proposed by Marr and Nishihara (1978). In that model, objects are represented schematically as complexes of generalized cones (surfaces generated by moving a cross-section along an axis, maintaining its shape but possibly varying its size). The human body, in particular, is represented as a hierarchy of generalized cones. Chapter 8 shows how these two approaches can be combined to yield a model of the body as a hierarchy of generalized cones linked by mechanical joints. I argue, first, that this model captures how we experience the space of our bodies and, second, that our experiencing the space of our bodies in this distinctive way is what ultimately grounds both the phenomenology of ownership and our judgments of ownership.

Chapter 9, "Bodily Ownership, Psychological Ownership, and Psychopathology," first published in a special issue of the *Review of Philosophy and Psychology* edited by Alexandre Billon, explores the relation between this general model of bodily ownership and discussions of psychological ownership—the phenomenon of taking one's thoughts, emotions, and other psychological states as one's own. In chapter 9 I term these φ-ownership (bodily) and ψ-ownership (psychological), respectively. The particular model of ψ-ownership I consider is that proposed by John Campbell in a number of papers. Reflecting on cases of schizophrenia (and other psychopathologies), Campbell proposes fractionating ψ-ownership into two components: a self-ascriptive component, on the one hand, and a causal component, on the other. One can think of those two dimensions of ownership as corresponding to the following two different types of judgment of ownership:

(1) "I am thinking this thought"

(2) "I am the producer of this thought"

Campbell's point is that schizophrenic patients suffering from delusions of thought insertion sometimes make judgments of the first type while rejecting judgments of the second type—they can think of themselves as thinking thoughts that they did not themselves produce.

On the view laid out in chapter 9, φ-ownership and ψ-ownership are distinct phenomena for which different explanations need to be offered. They are closely related in various ways, however. As I bring out, each presupposes the other. Our awareness of our own bodies and our awareness of our ongoing thoughts, emotions, and feelings are complementary elements of a single, embodied perspective on the world. Both φ-ownership and ψ-ownership are parts of what it is to be a bodily self, and for that reason one would expect there to be a deep commonality between them. As chapter 9 brings out, this commonality emerges from the fundamental role of agency in the two types of ownership.

Agency is at the heart of the model of φ-ownership that I have developed because it derives ownership from the spatial content of bodily awareness, and the spatial content of bodily awareness brings with it awareness of the agent's agential abilities. It is not just that the limits of the body are the limits of what is directly responsive to the will; the key variables for specifying both A-location and B-location are also given in terms of the agent's capacities for movement (since limbs and other effectors are manipulated through joints). Likewise, for the reasons I brought out earlier, agency is central to Campbell's model of ψ-ownership, which incorporates the idea that (in the normal case) ownership of one's thoughts goes beyond simple self-ascription and incorporates taking oneself to be (causally) responsible for the thought. Taking both φ-ownership and ψ-ownership into account, therefore, to experience oneself as a bodily self is to experience oneself as an agent.

The final essay in this volume takes a broader perspective on the issue of agency. Chapter 10, "The Bodily Self, Commonsense Psychology, and the Springs of Action," appears here for the first time, although it draws on elements of two previously published papers. It programmatically suggests how the general picture of the bodily self that has emerged from the essays reprinted here might be extended to modeling action and how it is explained. Let me explain the analogy and the suggestion.

The earlier essays in this volume have all, in one way or another, explored how full-fledged, conceptual self-consciousness rests on a multi-layered complex of forms of nonconceptual self-consciousness. These forms of nonconceptual self-consciousness are so omnipresent and pervasive that they can easily seem invisible. But the moral of the discussion is that our sophisticated abilities to think and speak about ourselves rest on a bed of much more primitive self-specifying representations. One way of framing this idea would be to say that the domain of conceptual self-consciousness turns out to be much narrower than it has typically been taken to be. It is not just that we can represent ourselves wordlessly and without concepts. It turns out that these representations guide and structure much (if not most) of our activity as we navigate the physical world. The bodily self, one might say, is primary.

So now, with this general picture in mind, consider standard models of the springs of action. Within philosophy and cognitive science, action is often understood in a highly conceptual way. That is to say, the springs of action are taken to be beliefs, desires, and other propositional attitudes, with the general idea being that action is caused by desires (or comparable pro-attitudes) and guided by belief (or comparable information states). Within philosophy, this way of thinking about action has a long and distinguished history, going back at least as far as Aristotle's discussion of the practical syllogism. More recently, it finds a very clear expression in the distinction between modular and central processing that Jerry Fodor, among others, sees as key to contemporary cognitive science. Central processing is the domain of the propositional attitudes, of practical reasoning and decision making. Intentional actions (that is to say, those not governed by reflex or habit) emerge from central processing. Since it is standard to think of beliefs and other propositional attitudes as having conceptual contents, this picture is one on which the springs of action fall within the domain of the conceptual.

This dominant way of thinking about the springs of action goes hand in hand with a model of social understanding and social coordination. According to this model, we navigate the social world by tacitly applying a conceptual understanding of how beliefs, desires, and other propositional attitudes work. The model can be developed in various ways. So, the conceptual understanding might take the form of an implicit theory (as proposed by so-called theory theorists) or it might be built into simulation mechanisms. But the common thread is that the conceptual framework of propositional attitude psychology (also known as folk psychology, or commonsense psychology) enables and structures our social interactions.

It is unsurprising that the two models go hand in hand, for it is natural to try to explain things in terms of what one thinks causes them. And, for that very reason, it seems unpromising to take issue with one without taking issue with the other. Accordingly, in chapter 10 I tackle both. The discussion is programmatic, designed to prime the pump, as it were, by pointing to a range of phenomena that fall outside the domain of commonsense psychology and propositional attitudes (from both an etiological point of view and an explanatory one).

First, I point toward ways of thinking about the springs of action that do not engage the propositional attitudes. As far as the etiology of action is concerned, human organisms act within the world in virtue of how they represent the world. But there often seems to be a fundamental lack of fit between our best models of the representations that generate behavior and the model of representation built into propositional attitude psychology. Evidence for this lack of fit comes from range of sources, from neural network modeling to detailed studies of action control and perceptual processing. Second, and correlatively, I explore tools for achieving social understanding and social coordination that bypass the propositional attitudes. These range from direct perception of emotions to game-theoretic heuristics (such as tit-for-tat in the iterated prisoner's dilemma) and what AI theorists term scripts and frames.

This introduction has brought out some of the common themes that run through all the chapters. In contrast, the book ends with an afterword that seeks to identify some of the principal avenues for further inquiry. If there is one unifying theme for this volume, it is that the fully conceptual understanding that we have of ourselves and others rests upon the complex underpinnings of many types and levels of nonconceptual (self-) awareness. Thinking through the implications of this will require reconfiguring a number of fundamental concepts, most obviously perhaps the concept of rationality. Our notion of rationality is closely tied to paradigms of highly reflective and self-aware thinking. As we begin to see, though, that the scope of such self-aware reflection is much narrower than standardly thought, it becomes pressing to ask how, if at all, standards of rationality can be applied to the actions and reactions of the bodily self. In an important sense, therefore, the message of this book is a challenge and a question: Now that the scope and importance of the nonconceptual bodily self is (I hope) clearly in view, how do we need to change the basic evaluative framework that we apply to human thinking and human behavior?

References

Anscombe, G. E. M. 1957. *Intention*. Oxford: Blackwell.

Anscombe, G. E. M. 1962. On sensations of position. *Analysis* 22:55–58.

Anscombe, G. E. M. 1975. The first person. In *Mind and Language*, ed. S. Guttenplan. Oxford: Clarendon Press.

Bermúdez, J. L. 1994. Peacocke's argument against the autonomy of nonconceptual representational content. *Mind & Language* 9:402–418.

Bermúdez, J. L. 1998. *The Paradox of Self-Consciousness*. Cambridge, MA: MIT Press.

Bermúdez, J. L. 2017. *Understanding "I": Language and Thought*. Oxford: Oxford University Press.

Bermúdez, J. L., and A. Cahen. 2015. Mental content, nonconceptual. *Stanford Encyclopedia of Philosophy*. http://plato.stanford.edu.

Bermúdez, J. L., A. J. Marcel, and N. Eilan, eds. 1995. *The Body and the Self*. Cambridge, MA: MIT Press.

Davidson, D. 1986. A coherence theory of truth and knowledge. In *Truth and Interpretation: Perspectives on the Philosophy of Donald Davidson*, ed. E. Lepore, 307–319. Oxford: Blackwell.

Gibson, J. J. 1966. *The Senses Considered As Perceptual Systems*. Boston: Houghton Mifflin.

Gibson, J. J. 1979. *The Ecological Approach to Visual Perception*. Boston: Houghton Mifflin.

Marr, D., and H. K. Nishihara. 1978. Representation and recognition of the spatial organization of three-dimensional shapes. *Proceedings of the Royal Society of London* 200:269–294.

McDowell, J. 1994. *Mind and World*. Cambridge, MA: Harvard University Press.

Merleau-Ponty, M. 1962. *The Phenomenology of Perception*. London: Routledge.

Peacocke, C. 1992. *A Study of Concepts*. Cambridge, MA: MIT Press.

Peacocke, C. 1994. Nonconceptual content: Kinds, rationales, and relations. *Mind & Language* 9:419–429.

Peacocke, C. 1999. *Being Known*. Oxford: Oxford University Press.

Peacocke, C. 2002. The relations between conceptual and nonconceptual content (Postscript to reprint of Peacocke 1994). In *Essays on Nonconceptual Content*, ed. Y. Guenther. Cambridge, MA: MIT Press.

Shoemaker, S. 1996. *The First-Person Perspective and Other Essays*. Cambridge University Press.

Strawson, P. F. 1975. *The Bounds of Sense: An Essay on Kant's "Critique of Pure Reason,"* vol. 18. New York: Routledge.

1 Nonconceptual Self-Consciousness and Cognitive Science

Philosophy and the cognitive sciences have an uneasy relationship.[1] Fruitful engagement is rare in either direction.[2] This is partly the inevitable result of the division of academic labors. But there is also a deeper reason. The dominant methodological conception governing work in the cognitive sciences involves a distinction of levels of explanation (see the papers in Bermúdez and Elton 2000). Marr's theory of vision has often been held up as a model that the cognitive sciences in general ought to follow—mainly because it is one of the very few worked out and satisfying theoretical treatments of a cognitive capacity that cognitive science has so far produced. As is well known, Marr's approach to the study of the visual system is top down (Marr 1982). He starts with an abstract specification of the computational tasks that the visual system has to perform, hypothesizes a series of algorithms that could carry out these computational tasks, and then speculates about the implementation of those algorithms at the neural level. Each of the levels of explanation at which the theory operates is relatively autonomous, although the algorithmic level models the realization of the functions identified at the computational level and the implementational level explains how the functions identified at the algorithmic level are realized. The resulting theory is a dazzling achievement. But there are hidden implications in taking it as a general paradigm for cognitive science. Taking

1. I have made a significant number of changes to this essay for publication in the current volume, both to update some of the discussion and to reduce overlap with other essays.

2. This essay was originally published in 2000, and things have changed for the better since then. The methodological obstacles identified below are still there, but more philosophers and cognitive scientists are successfully overcoming them.

it as a paradigm makes it natural to think, for example, that the place of philosophy is at the computational level and, correspondingly, that the place of cognitive neuroscience is at the implementational level. The result, of course, is that the two disciplines are effectively insulated from each other by the intervening algorithmic level of explanation.

There is an obvious problem, however, with generalizing Marr's approach. The problem is that the distinction of levels of explanation really makes sense only where one can identify a clear computational task or set of tasks that need to be carried out. But it is not clear that this can be done outside the restricted domain of encapsulated modules—such as the early visual system, the language-parsing system or the face recognition system. Fodor, the most articulate defender of this methodological approach, has clearly appreciated this, and drawn the drastic conclusion that cognitive science cannot hope to shed any light on the so-called "central processes" of cognition. A more sensible lesson to draw, I think, is that outside this restricted domain a more interactive conception of the relation between the levels of explanation is appropriate. There must be constraints on theorizing at the computational and algorithmic levels. On the top-down approach these constraints emerge from clearly defined computational tasks. But where there are no such computational tasks explanation cannot be purely top down. There must be constraints and programmatic suggestions moving in both directions (Bermúdez 1995a,b, 2000).

The difficulty in putting this program into practice is identifying the points of contact between philosophical concerns and, say, neuroscientific concerns. What I want to do in this paper is to identify some of the areas where cognitive scientific and philosophical issues intersect in the study of self-consciousness—a form of cognition about as far as it is possible to get from the encapsulated modules where top-down analyses can be so profitably applied.[3]

1   The Paradox of Self-Consciousness

In thinking about self-consciousness we need to start with the phenomenon of first-person thought. Most, if not all, of the higher forms of

3. For more discussion of levels of explanation in cognitive science, see the discussion of what I call the Integration Challenge in chapter 4 of my book *Cognitive Science: An Introduction to the Science of the Mind* (Bermúdez 2014).

self-consciousness presuppose our capacity to think about ourselves. Consider, for example, self-knowledge, the capacity for moral self-evaluation and ability to construct a narrative of our past. Although much of what we think when we think about ourselves involves concepts and descriptions also available to us in our thoughts about other people and other objects, our thoughts about ourselves also involve an ability that we cannot put to work in thinking about other people and things—namely, the ability to apply those concepts and descriptions uniquely to ourselves. I shall follow convention in referring to this as the capacity to entertain "I"-thoughts.

"I"-thoughts of course involve self-reference, but it is self-reference of a distinctive kind. Consider the following two ways in which I might entertain thoughts that refer to myself:

(1) JLB thinks: JLB is about to be attacked by a poisonous spider
(2) JLB thinks: I am about to be attacked by a poisonous spider

It is clear that these are very different thoughts, even though they are both thoughts about the same person, namely me. If I am suffering a temporary attack of amnesia that has led me to forget my own name I can think the first thought with equanimity. Not so the second.

This property of "I"-thoughts is sometimes described as their *immunity to error through misidentification*, where this means (roughly) that one cannot think an "I"-thought without knowing that it is in fact about oneself (Shoemaker 1968; Evans 1982). This feature of "I"-thoughts is closely tied to the well-known linguistic property of the first-person pronoun, namely, that the first-person pronoun "I" always refers to the person uttering it. The guaranteed reference of "I" does not secure the immunity to error through misidentification of the thoughts expressed through "I"-sentences, because many "I"-sentences express thoughts that lack the immunity property. The connection between the immunity property and guaranteed reference is more subtle. When we have a sentence of the form "I am *F*" expressing a thought that is immune to error through misidentification, the fact that the sentence is about me is not fixed by any form of identification. So (one might reasonably think) all that there is available to fix the reference of "I" is the reference rule governing the first-person pronoun.

Combining the immunity to error through misidentification of "I"-thoughts with the guaranteed reference of the first-person pronoun suggests the following deflationary account of self-consciousness:

(A) Once we have an account of what it is to be capable of thinking "I"-thoughts we will have explained everything that is distinctive about self-consciousness.

(B) Once we have an account of what it is to be capable of thinking thoughts that are immune to error through misidentification we will have explained everything that is distinctive about the capacity to think "I"-thoughts.

(C) Once we have explained what it is to master the semantics of the first-person pronoun (e.g., via mastery of some version of the token-reflexive rule that a given utterance of "I" always refers to the person uttering it), we will have explained everything that is distinctive about the capacity to think thoughts that are immune to error through misidentification.

The problem with the deflationary view that I explored in my book *The Paradox of Self-Consciousness* (Bermúdez 1998) is that first-person self-reference is itself dependent upon "I"-thoughts in a way that creates two forms of vicious circularity, which collectively I term the paradox of self-consciousness. The first type of circularity (*explanatory circularity*) arises because the capacity for self-conscious thought must be presupposed in any satisfactory account of mastery of the first-person pronoun. I cannot refer to myself as the producer of a given token of "I" without, for example, knowing that I intend to refer to myself—which is itself a self-conscious thought of the type that we are trying to explain. The second type of circularity (*capacity circularity*) arises because this interdependence rules out the possibility of explaining how the capacity either for self-conscious thought or for linguistic mastery of the first-person pronoun arises in the normal course of human development. It does not seem possible to meet the following constraint:

The Acquisition Constraint   If a given psychological capacity is psychologically real, then there must be an explanation of how it is possible for an individual in the normal course of human development to acquire that capacity.

Neither self-conscious thought nor linguistic mastery of the first-person pronoun is innate, and yet each presupposes the other in a way that seems to imply that neither can be acquired unless the other capacity is already in place.

2 Escaping the Paradox of Self-Consciousness

The strategy that I developed in *The Paradox of Self-Consciousness* for escaping the paradox involves making a clear distinction between (a) those forms of full-fledged self-consciousness that presuppose mastery of the first-person concept and linguistic mastery of the first-person pronoun, and (b) those forms of *primitive* or *nonconceptual self-consciousness* that do not require any such linguistic or conceptual mastery. It is these nonconceptual forms of self-consciousness that allow us to escape both the types of circularity just identified.

The domain of self-consciousness is far wider than it has been held to be by philosophers. Self-consciousness has often been thought to be the highest form of human cognition, and many philosophers, famous and not so famous, have correspondingly thought that a philosophical account of self-consciousness would be the Archimedean point for a satisfactory account of human thought. But the premise is flawed. Self-consciousness is something we share with prelinguistic infants and with many members of the animal kingdom (Hurley 1998). The highly conceptual forms of self-consciousness emerge from a rich foundation of nonconceptual forms of self-awareness. As I will try to bring out, recognizing this builds a bridge between philosophical interests and neuroscientific ones.[4]

Pursuing this strategy involves rejecting what might be termed the classical view of content. In particular, it involves rejecting the following thesis:

The Conceptual Requirement Principle The range of contents that it is permissible to attribute to a creature is directly determined by the concepts that creature possesses.

Roughly speaking, it is because concepts are language dependent and yet there exist strong reasons for ascribing thought-contents to nonlinguistic creatures that we have to accept the existence of nonconceptual contents (Bermúdez 1994, 1995c, 1998). A nonconceptual content is one that can be ascribed to a thinker without that thinker having to possess the concepts required to specify that content. I defend the claim (which I term the

---

4. The interdisciplinary dimension of the idea of nonconceptual self-consciousness is also very much at the forefront of Susan Hurley's work on the self in chap. 4 of her 1998 book.

Priority Principle) that concepts can only be possessed by language-users. Nonlinguistic thoughts can only be thoughts with nonconceptual content, because concepts are essentially linguistic phenomena.

The constitutive connection between concepts and language is a function of the conditions on the individuation of concepts—which in turn are conditions on what it is to possess or grasp a concept. Any acceptable account of what it is to possess a concept will have to include certain specifications of circumstances in which it is appropriate to apply that concept. But this is not all. Concepts form part of, and are individuated by their role in, the contents of propositional attitudes. Part of what it is to possess a given concept is that one should be able to recognize that certain circumstances give one good reasons to take particular propositional attitudes to contents containing that concept. Moreover, concept mastery is also evidenced in dispositions to make and to accept as legitimate or justified certain inferential transitions between judgments.

The plausibility of the Priority Principle emerges from the constraints on being able to appreciate rational grounds for certain inferences.[5] It is certainly true that it is possible to be justified (or warranted) in making a certain inferential transition without being able to provide a justification (or warrant) for that inferential transition. It is a familiar epistemological point, after all, that there is a difference between being justified in holding a belief and justifying that belief. What does not seem to be true is that it is possible to distinguish between justified and unjustified inferential transition in the case of a subject who is not capable of providing any justifications at all for any inferential transitions. But providing justifications is a paradigmatically linguistic activity. This is so for two reasons. First, providing justifications is a matter of identifying and articulating the reasons for a given classification, inference, or judgment. It is a paradigmatically social, and consequently linguistic, activity. Second, mere sensitivity to the truth of inferential transitions involving a given concept is not enough for possession of that concept. Rational sensitivity is required, and rational sensitivity comes only with language mastery. This is so because critical reflection on one's own thinking requires intentional ascent. That is, critical reflection requires being able to take one's own thoughts as objects of thought, and we have no understanding of how this can take

5. For a more nuanced version of the argument that follows, see Bermúdez 2010.

place except where the thoughts in question have a linguistic vehicle (Bermúdez 2003).

If the Priority Principle is true, so that there can be no concepts without language, it follows that, if we have good reason to ascribe content-bearing psychological states to nonlinguistic creatures, then the contents of those states will be nonconceptual. The attribution of representational states with nonconceptual content to nonlinguistic creatures is an instance of inference to the best explanation. As such it is subject to the constraints associated with inference to the best explanation—that is, constraints of simplicity, explanatory power, and parsimony. In particular, it is only to be entered into when simpler explanations that do not appeal to representational states are demonstrably inadequate. I take it as a viable working hypothesis, strongly supported by work in contemporary cognitive ethology and developmental psychology, that we do need to give psychological explanations of the behavior of nonlinguistic creatures—and consequently that there are psychological states with nonconceptual content.

Nonetheless, many philosophers would be prepared to countenance the possibility of nonconceptual content without accepting that there might be nonconceptual first person contents or "I"-thoughts. If the theory of nonconceptual content is to solve the paradox of self-consciousness, the possibility of nonconceptual first-person contents, and hence the possibility of nonconceptual self-consciousness, must be independently motivated. This requires identifying forms of behavior in prelinguistic or nonlinguistic creatures for which inference to the best understanding or explanation demands the ascription of states with nonconceptual first-person contents. I carry out this strategy in four domains:

(a) perceptual experience
(b) somatic proprioception (bodily self-awareness)
(c) self–world dualism in spatial reasoning
(d) psychological interaction

3 The Self of Ecological Optics

3.1

One of J. J. Gibson's great insights in the study of visual perception was that the very structure of visual perception contains *propriospecific* information about the self, as well as *exterospecific* information about the distal environment (Gibson 1979). Visual perception incorporates a first-person perspective in the information it picks up about the world. This is the basis of nonconceptual self-awareness, the foundation on which all forms of self-awareness are built.

In his book *The Senses Considered as Perceptual Systems* (Gibson 1966), Gibson identifies what he calls the "fallacy of ascribing proprioception to proprioceptors." This is the fallacy (he claims) of making a sharp distinction between outwardly directed *exteroceptors* (i.e., the five senses of sight, touch, smell, taste, and hearing) and inwardly directed *proprioceptors* (i.e., receptors in muscles, joints, and the inner ear providing information about bodily position and movement) and *interoceptors* (receptors in the visceral organs providing information about homeostatic states such as hunger and thirst). On the view that Gibson is attacking, information about the self can come only from proprioceptors and interoceptors. The job of the exteroceptors is solely to provide information about the external world.

On Gibson's view, each of the exteroceptive senses brings with it a distinctive type of proprioception. Here are some representative passages for touch and hearing.

Cutaneous proprioception "The skin is action-sensitive whenever the individual makes contact with something, or grasps or clings to it, or makes contact with himself" (Gibson 1966, 37).

Auditory proprioception "The organ registers any sounds made by action, as in walking, eating, vocalizing, or speaking, and by tool-using, as in hammering, typing, or music-making" (Gibson 1966, 37).

Vision, though, is the principal source of propriospecific information. Gibson studies visual proprioception in insightful detail in his book *The Ecological Approach to Visual Perception* (Gibson 1979).

What is particularly significant in Gibson's analysis of visual proprioception (as compared to cutaneous or auditory proprioception) is his bold suggestion that visual perception involves direct perception of the self. Here is a representative passage:

When a point of observation is occupied, there is also optical information to specify the observer himself, and this information *cannot* be shared by other observers. For the body of the animal who is observing temporarily conceals some portion of the environment in a way that is unique to that animal. I call this information *propriospecific* as distinguished from *exterospecific*, meaning that it specifies the self as distinguished from the environment. (Gibson 1979, 104)

His analysis of visual proprioception begins with the concept of a field of view. This is the solid angle of ambient light that can be registered by the visual system. Gibson emphasizes that the field of view is bounded in a way that is perceptibly manifest. He evocatively comments: "Ask yourself what it is you see hiding the surroundings as you look out upon the world—not darkness surely, not air, not nothing, but the ego!" (Gibson 1979, 105). He illustrates this with an updated version of a famous diagram drawn by Ernst Mach with the title "The visual ego."

In addition to the oval boundaries of the field of view, Gibson identifies a range of bodily parts that function as *occluding edges*, hiding regions of the environment. The nearest are the eye sockets, eyebrows, nose, and cheekbones. And then come the bodily extremities—arms, legs, hands, and feet. These are not occluding edges, but they behave in a very distinctive way that leads Gibson to refer to them as "subjective objects" (Gibson 1979, 113). A solid angle is an angle with its base at a perceived object and its apex at the eye. All objects can present a range of solid angles in the field of view, but the bodily extremities are distinctive in that the solid angles they subtend cannot be reduced beyond a certain minimum.

A second type of propriospecific information in field of view is information about movement derived from patterns of optic flow (and nonflow) as perspective changes relative to an invariant structure. Invariants in the

optic array include the contrast between earth and sky at the horizon, and the texture of the earth. Optic flow starts from a center in the field of view that is itself stationary. This point is the aiming point of locomotion—we steer, according to Gibson, by keeping the focus of optic flow on the destination, so that the solid angle it subtends expands to its maximum. He comments:

The moving self and the unmoving world are reciprocal aspects of the same perception. ... One experiences a rigid world and a flowing array. The optical flow of the ambient array is almost never perceived as motion; it is simply *experienced as kinesthesis*, that is *egolocomotion*. (Gibson 1979, 115)

Unlike the kinesthetic information derived from proprioceptors in muscles and joints, visual kinesthesis works equally well for passive motion. An illustration comes from "moving room" experiments where subjects placed on the stationary floors of rooms with walls and ceilings that move backward and forward on the saggital plane report that they feel the sensation of moving (Lishman and Lee 1973).

The theory of ecological optics identifies a third form of self-specifying information existing in the field of vision. This is due to the direct perception of a class of higher-order invariants that Gibson terms *affordances*. It is in the theory of affordances that we find the most sustained development of the ecological view that the fundamentals of perceptual experience are dictated by the organism's need to navigate and act in its environment. The basic premise from which the theory of affordances starts is that objects and surfaces in the environment have properties relevant to the abilities of particular animals, in virtue of which they allow different animals to act and react in different ways.

According to Gibson, information specifying affordances is available in the structure of light to be picked up by the creature as it moves around the world. The possibilities that the environment affords are not learned through experience, and nor are they inferred. They are directly perceived as higher-order invariants. And of course, the perception of affordances is a form of self-perception—or, at least, a way in which self-specifying information is perceived. The whole notion of an affordance is that of environmental information about one's own possibilities for action and reaction.

Recognizing the existence of the "ecological self," as it has come to be known (Neisser 1988, 1999), is the first step in resolving the paradox of self-consciousness. It removes the need to explain how infants can "boot-strap" themselves into the first-person perspective. The evidence is overwhelming that nonconceptual first-person contents are available more or less from the beginning of life. Illustrations are to be found in:

• the ability of neonates to distinguish tape recordings of themselves crying from recordings of other newborn babies crying (Martin and Clark 1982);
• the evidence that new born babies are able to imitate facial expressions before they have any visual information as to the nature and form of their own facial expressions (Meltzoff and Moore 1977);
• the ability of infants to calibrate their reaching behavior to the distance separating them from an object and to adapt the speed of their reach to the speed of a moving object (Field 1976; Von Hofsten 1982); and
• the sensitivity of infants to the moving room. Even pre-locomotive infants make compensatory head movements in response to the perceived loss of balance (Lee and Aronson 1974; Butterworth and Hicks 1977; Pope 1984)

Developing this notion of the ecological self allows a more nuanced view of infant self-consciousness in particular, and infant cognition in general. Reacting against traditional ideas of the infant mind as a tabula rasa, many contemporary theorists have proposed that even very young infants are "little scientists," tacitly deploying the principles of a theory of mind that is basically continuous with that used by older children and adults (see, e.g., Gopnik and Meltzoff 1997). Ecological self-consciousness offers a middle path between these two extremes, pointing to a clear sense in which infants (and nonlinguistic creatures in general) can be described as genuinely self-aware in ways that are shared by language-using creatures—while at the same time making clear how primitive this form of self-awareness is relative to full-fledged linguistic self-consciousness.

Let me turn now to considering some of the implications of this type of nonconceptual self-consciousness for the cognitive science of vision.

3.2

The neural underpinnings of this form of self-specifying information in visual perception have been fairly closely studied by neuroscientists and experimental psychologists. Particularly relevant here is the proposal, currently under much discussion, that there are two distinct cortical pathways in the human visual system, each carrying distinct types of information (Ungerleider and Mishkin 1982; Goodale and Milner 1992). The distinction between the information carried by the dorsal and the ventral pathways respectively has been conceptualized in different ways. Mishkin and Ungerleider see it as a distinction between information about the spatial relations in which an object might stand to the perceiver and information that allows the recognition of objects. Goodale and Milner, in contrast, take the distinction to be between visuomotor information about the "extrinsic" properties of objects (their spatial position, orientation, height, and so forth) and recognitional information about the "intrinsic" properties of objects (their color, shape, and so on).

Perhaps the crucial question to be asked from a philosophical point of view of the 'two-pathways hypothesis' is how it maps onto the phenomenology of perception. Milner and Goodale have taken the extreme view that perception for the online control of action is dependent upon the "dorsal stream," the neural pathway from the striate cortex to the posterior parietal cortex. On their view, perceptually governed action controlled by information in the dorsal stream is typically not accompanied by conscious awareness.[6] Unlike the information subserving perceptual identification, the self-specifying and relational information required for action is picked up nonconsciously. It seems to me, however, that this hypothesis gives a very skewed perspective on the phenomenology of perception, one that ignores Gibson's insights into the interdependence of propriospecific and exterospecific information in visual perception. Let us suppose that the action-based self-specifying information that Gibson discusses at the phenomenological level in terms of affordances and invariants in optical flow is carried in the dorsal stream (McCarthy 1993)—even though there is a sense in which the basic concept of an affordance seems to straddle the distinction between "where" and "what," or between "recognition" and "pragmatic." Then Goodale and Milner's interpretation of the phenomenological significance of the two processing pathways clearly has the consequence that we do not consciously perceive the spatial relations in which we stand to objects, or the possibilities for action and reaction that

6. For a philosophical version of this claim, see Clark 2001, and for critical discussion see Briscoe 2009.

they afford. But this cannot be correct, given Gibson's insightful analysis of visual proprioception.

This is not intended, of course, as a critique of the two-pathways hypothesis construed as a claim about how information is processed in different neural pathways—although it would be unwise to ignore the recent work suggesting that the two visual pathways actually collaborate in the control of action (Jeannerod 1997).[7] The point is rather that a proper understanding of the role of perceptual experience as a form of self-consciousness can, and should, constrain how we interpret such claims at the level of conscious phenomenology.

4 Somatic Proprioception and the Bodily Self

4.1

Gibson's insights into the structure of visual perception were partly vitiated by his insistence on downplaying the importance of somatically derived information about the self. Visual kinesthesis and the perceptual invariants stressed by Gibson are adequate for distinguishing self-movement from movement of the environment, but they are unable to distinguish passive self-movement from active self-movement. They can inform the subject of his movement relative to the environment, but (crudely speaking) they do not tell him whether or not he is moving under his own steam. A different form of self-awareness is required at this point—the bodily self-awareness of proprioception.[8]

A particularly vivid illustration of the importance of these forms of proprioceptive information comes from the documented cases of complete deafferentation—patients who have effectively lost all bodily sensation, either from below the neck in the case of Jonathan Cole's patient IW or from below the jaw in Jacques Paillard's patient GL (Cole and Paillard 1995). Although IW, unlike GL, can walk, everything he does has to be performed

---

7. See also Jacob and Jeannerod 2003 and my review of that book (Bermúdez 2007).

8. I am referring here only to the conscious, personal-level forms of proprioception. Subpersonal mechanisms for providing body-relative information, such as efference copy, do not count as forms of proprioceptive self-consciousness—although of course they are vital elements in the subpersonal underpinnings of proprioceptive self-consciousness.

under visual control. Without visual feedback he is incapable of orienting himself and acting. So much so that he sleeps with the light on—if he woke up in the dark he would have no idea where his body was and would never be able to find the light switch. It is interesting, furthermore, to watch a video of him walking. His head is bent forward and pointing downward so that he can keep his legs and feet in sight constantly.

There is a popular sense of "self-conscious" on which IW seems to be more self-conscious than we are, for the simple reason that everything he does requires his full attention. But this is not the sense of "self-consciousness" in which I am interested. What is striking about deafferented subjects is how the subjective sense of the body as a bounded spatial entity responsive to the will collapses in the absence of somatic proprioception and can only be partially reestablished with great artificiality and great difficulty. IW and GL are self-conscious in the popular sense precisely because they fail to be self-conscious in a more primitive and fundamental sense.

4.2

What is this more primitive and fundamental form of self-consciousness that we derive from somatic proprioception?

(1) At the simplest level, somatic proprioception is a form of self-consciousness simply in virtue of providing information about the embodied self. This is not particularly interesting, although it is worth noting that proprioception gives information about the embodied self that is *immune to error through misidentification* in the sense discussed earlier. It cannot be the case that one receives proprioceptive information without being aware that the information concerns one's own body.

(2) More importantly, somatic proprioceptive information provides a way of registering the boundary between self and nonself. To appreciate this we need to note that there is an important variation among the information systems that provide information about the body. Some provide information *solely* about the body (e.g., the systems providing information about general fatigue and nutrition). The vestibular system, in contrast, is concerned with bodily balance and hence with the relation between the body and the environment. Other systems can be deployed to yield information either about the body or about the environment. Receptors in the hand sensitive to skin stretch, for example, can provide information about the hand's shape and disposition at a time, or about the shape of small

objects. Similarly, receptors in joints and muscles can yield information about how the relevant limbs are distributed in space, or, through haptic exploration, about the contours and shape of large objects.

These latter information systems, underpinning the sense of touch, yield a direct sense of the limits of the body—and hence of the limits of the self. This is one step further in the development of what might be termed self–world dualism that comes with the self-specifying information in visual perception. The self of visual perception, the ecological self, is schematic and geometrical. Its properties are purely spatial, defined by patterns in the optic flow. It is only in virtue of the sense of touch that the body is experienced as a solid and bounded entity in the world.

(3) The final feature of proprioceptive self-awareness extends this sense of the body as an object. Through feedback from kinesthesia, joint-position sense, and the vestibular system we become aware of the body as an object responsive to the will. Proprioception gives us a sense of the embodied self not just as spatially extended and bounded, but also as a potentiality for action.

In this context it might be helpful to point to the role of proprioceptively derived information in the construction of the cross-modal egocentric space within which action takes place. It is well known that lesions to the posterior parietal cortex produce spatial deficits in primates, human and nonhuman, and the inference frequently drawn is that the posterior parietal cortex is the brain area where the representation of space is computed. Recent neurophysiological work based on recordings from single neurons has suggested that the distinctive contribution of the posterior parietal cortex is the integration of information from various modalities to generate coordinate systems (Andersen 1995). Information about visual stimuli is initially transmitted in retinal coordinates. Calibrating this with information about eye position yields head-centered coordinates and further calibration with proprioceptively derived information yields a body-centered frame of reference. The distal targets of reaching movements are encoded on this modality-free frame of reference, as are motor commands.[9]

At the same time, cognitive science has yielded great insights into the different information systems and channels subserving somatic

9. For further discussion of the relation between bodily self-consciousness and frames of reference, see particularly chapter 8 in this volume.

proprioception, as well as the neural mechanisms supporting representation of the body. Directly relevant to self-consciousness, robust experimental paradigms have emerged for studying the structure of bodily experience, particularly the experience of ownership (what it is to experience one's body as one's own). The first such paradigm was the rubber hand illusion, first demonstrated by Botvinick and Cohen (1998). This was subsequently extended to generate illusions of ownership at the level of the body as a whole (for reviews see Tsakiris 2010, Serino et al. 2013, and Kilteni et al. 2015). This research has operationalized aspects of bodily experience that had previously been explored either from a purely theoretical perspective or as they are distorted in neurological disorders such as unilateral spatial neglect.[10]

5 Points of View

5.1

The nonconceptual first-person contents implicated in somatic proprioception and the pickup of self-specifying information in visual perception provide very primitive forms of nonconceptual self-consciousness, albeit ones that can plausibly be viewed as in place from birth or shortly afterward. A solution to the paradox of self-consciousness, however, requires showing how we can get from these primitive forms of self-consciousness to the full-fledged self-consciousness that comes with linguistic mastery of the first-person pronoun. This progression will have to be both logical (in a way that will solve the problem of explanatory circularity) and ontogenetic (in a way that will solve the problem of capacity circularity). Clearly, this requires that there be forms of self-consciousness that, while still counting as nonconceptual, are nonetheless more developed than those yielded by somatic proprioception and the structure of exteroceptive perception—and, moreover, that it be comprehensible how these more developed forms of nonconceptual self-consciousness should have "emerged" out of basic nonconceptual self-consciousness.

The dimension along which forms of self-consciousness must be compared is the richness of the conception of the self that they provide. Nonetheless, and as we have seen in the case of somatic proprioception, a crucial

10. For further discussion, see particularly chapters 7 and 8 in this volume.

element in any form of self-consciousness is the way it makes it possible for the self-conscious subject to distinguish between self and environment. In this sense self-consciousness is essentially a contrastive notion. One implication of this is that a proper understanding of the richness of the conception of the self which a given form of self-consciousness provides requires taking into account the richness of the conception of the environment with which it is contrasted. In the case both of somatic proprioception and of the pickup of self-specifying information in exteroceptive perception, a relatively impoverished conception of the self is associated with a comparably impoverished conception of the environment. One prominent limitation is that both are synchronic rather than diachronic. The distinction between self and environment that they offer is a distinction that is effective at a time but not over time. The contrast between propriospecific and exterospecific invariants in visual perception, for example, provides a way in which a creature can distinguish between itself and the world at any given moment, but this is not the same as a conception of oneself as an enduring thing distinguishable over time from an environment that also endures over time.

To capture this diachronic form of self–world dualism we can employ the notion of a nonconceptual point of view (Bermúdez 1995b, reprinted as chapter 2 in this volume). Having a nonconceptual point of view on the world involves taking a particular route through the environment in such a way that one's perception of the world is informed by an awareness that one is taking such a route. This diachronic awareness that one is taking a particular route through the environment involves two principal components—a *nonsolipsistic component* and a *spatial awareness component*.

1. The nonsolipsistic component is a subject's capacity to draw a distinction between his experiences and what those experiences are experiences of, and hence his ability to grasp that an object exists at times other than those at which it is experienced. This requires the exercise of recognitional abilities involving conscious memory and can be most primitively manifested in the feature-based recognition of places. This is the beginning of an understanding of the world as an articulated, structured entity.

2. The spatial awareness component of a nonconceptual point of view can be glossed in terms of possession of an integrated representation

of the environment over time—an understanding not just of how the articulated components of the external world fit together spatially, but also of the perceiver's own spatial location in the world as a moving perceiver and agent.

That a creature possesses such an integrated representation of the environment is manifested in three central cognitive/navigational capacities:

• the capacity to think about different routes to the same place;
• The capacity to keep track of changes in spatial relations between objects caused by its own movements relative to those objects; and
• the capacity to think about places independently of the objects or features located at those places.

Powerful evidence from both ethology and developmental psychology indicates that these central cognitive/navigational capacities are present in both nonlinguistic and prelinguistic creatures (Bermúdez 1998, §8.4).

5.2

This conception of a nonconceptual point of view provides a counterbalance to important work on animal representations of space and their neurophysiological coding. Chapters 5 and 6 of Gallistel's *The Organization of Learning* defend the thesis that all animals from insects upward deploy cognitive maps with the same formal characteristics in navigating around the environment. Gallistel argues that the cognitive maps that control movement in animals all preserve the same set of geometric relations within a system of earth-centered (*geocentric)* coordinates. These relations are metric relations. The distinctive feature of a metric geometry is that it preserves all the geometric relations between the points in the coordinate system. Gallistel's thesis is that, although the cognitive maps of lower animals have far fewer places on them, they record the same geometrical relations between those points as humans and other higher animals. Moreover, he offers a uniform account of how such metric cognitive maps are constructed in the animal kingdom. Dead reckoning (the process of keeping track of changes in velocity over time) yields an earth-centered representation of vantage points and angles of view that combines with current perceptual experience of the environment to yield an earth-centered cognitive map.

Without, of course, wishing to challenge Gallistel's central thesis that all animal cognitive maps from insects up preserve geometric relations, it nonetheless seems wrong to draw the conclusion that all animals represent space in the same way. Just as important as how animals represent spatial relations between objects is how they represent their own position within the object-space thus defined. And it is here, in what we should think of as not just their awareness of space but also their awareness of themselves as spatially located entities, that we see the major variations and the scale of gradations that the theorists whom Gallistel is criticizing have previously located at the level of the cognitive map.

6 Psychological Self-Awareness

Possession of a nonconceptual point of view manifests an awareness of the self as a spatial element moving within, acting upon, and being acted upon by the spatial environment. This is far richer than anything available through either somatic proprioception or the self-specifying information available in exteroceptive perception. Nonetheless, like these very primitive forms of self-consciousness, a nonconceptual point of view is largely awareness of the material self as a bearer of physical properties. This limitation raises the question of whether there can be a similarly nonconceptual awareness of the material self as a bearer of psychological properties.

There appear to be three central psychological properties defining the core of the concept of a psychological subject—the property of being a perceiver, the property of being an agent, and the property of being a bearer of reactive attitudes. Research on the social cognition of infants shows that there are compelling grounds for attributing to prelinguistic infants in the final quarter of the first year awareness of themselves as bearers of all three of these properties.

Psychological self-awareness as a perceiver is manifested in the phenomenon of *joint selective visual attention*, where infants (a) attend to objects as a function of where they perceive the attention of others to be directed (Scaife and Bruner 1975; Bruner 1975), and (b) direct another individual's gaze to an object in which they are interested (Leung and Rheingold 1981; Stern 1985). In (b), for example, the infant tries to make the mother recognize that he, as a perceiver, is looking at a particular object, with the eventual aim that her recognition that this is what he is trying to do will cause the mother to look in the same direction.

Psychological self-awareness as an agent is manifested in the collaborative activities that infants engage in with their caregivers (*coordinated joint engagement*). Longitudinal studies (e.g., Trevarthen and Hubley 1978) show infants not just taking pleasure in their own agency (in the way that many infants show pleasure in the simple ability to bring about changes in the world, like moving a mobile), but also taking pleasure in successfully carrying out an intention—a form of pleasure possible only for creatures aware of themselves as agents. When, as it frequently is, the intention successfully carried out is a joint intention, the pleasure shared with the other participants reflects an awareness that they too are agents.

Psychological self-awareness as a bearer of reactive attitudes is apparent in what developmental psychologists call *social referencing* (Klinnert et al. 1983). This occurs when infants regulate their own behavior by investigating and being guided by the emotional reactions of others to a particular situation. The infant's willingness to tailor his own emotional reactions to those of his mother presuppose an awareness that both he and she are bearers of reactive attitudes.

7   Solving the Paradox of Self-Consciousness

The four types of primitive or nonconceptual self-awareness provide the materials for resolving the paradox of self-consciousness. The problem of explanatory circularity can be blunted by giving an account of what it is to have mastery of the first-person pronoun that shows how the relevant first-person thoughts implicated in such mastery can be understood at the nonconceptual level.

Consider the following plausible account of the communicative intent governing intentional self-reference by means of the first-person pronoun.

An utterer **U** utters "I" to refer to himself* iff **U** utters "I" in full comprehension of the token-reflexive rule that tokens of "I" refer to their producer and with the tripartite intention:

(i)   that some audience A should have their attention drawn to him*,
(ii) that A should be aware of his* intention that A's attention should be drawn to him*, and

(iii) that the awareness mentioned in (ii) should be part of the explanation for A's attention being drawn to him*.

Each of the three clauses of the tripartite intention is a first-person thought, in virtue of the presence in each of them of the indirect reflexive pronoun he* (which, following Castañeda [1966] and others, I am using to capture *in oratione obliqua* what would be said using "I" *in oratione recta*). Each of the first-person thoughts (i)–(iii) can be understood at the nonconceptual level.

The first clause in the tripartite intention is that the utterer should utter a token of "I" with the intention that some audience should have their attention drawn to himself*. There are two key components here. The first component is that the utterer should intend to draw another's attention to something. That this is possible at the nonconceptual level is clearly shown by the discussion of joint selective visual attention. The second component is that the utterer should be aware of himself* as a possible object of another's attention. This is largely a matter of physical self-consciousness. The materials here are provided by proprioceptive self-consciousness and the various forms of bodily self-consciousness implicated in possession of a nonconceptual point of view.

Moving on to the second clause, the requirement here is that the utterer of "I" should intend that his audience recognize his* intention to draw their attention to him*. This is a reflexive awareness of the intention in the first clause. The real issue it raises is one about how iterated psychological states can feature in the content of intentions. This occurs whenever there is recognition of another's intention that one should do something. Recognitional states like these play a crucial role in the cooperative games and projects that are so important in infancy after the last quarter of the first year. An important source of infants' pleasure and enjoyment is their recognition that they have successfully performed what their mothers intended them to—and this implicates an embedding of a first-person content within a first-order iteration.

In the third clause the utterer of "I" needs to understand how the satisfaction of the first clause can causally bring about the satisfaction of the second clause. The causal relation of bringing-it-about-that is integral to the notion of a nonconceptual point of view and to the self-awareness that it implicates. Possession of a nonconceptual point of view involves an awareness of the self as acting upon and being acted upon by the spatial environment. Certainly, there is a distinction to be made between physical causation and psychological causation, but both coordinated joint engagement and joint visual attention involve a comprehension that one's intentions can be effective in bringing about changes in the mental states of others.

This resolution of the problem of explanatory circularity also shows how we may resolve the problem of capacity circularity. The solution is similar in general form to the solution to the problem of explanatory circularity. Suppose we read the above specification of the communicative intent governing the correct use of the first-person pronoun as offering conditions on learning the proper use of the token reflexive rule—as opposed to an intention that must be satisfied on any occasion of successful communication. If that suggestion is accepted then the solution to the problem of explanatory circularity gives, first, a clear specification of a set of first-person thoughts that must be grasped by anybody who successfully learns the first-person pronoun and, second, an illustration of how those first-person thoughts are of a kind that can be nonconceptual. Of course, a detailed ontogenetic story needs to be told about how the nonconceptual first-person contents implicated in mastery of the first-person pronoun can emerge from the basis of ecological and bodily self-awareness, but there is no longer a principled reason for thinking that no such story can be forthcoming.

8   Conclusion

Let me return to the methodological reflections with which I began. I sketched out what I take to be a dominant approach to the methodology of cognitive science—the top-down approach that clearly distinguishes the computational, algorithmic and implementational levels of explanation. As I suggested, this approach really seems applicable only where there are clearly defined identifiable, computational tasks, and consequently it is only going to work for "peripheral" rather than "central" cognitive processes. The corollary, as Fodor has clearly seen, is that we can expect little illumination of "central" processes from the cognitive sciences. What I've tried to sketch out is an alternative approach, one where the distinction of levels of explanation does not correspond to a division of explanatory labor. I have explored how attending to a particular philosophical puzzle about self-consciousness, perhaps the paradigm "central" cognitive process, brings out the importance of forms of self-consciousness that look as if they can only be understood by a more interactive collaboration between disciplines whose spheres of competence are so clearly separated on the conventional view. I hope I have done enough to give the sense of a genuine alternative to the mainstream methodology of cognitive science.

Acknowledgments

The original version of this essay was presented at the UNAM Centro de Neurobiología in Querétaro, Mexico; at the Institut des Sciences Cognitives in Lyon; at the International Workshop on Self and Self-Consciousness, organized by the Seminar für Logik und Grundlagenforschung at the University of Bonn; and at the Conference on Consciousness and Art, organized by Erik Myin at the Vrije Universiteit Brussel. I am grateful to audiences on those occasions for valuable comments. Work on the essay, and attendance at those meetings, was made possible by a visiting appointment at CREA, Ecole Polytechnique, Paris, and a European Research Fellowship from the Royal Society of Edinburgh and Caledonian Research Foundation. I am very grateful to my colleagues at Stirling for allowing me to take a year's leave of absence. Many thanks also to Erik Myin for careful and useful comments on previous versions of this essay.

References

Andersen, R. A. 1995. Coordinate transformations and motor planning in posterior parietal cortex. In *The Cognitive Neurosciences*, ed. M. Gazzaniga. Cambridge, MA: MIT Press.

Bermúdez, J. L. 1994. Peacocke's argument against the autonomy of nonconceptual content. *Mind & Language* 9:203–218.

Bermúdez, J. L. 1995a. Syntax, semantics and levels of explanation. *Philosophical Quarterly* 45:361–367.

Bermúdez, J. L. 1995b. The notion of a nonconceptual point of view. In *The Body and the Self*, ed. J. L. Bermúdez, J. Marcel, and N. Eilan. Cambridge, MA: MIT Press.

Bermúdez, J. L. 1995c. Nonconceptual content: From perceptual experience to subpersonal computational states. *Mind & Language* 10:333–369.

Bermúdez, J. L. 1998. *The Paradox of Self-Consciousness*. Cambridge, MA: MIT Press.

Bermúdez, J. L. 2000. A difference without a distinction. In "Personal and Subpersonal Explanation," special issue, *Philosophical Explorations* 2, ed. J. L. Bermúdez and N. Elton.

Bermúdez, J. L. 2003. *Thinking without Words*. Oxford: Oxford University Press.

Bermúdez, J. L. 2007. From two visual systems to two forms of content? *Psyche* 13.

Bermúdez, J. L. 2010. Two arguments for the language-dependence of thought. *Grazer Philosophische Studien* 81:37–54.

Bermúdez, J. L. 2014. *Cognitive Science: An Introduction to the Science of the Mind*. 2nd ed. Cambridge: Cambridge University Press.

Bermúdez, J. L., and M. E. Elton, eds. 2000. Personal and subpersonal explanation. Special issue, *Philosophical Explorations* 2.

Bermúdez, J. L., A. J. Marcel, and N. Eilan, eds. 1995. *The Body and the Self*. Cambridge, MA: MIT Press.

Botvinick, M., and J. Cohen. 1998. Rubber hands "feel" touch that eyes see. *Nature* 391:756.

Briscoe, R. 2009. Egocentric spatial representation in action and perception. *Philosophy and Phenomenological Research* 79:423–460.

Bruner, J. S. 1975. The ontogenesis of speech acts. *Journal of Child Language* 2:1–19.

Butterworth, G. E., and L. Hicks. 1977. Visual proprioception and postural stability in infancy: A developmental study. *Perception* 6:255–262.

Castañeda, H.-N. 1966. "He": A study in the logic of self-consciousness. *Ratio* 8:130–157.

Clark, A. 2001. Visual experience and motor action: Are the bonds too tight? *Philosophical Review* 110:495–519.

Cole, J., and J. Paillard. 1995, Living without touch and peripheral information about body position and movement: Studies with deafferented subjects. In *The Body and the Self*, ed. J. L. Bermúdez, A. J. Marcel, and N. Eilan. Cambridge, MA: MIT Press.

Eilan, N., R. McCarthy, and M. W. Brewer, eds. 1993. *Spatial Representation: Problems in Philosophy and Psychology*. Oxford: Blackwell.

Evans, Gareth. 1982. *The Varieties of Reference*. Oxford: Clarendon Press.

Field, J. 1976. Relation of young infants' reaching behaviour to stimulus distance and solidity. *Developmental Psychology* 12:444–448.

Fodor, J. A. 1983. *The Modularity of Mind*. Cambridge, MA: MIT Press.

Gallistel, C. R. 1990. *The Organization of Learning*. Cambridge, MA: MIT Press.

Gibson, J. J. 1966. *The Senses Considered as Perceptual Systems*. Boston: Houghton Mifflin.

Gibson, J. J. 1979. *The Ecological Approach to Visual Perception*. Boston: Houghton Mifflin.

Goodale, M. A., and A. D. Milner. 1992. Separate visual pathways for perception and action. *Trends in Neurosciences* 15:20–25.

Gopnik, A., and A. Meltzoff. 1997. *Words, Thoughts, and Theories*. Cambridge, MA: MIT Press.

Hurley, Susan. 1998. *Consciousness in Action*. Cambridge, MA: Harvard University Press.

Jacob, P., and M. Jeannerod. 2003. *Ways of Seeing: The Scope and Limits of Visual Cognition*. New York: Oxford University Press.

Jeannerod, M. 1997. *The Cognitive Neuroscience of Action*. Oxford: Blackwell.

Kilteni, K., A. Maselli, K. P. Kording, and M. Slater. 2015. Over my fake body: Body ownership illusions for studying the multisensory basis of own-body perception. *Frontiers in Human Neuroscience* 9:141.

Klinnert, M. D., J. J. Campos, and J. F. Sorce. R, N. Emde, and M. Svejda. 1983. Emotions as behaviour regulators: Social referencing in infancy. In *Emotion: Theory, Research, Experience*, ed. R. Plutchik and H. Kellerman. Boston: Academic Press.

Lee, D. N., and E. Aronson. 1974. Visual proprioceptive control of standing in human infants. *Perception & Psychophysics* 15:529–532.

Leung, E., and H. Rheingold. 1981. Development of pointing as a social gesture. *Developmental Psychology* 17:215–220.

Lishman, J. R., and D. N. Lee. 1973. The autonomy of visual kinaesthetics. *Perception* 2:287–294.

McCarthy, R. A. 1993. Assembling routines and addressing representations: An alternative conceptualization of "what" and "where" in the human brain. In *Spatial Representation: Problems in Philosophy and Psychology*, ed. N. Eilan, R. McCarthy, and M. W. Brewer. Oxford: Blackwell.

Marr, D. 1982. *Vision*. San Francisco: W. H. Freeman.

Martin, G. B., and R. D. Clark. 1982. Distress crying in neonates: Species and peer specificity. *Developmental Psychology* 18:3–9.

Meltzoff, A. N., and M. K. Moore. 1977. Imitation of facial and manual gestures by human neonates. *Science* 198:75–78.

Neisser, U. 1988. Five kinds of self-knowledge. *Philosophical Psychology* 1:35–59.

Neisser, U. 1999. The ecological self and its metaphors. *Philosophical Topics* 26:201–215.

Pope, M. J. 1984. Visual proprioception in infant postural development. PhD thesis, University of Southampton.

Ramachandran, V. S. 1994. Phantom limbs, neglect syndromes, repressed memories, and Freudian psychology. *International Review of Neurobiology* 37:291–333.

Scaife, M., and J. S. Bruner. 1975. The capacity for joint visual attention in the infant. *Nature* 253:265–266.

Serino, A., A. Alsmith, M. Costantini, A. Mandrigin, A. Tajadura-Jimenez, and C. Lopez. 2013. Bodily ownership and self-location: Components of bodily self-consciousness. *Consciousness and Cognition* 22:1239–1252.

Shoemaker, S. 1968. Self-reference and self-awareness. *Journal of Philosophy* 65:555–567.

Stern, D. 1985. *The Interpersonal World of the Infant*. New York: Basic Books.

Trevarthen, C., and P. Hubley. 1978. Secondary intersubjectivity: confidence, confiding and acts of meaning in the first year. In *Action, Gesture, Symbol: The Emergence of Language*, ed. A. Lock. London: Academic Press.

Tsakiris, M. 2010. My body in the brain: A neurocognitive model of body-ownership. *Neuropsychologia* 48:703–712.

Ungerleider, M., and L. Mishkin. 1982. Two cortical visual systems. In *Analysis of Visual Behavior*, ed. D. J. Ingle, M. A. Goodale and R. J. W. Mansfield. Cambridge, MA: MIT Press.

Von Hofsten, C. 1982. Foundations for perceptual development. *Advances in Infancy Research* 2:241–261.

2 Ecological Perception and the Notion of a Nonconceptual Point of View

There are many distinct layers of self-consciousness. Obvious examples are the capacity to think of one's body as one's own; to recognize oneself as the bearer of mental states; to master the grammar of the first-person pronoun; to view oneself an one object in the world among others, or as one person in the world among others; to have memories about one's past self; to construct autobiographical narratives; to formulate long-term plans and ambitions. Whichever one of these one is considering, however, it is tempting to think of it as somehow parasitic on a more primitive and already-existing form of self-awareness. So, for example, it seems intuitively hard to imagine that one could formulate long-term plans without having some sort of autobiographical narrative at one's disposal or, indeed, that one could formulate such an autobiographical narrative without having a stock of memories about one's past self. If this is so, however, and if a regress is to be avoided, then it seems plausible to suppose that all these layers must eventually be grounded in a form of self-awareness primitive enough not to depend on a more basic self-awareness.

One of the attractions of the Gibsonian concept of ecological perception is that it seems to provide us with a basic level of self-awareness that could serve as a core for such comprehensive accounts of the phenomenon (or phenomena) of self-consciousness. On the ecological understanding of perception, a form of sensitivity to self-specifying information is built into the very structure of perception from the earliest stages of infancy in such a way that, as Gibson famously put it, all perception involves coperception of the self and the environment. In this essay I propose to explore the implications of this suggestion. I will argue that by starting with ecological perception and seeing how it needs to be built up, we can reach an understanding of the features that a basic form of self-awareness must incorporate.

1   The Ecological View of Perception

For many psychologists and philosophers the five senses are directed "out-ward"—they are exteroceptive or exterosensitive, designed to inform us about objects and events in the world. They can, of course, be turned on oneself, as, for example, when one looks at oneself through a mirror, but doing this provides a distinct sort of information about oneself, informa-tion that objectifies the body, failing to do justice to the sense in which the subject of perception is also the object of perception. This objectifying form of perceiving oneself is often contrasted with the form of self-perception from within, gained through what has been termed a "body sense." Recep-tors in the skin, muscles, tendons, and joints, operating in conjunction with the vestibular system, yield proprioceptive information about bodily position and movement that is crucial in orienting and acting within the world. This has led to a firm distinction in both operation and function, with the five exteroceptive senses deemed to provide information about the external world, while the proprioceptive system provides information about the self, in particular about bodily posture and movement.

It is instructive to view the Gibsonian theory of ecological perception as challenging precisely such a strict distinction between proprioceptive and exteroceptive senses (see also Neisser 1988, 1991). Gibson claims that the five ostensibly outward-directed senses provide both exteroceptive and pro-prioceptive information, rejecting the traditional division of labor between the five exteroceptive senses and proprioceptive body sense.

A deep theoretical muddle is connected with proprioception. ... In my view, pro-prioception can be understood as egoreception, as sensitivity to the self, not as one special channel of sensations or as several of them. I maintain that all the perceptual systems are propriosensitive as well as exterosensitive, for they all provide infor-mation in their various ways about the observer's activities. ... Information that is specific to the self is picked up as such, no matter what sensory nerve is delivering impulses to the brain. (Gibson 1979, 115)

Although propriospecific and exterospecific information are distinct types of information, they are simultaneously available to each sense, rather than each being the province of a distinct sensory system.

Perhaps the most basic form of propriospecific information arises through the structure imposed upon the visual array by the perceiver's body. As Gibson stresses, every animal has a field of view that is bounded by its body, and the particular way in which each animal's body blocks out aspects of its environment is unique to that animal. "Ask yourself what it is you see hiding the surroundings as you look out upon the world—not darkness, surely, not air, not nothing, but the ego" (Gibson 1979, 112). In this limited but important sense the self is actually present in visual perception, as the frame of the field of view, as what surrounds and gives it structure.

A second type of propriospecific information emerges through what Gibson terms *visual kinesthesis*. This is how he thinks the visual system solves the fundamental challenge created by the subject's movement through the environment. How can the massively changing visual inputs generated by movement be parsed and interpreted so that subjects perceive that it is they themselves who are moving through a broadly stationary environment? How can the visual system separate out and compensate for those changes in visual information that are due to the subject's own movement? Gibson's basic idea is that the visual system solves this problem through sensitivity to patterns in the optical array, and in particular the interplay between flow in the array (specifying movement) and nonflow (specifying rest). Invariant features of the optical array specify, for example, the aiming point of locomotion, which is the stationary point from which the optical flow originates. Relative to those invariants, the optical flow can indicate, for example, the speed with which a goal is being reached—think of the base of a solid angle at an object as an invariant, and the rate at which that angle increases as an indication of speed. This interplay between flow and nonflow can be manipulated, as in the moving-room experiments where subjects are placed on the solid floors of rooms with independently moveable walls (Lishman and Lee 1973; Lee and Aronson 1974). Young children sway and lose their balance as they try to compensate for their own apparent movement, when the walls are moved in the saggital plane.

The third relevant form of self-specifying information available in the environment is encapsulated in the Gibsonian notion of *affordances*: "At any given moment the environment affords a host of possibilities: I could grasp that object, sit on that chair, walk through that door. These are examples of *affordances*: relations of possibility between actors and environments. It is affordances that animals most need to see: here is prey that I might eat, a predator who might possibly eat me, a tree I might climb to escape him" (Neisser 1991, 201). The claim here is that the perception of affordances is relativized to the perceiving subject, so that, for example, in looking at a window one perceives not just an aperture but an aperture that presents the possibility of one's looking through it. The ecological suggestion is that the perception of affordances is partly a mode of self-perception. Furthermore, it is such constitutively. The whole notion of an affordance rests on relating environmental information to one's own possibilities for action and reaction.

2   Ecological Perception and the Notion of Point of View

Ecological self-perception falls a long way short of full-fledged self-consciousness. There is a crucial difference between having information about oneself as part of one's ecological experience and being fully self-conscious, where full-fledged self-consciousness is taken to involve the capacity to entertain "I" thoughts or to maintain some form of detached perspective on oneself. Neither of these two sophisticated capacities is required for ecological self-perception to take place. What the ecological approach might more plausibly be argued to provide is a way of understanding the notion of a point of view on the world. The most developed account of this notion has been offered by Strawson in his discussion of Kant's Transcendental Deduction in *The Bounds of Sense*, where he suggests it as a necessary but not sufficient strand in a complete account of self-consciousness. I will consider his position in some detail because it sets the framework for this essay.

Strawson argues that possession of a point of view rests on the possibility of a subject's experiences being such "as to determine a distinction between the subjective route of his experiences and the objective world through which it is a route" (Strawson 1966, 104). That a subject's experiences contain such a distinction over time is what yields the subject's point of view on the world:

A series of experiences satisfying the Kantian provision has a certain double aspect. On the one hand it cumulatively builds up a picture of the world in which objects and happenings (with their particular characteristics) are presented as possessing an objective order, an order which is logically independent of any particular experiential route through the world. On the other hand it possesses its own order as a series of experiences of objects. If we thought of such a series of experiences as continuously articulated in a series of detailed judgments, then, taking their order and content together, those judgments would be such as to yield, on the one hand, a (potential) description of an objective world and on the other the chart of the course of a single subjective experience of that world. (Strawson 1966, 105–106)

Strawson's conception of a point of view is intended to draw together two distinct (sets of) conceptual capacities: the capacity for the self-ascription of experiences and the capacity to grasp the objectivity of the world. Why do they need to be brought together?

Strawson is considering the question, What conditions have to be fulfilled for experience to be possible? He approaches it through the hypothesis that there might be an experience whose objects were sense data, "red, round patches, brown oblongs, flashes, whistles, tickling sensations, smells" (1966, 99). This would not count as anything recognizable as experience, he maintains, because it would not permit any distinction to be drawn between a subject's experiences and the objects of which they are experiences. In such a case, the *esse* of the putative "objects of experience" would be their *percipi*. There would be no distinction between the order of experiences and the order of the objects of experience, and this, according to Strawson, effectively means that we cannot talk either about objects of experience or about a subject of experience, and hence we cannot talk about experience at all.

The general idea is that no creature can count as a subject of experience unless it is capable of drawing certain very basic distinctions. What is important about a point of view, as Strawson conceives it, is that experience that reflects a temporally extended point of view on the world will ipso facto permit those basic distinctions to be drawn, and this is so because experience reflecting a point of view has the double aspect outlined in the passage quoted earlier. Experience reflecting a point of view just is experience that permits the right sort of distinctions to be drawn between a subject's experiences and the objects of which they are experiences.

Suppose we grant that such a purely sense-datum "experience" is impossible. And suppose we also grant that experience with the sort of double aspect that he describes qualifies as genuine experience by making available the sorts of distinctions that could not be drawn in a purely sense-datum experience. This still leaves open an important question. Are the capacity to ascribe experiences to oneself and the capacity to grasp the objectivity of the world necessary conditions of any possible experience that has the dual structure impossible in a putative sense-datum experience?

One reason for thinking that these conceptual capacities might not be necessary conditions is provided by research on object representation in infancy. Much recent work in developmental psychology strongly suggests that very young infants are capable of primitive forms of object representation which involve, for example, the capacity to perceive object unity and to employ certain basic principles of physical reasoning, such as the principle that objects move on single connected paths (Spelke 1990; Spelke and Van de Walle 1993). Such a level of object representation does not demand a conceptual grasp of causality or of the connectedness of space, and hence does not involve possessing the sort of comprehension of the objectivity of the world built into Strawson's notion of a point of view. Nor, of course, does it involve having a theoretical grip on objects and the principles of naive physics.

It would be rash to suggest that these experiments alone provide evidence that the infants have anything like a point of view, but they at least suggest the need to formulate the basic distinction at the heart of the notion of a point of view in such a way that it does not come out as a matter of definition that the infants cannot have experience that reflects a point of view. Just as there are ways of representing objects that do not require mastery of the relevant concepts, might there not be ways in which a creature's experience could incorporate the basic distinction at the heart of the notion of a point of view without a conceptual grasp of the distinction? In this essay I would like to suggest that there are indeed such ways. Before going any further, however, I need a way of understanding that basic distinction that at least leaves this possibility open.

If we formulate the central distinction as one between subjective experience and what that subjective experience is experience of, we capture what seems to be the crucial feature missing in the hypothesized purely sense-datum experience, without immediately demanding any relevant conceptual capacities on the part of the subject. Using this as the central notion, we can reformulate the original characterization: having a temporally extended point of view on the world involves taking a particular route through space-time in such a way that one's perception of the world is informed by an awareness that one is taking such a route, where such an awareness requires being able to distinguish over time between subjective experience and what it is experience of.

The matter can be further clarified by adverting to the concept of a *non-solipsistic consciousness*, which Strawson introduces in *Individuals*. There he refers to "the consciousness of a being who has a use for the distinction between himself and his states on the one hand, and something not himself or a state of himself, of which he has experience, on the other" (1959, 69). We can see the notion of a point of view as fleshing out what experience must be like for any creature that is to count as nonsolipsistic in this sense. Putting it like this brings out why one might expect the notion of a point of view to play a foundational role in a comprehensive account of self-consciousness. The thought would be that being a nonsolipsistic consciousness is the most basic form of self-awareness, and since the notion of a point of view is put forward to capture what experience must be like to support such a nonsolipsistic consciousness, it would seem that here, if anywhere, we have the sort of primitive form of self-awareness that would anchor an account of self-consciousness as a whole.

Because this new formulation is trying to sidestep any demand for sophisticated concept mastery, we can term it the *nonconceptual point of view*. The notion of the nonconceptual at work here can be elucidated with reference to current work on representational content. It has been suggested by various writers on the philosophy of content that it is theoretically legitimate to refer to mental states that represent the world but do not require the bearer of those mental states to possess the concepts required to give a correct specification of the way in which they represent the world (Cussins 1990; Peacocke 1992). The most plausible candidates for such states are perceptual states and subpersonal computational states. For present purposes, only the former is relevant. The notion of nonconceptual content as applied to perceptual states is a reaction to the idea dominating much philosophy of perception that all perceptual experience is structured by the concepts possessed by the perceiver. Now, as formulated, the notion of nonconceptual content is neutral on the question of whether the bearer of the appropriate states possesses any concepts at all, because it is nonconceptual in virtue of the fact that the bearer is not required to possess the concepts involved in specifying it. So a point of view will be nonconceptual just in case a creature can be ascribed such a point of view without it being ipso facto necessary to ascribe to it mastery of the concepts required to specify the way in which its experience reflects a point of view. Nonetheless, it is important to distinguish between a conception of *autonomous* nonconceptual content, which does not require that a creature to which it is attributed possess any concepts at all, and a conception of nonconceptual content, which denies that a creature possessing no concepts at all can be in contentful states (Peacocke 1992, 90; Bermúdez 1994). I am interested in the former.

Of course, the possibility of formulating the notion of a point of view so that no relevant conceptual requirements are built into it does not mean that it is possible to have a point of view in the absence of those concepts. It is not ruled out by definition any longer, but there might be other reasons to rule it out. Nonetheless, on this weaker formulation of the notion of a nonconceptual point of view, it seems promising to elucidate it through the idea of ecological self-perception. No special argument is needed to show that it is possible to have a nonconceptual point of view, it might be suggested, because such a nonconceptual point of view is built into the very structure of perception. The propriospecific information involved in all exteroception seems to be information about the spatiotemporal route that one is taking through the world, as is particularly apparent in visual kinesthesis. One has, it might seem, a continuous awareness of oneself taking a particular route through the world that does not require the exercise of any conceptual abilities, in virtue of having a constant flow of information about oneself qua physical object moving through the world. On this view, ecological coperception of self and environment is all that is needed for experience with a nonconceptual point of view.

Before evaluating this possibility, it is worth being more explicit about why a point of view has been described as temporally extended. The reason is that a creature whose experience takes place completely within a continuous present (i.e., who lacks any sense of past or future) will not be capable of drawing the fundamental nonsolipsistic distinction between its experience and what it is experience of. We can bring this out by reflecting that being able to make this distinction rests on an awareness that what is being experienced exists independently of any particular experience of it. Such a grasp of independent existence itself involves an understanding that what is being experienced at the moment either has existed in the past, or will exist in the future, that what is being experienced at the present moment has an existence transcending the present moment. By definition, however, a creature that experiences only a continuous present cannot have any such understanding.

The important question, therefore, seems to be, What form must experience take if it is to incorporate an awareness that what is being experienced does not exist only when it is being experienced? Alternatively put, what must the temporal form of any such experience be? Clearly, such an awareness would be incorporated in the experience of any creature that had a grasp of the basic temporal concepts of past, present, and future, but we are looking for something at a more primitive level. What I would suggest is that certain basic recognitional capacities offer the right sort of escape from the continuous present without demanding conceptual mastery. Consider the act of recognizing a particular object. Because such an act involves drawing a connection between one's current experience of an object and a previous experience of it, it brings with it an awareness that what is being experienced has an existence transcending the present moment.

But it is important to specify what it is that the recognitional capacities are being exercised on. A creature could recognize an experience as one that it has previously experienced without any grasp of the distinction between experience and what it is experience of. Clearly, the recognitional capacities must be exercised on something extraneous to the experiences themselves. But what? Physical objects are an obvious candidate, and any creature that could recognize physical objects would have experience that involved drawing the right sort of distinctions. However, one might wonder whether the distinctions could be drawn at a level of experience that does not involve objects. The answer one gives here depends on one's ontological position on the issue of whether there are "things" that can be reidentified and recognized but are not physical objects. Many philosophers would deny this (including Strawson 1959, chap. 1). The debate is too tortuous to go into here, and I merely state my position without attempting to defend it. There are indeed "things" that can be reidentified and recognized and are neither physical objects nor require experience of physical objects for their recognition. These "things" are places, which can be recognized in terms of distinctive features holding at those places even by a creature that has no grasp on the notion of a physical object (Campbell 1993).

If this is right, we seem in a position to argue that any creature being ascribed a point of view must be capable of exercising the basic capacity to recognize places. If a creature can recognize a particular place, we have a nonsolipsistic consciousness, because we have an object of experience that is grasped as existing independently of a particular experience of it. By the same token, in the absence of such a recognitional capacity (and assuming that there is no grasp of basic temporal concepts nor a capacity to recognize physical objects), it does not seem appropriate to speak of a point of view in the sense under discussion. This yields a strong sense in which a point of view is temporally extended. It is temporally extended not just in that it must extend over time but also in that it must involve the use of memory and recognition to register the passing of time.

It is useful at this point to make a distinction between two types of memory. There are, on the one hand, instances of memory in which past experiences influence present experience, but without any sense on the part of the subject of having had the relevant past experiences, and, on the other, instances in which past experiences not only influence present experience but also the subject is in some sense aware of having had those past experiences. In the former case what licenses talk of memory is the fact that a subject (or an animal, or even a plant) can respond differentially to a stimulus as a function of prior exposure to that stimulus or to similar stimuli. This is not to deny that such memory can be extremely complex. Quite the contrary, such memory seems to be central to the acquisition of any skill, even the most developed. The differential response does not have to be simple or repetitive. Nonetheless, we can draw a contrast between memory at this level and the various forms of memory that do involve an awareness of having had the relevant past experiences, as, for example, when a memory image comes into one's mind or one successfully recalls what one did the previous day. Clearly, there are many levels of such memory (which I shall term "conscious memory"), of which autobiographical memory is probably the most sophisticated. One thing that these forms of conscious memory all have in common, however, is that previous experience is consciously registered, rather than unconsciously influencing present experience. The distinction is a crude one, precisely because the term "conscious memory" is so hazy, but it will be sharpened up below.

It follows from our discussion of the notion of a point of view that the place recognition it requires must involve some conscious registration of having been there. Reflect on the case of a creature, perhaps a swallow, that is perfectly capable of performing complicated feats of navigation that involve finding its way back to its nest or back to the warmer climes where it spends the winter but nonetheless does not in any sense consciously recognize the places that it repeatedly encounters. This is not a case, I think, in which one would want to claim that the creature has the appropriate awareness of the route that it is taking through space-time, although it is sensitive to certain facts about that route, because those facts clearly determine behavior (facts, for example, about how to get from one place to another and then back to where it started from). Yet if the creature is credited with exactly the same behavior, only this time accompanied by some form of conscious recognition of the relevant places, the situation seems fundamentally different. Insofar as it recognizes a place, it is aware of having been there before, and insofar as it recognizes having been at a place before, it has the beginning of an awareness of movement through space over time. It is emerging from a continuous present and moving toward possession of a temporally extended point of view.

This enables us to evaluate the suggestion that an ecological analysis of perception shows that a temporally extended point of view is built into the structure of perception. Does ecological self-perception involve anything like conscious memory? If it does, then we will be in a stronger position to claim that the two notions are very intimately connected (although, as stressed above, conscious place recognition is a necessary rather than sufficient condition of possessing a temporally extended point of view).

On the ecological view, perception is fundamentally a process of extracting and abstracting invariants from the flowing optical array. Organisms perceive an environment that has both persisting surfaces and changing surfaces, and the interplay between them allows the organism to pick up the sort of information that specifies, for example, visual kinesthesis. The key to how that information is picked up is the idea of direct perception. The mistake made by existing theories of perception, according to Gibson, is construing the process of perception in terms of a hierarchical processing of sensory inputs, with various cognitive processes employed to organize and categorize sensations. A crucial element of this serial processing is bringing memories to bear on present experience. Gibson rejects this. Accepting that present experience is partly a function of past experience, he firmly denies that this sensitivity to past experience is generated by processing memories and sensations together. His alternative account rests on the idea that the senses, as perceptual systems, become more sensitive over time to particular forms of information as a function of prior exposure. Although Gibson was rather polemical about what he termed "the muddle of memory," it would seem that his account involves the first notion of memory discussed above, namely a differential response to stimuli as a function of past experience. Gibson's position seems to be that conscious recognition is not implicated in ecological perception, although it might or might not develop out of such ecological perception. It is perfectly possible for a creature to have experience at the ecological level without any conscious recognitional capacities at all. If, then, the exercise of a capacity for conscious place recognition is a necessary condition of having experience that involves a temporally extended point of view, it seems that the dual structure of experience involved in the ecological coperception of self and environment must be significantly enriched before yielding a point of view.

Of course, this does not mean that we should abandon the basic idea of ecological perception; rather, it means that the materials offered by Gibson's own account need to be supplemented if they are to be employed in the theoretical project under discussion, and it is perfectly possible that Gibson's concepts of information pickup and direct resonance to information in the ambient environment will have a crucial role to play in such an extension of the basic way in which ecological perception is sensitive to past experience (as they are, for example, in the account of perception and memory developed in Neisser 1976). The point is that, as it stands, the Gibsonian account cannot do all the work it was earlier suggested it might be able to do. The suggestion was that the Gibsonian account of ecological perception could show how something like a nonconceptual point of view is reflected in the very structure of perception. It now seems, however, that this will not be achieved until the appropriate capacity for conscious place recognition is added to the ecological coperception of self and environment. In the next section I will further discuss the constraints that this imposes upon the notion of a point of view.

3   Awareness of Action and Points of View

The discussion in the previous section stressed the importance of place recognition in yielding a sense of objects of experience existing independently of their being experienced. But surely, it might be argued, place recognition involves more than this. A creature recognizing a particular place is aware not only that that place has existed in the past but also that it itself has been there before. How, it might be asked, could it have the former without the latter, since the capacity for place recognition seems to rely on both a sense of the transtemporal identity of places and a sense of the transtemporal identity of the self.

This intuition has been emphatically endorsed by Christopher Peacocke, who makes the stronger claim that any genuine attribution to a creature of a capacity for place recognition (which he terms place reidentification) entails that the creature have mastery of the first-person concept. I have taken the liberty of schematizing the rather condensed discussion within which this claim emerges (1992, 90–92):

1. The attribution of genuine spatial representational content to a creature is justified only if that creature is capable of identifying places over time.
2. Identifying places over time involves reidentifying places.
3. Reidentifying places requires the capacity to identify one's current location with a location previously encountered.
4. Reidentifying places in this way involves building up an integrated representation of the environment over time.
5. Neither (3) nor (4) would be possible unless the subject possessed at least a primitive form of the first-person concept.

Peacocke's reason for maintaining (3) and (4) is that the existence of navigational abilities—however sophisticated, systematic, or structured—is not sufficient to compel the ascription of states with genuine spatial content. Simply being able to find one's way from one place to another is not enough. What is needed is some form of grasp of having been there before, and Peacocke places a strong requirement on any such grasp. The possibility of reidentifying places, he argues, requires the capacity to entertain thoughts or protothoughts of the form "I have been to this place before," and such thoughts could not be entertained by a creature lacking the first-person concept. The capacity for such thoughts goes hand in hand, for Peacocke, with the capacity to engage in spatial reasoning, where this "requires the subject to be able to integrate the representational contents of his successive perceptions into an integrated representation of the world around him, both near and far, past and present" (1992, 91). The thought seems to be that reidentifying places in the appropriate manner involves representing those places as existing unperceived within a spatial framework also constructed so that it is independent of any particular perception. The construction of this spatial framework implicates a rudimentary form of first-person thought, because it involves the subject's not only representing its own location within the framework but also grasping that the location can change over time. It involves "the subject's appreciating that the scene currently presented in his perception is something to which his own spatial relations can vary over time" (1992, 90).

This poses a serious threat to my argument. My account of what it is to possess a temporally extended point of view on the world has, as a necessary condition, the capacity for conscious place recognition. If Peacocke's argument is sound, then any creature possessing this capacity will possess a primitive form of the first-person concept, and this creates serious difficulties for the suggestion that an account of the notion of a point of view can be given at the nonconceptual level. Evidently, if experience reflecting a point of view involves possessing a form of the first-person concept, albeit a primitive one, then it cannot count as a form of autonomous nonconceptual content in the sense discussed earlier, because any creature with such experience will have to possess at least some concepts. But a stronger conclusion also follows: that such experience cannot be a form of nonconceptual content at all. This is so because the key distinction that the notion of a point of view is intended to capture is that between subjective experience and what it is experience of, and the concept of the first person will be involved in specifying how this distinction is manifest within the experience of any particular creature. Indeed, precisely this constraint characterizes the notion of a point of view: that it can be specified only in the first person.

One way of resisting this conclusion would be to deny the strong conditions that Peacocke places on the capacity for place reidentification. In particular, one might query the suggestion that place reidentification is only available to creatures who have the capacity to construct suitably integrated representations of their environment and to engage in spatial reasoning in a way that necessarily involves grasp of the first-person pronoun. This could be done, for example, by appealing to the notion of causally indexical comprehension developed by John Campbell (1993). Grasping a causally indexical notion is just grasping its implications for one's own actions. Examples of such causally indexical notions are that something is too heavy for me to lift, or that something else is within reach. As he points out, grasp of causally indexical notions may be linked with a reflective understanding of one's own capacities and of the relevant properties of the object. But, on the other hand, it need not be so linked: it makes sense to ascribe to creatures a grasp of such causally indexical notions without ascribing to them any grasp of notions that are not causally indexical (even though those non-causally indexical notions might be essential to characterize the causally indexical notions) because the significance of such notions is exhausted by their implications for perception and action. And as such, causally indexical mental states qualify as states with nonconceptual content.

In this context, then, one might attempt to defend the idea of a non-conceptual point of view by suggesting that the spatial abilities involved are causally indexical. Such an objection would maintain that we need not place the theoretical weight that Peacocke does on disengaged reflective and reasoning abilities. Rather, we should be looking at the way in which a creature interacts with its surroundings, because this will be how it manifests its grasp of the spatial properties of its environment (of the connectedness of places, for example). On such a view, a creature could possess an integrated representation of its environment in the absence of any capacity to reflect upon its interactions with its environment. If this line is pursued, then it seems to provide a way in which we can retain the idea of place reidentification without accepting Peacocke's claim that it implicates possession of a primitive form of the first-person concept—precisely because it denies Peacocke's central claim, that any creature capable of place reidentification must be capable of explicitly representing itself and its location in its surroundings.

The trouble with this suggestion, however, is that there is a strong tension between the idea of causally indexical content and my earlier insistence on the importance of conscious recognitional abilities. The idea of an awareness that is exhausted in its implications for perception and action does not mesh well with the account I have been developing of the essential features of experience reflecting a point of view. On the causally indexical conception of place reidentification, we ascribe to a creature a grasp of the spatial properties of its environment because its behavior is suitably complex and the relevant connections between perception and action seem to hold. It would seem, however, that appropriately complex behavior could exist at the primitive level of nonconscious memory and skill acquisition. On the causal indexicality account, the ability to track places and perform complicated feats of navigation of the sort regularly carried out by homing pigeons and migrating swallows would be good grounds for ascribing the relevant grasp of the spatial properties of the environment, but it does not implicate the sort of recognitional sense of the transtemporal identity of places that has been argued to be a crucial element in the notion of a point of view.

There seems, then, to be the following challenge for the idea of a non-conceptual point of view as developed in the first part of this essay. To keep the connection with conscious experience of the transtemporal identity of places that, I have argued, is required to distinguish a genuine point of view from the sort of capacity to distinguish proprioceptive and exteroceptive invariants evidenced in ecological perception, we need to reject the causally indexical account of place reidentification. In doing this we move toward understanding the representation of places in a way that is explicit and (relatively) disengaged, rather than exhausted in its implications for action. The question is whether this can be done without moving the notion of a point of view out of the realm of nonconceptual content altogether, as Peacocke does.

It would seem that the only way out here would be to resist Peacocke's suggestion that a primitive form of the first-person concept is involved in the type of spatial reasoning involved in place reidentification and recognition. Could there not be a way of representing the self that does not count as fully conceptual but nonetheless enables the subject to engage in basic reasoning about places? Toward the end of this essay I will suggest that this is indeed a possible direction. Before doing so, however, it is important to make clear that there are theoretical reasons driving such a move that are independent of the attractiveness of the notion of a nonconceptual point of view.

An initial worry that one might have with implicating the first-person concept in spatial reasoning is that doing so seems to link spatial reasoning with unwarrantedly sophisticated conceptual abilities. Matters can be focused here by asking whether a creature's mastery of the first-person concept involves the capacity to ascribe to itself psychological predicates. If mastery of the first-person concept does involve such a capacity, then one seems committed to the idea that spatial reasoning is available only to creatures capable of conceiving of other subjects of thought and experience, for the following reason. Suppose we take the ability to generalize as the mark of a genuine concept user, in the way suggested by Gareth Evans's

Generality Constraint, so that it is a condition on a creature's being credited with the thought a is F, and hence of possessing the concepts of a and F, that it be capable of thinking a is G for any property G of which it has a conception, and of thinking b is F for any object b of which it has a conception (Evans 1982, 100–105). Now if a creature's conceptual repertoire contains psychological predicates, it will have to be capable of generalizing them in the appropriate manner, and for obvious reasons, such generalization can take place only over other psychological subjects. So, on the assumption that mastery of the first-person concept requires the capacity to generalize psychological predicates, spatial reasoning is available only to subjects who have a relatively sophisticated grasp of folk psychology.

Nobody (I think) would want to maintain this. So a position like Peacocke's clearly requires a form of the first-person concept that does not implicate the capacity for the self-ascription of psychological predicates, and indeed, he stresses that it is supposed to be primitive. We could think of it as involving only the capacity to apply certain very basic temporal, spatial, and relational predicates, and hence as requiring only a very limited conceptual repertoire. Certainly, this would completely avoid the difficulty raised in the previous paragraph. One might, however, have doubts about such a proposal. One very general worry here would concern the ontogeny of self-consciousness. The proposed primitive form of the first-person concept is clearly intended to be ontogenetically primitive. That is, it will be the key to understanding an early, if not the earliest, form of self-conscious thought. But in employing such a concept, a creature would be thinking of itself only as a subject of spatial, relational, and temporal properties. It would be thinking of itself just as a physical object. The ontogenetic story to be told here would then be one in which the higher forms of self-consciousness emerge from such a restricted but nonetheless detached mode of presentation of the self. And the worry that one might have would be that this gets the ontogenetic order the wrong way round: the capacity to think of oneself as a physical object (thought in which one features as one object among others) does not emerge until relatively late in the developmental process.

A satisfactory development of this line of argument awaits a satisfactory account of the ontogenesis of self-conscious thought. But someone tempted by it might find additional support in reflecting on Gareth Evans's account of how first-person thought meets the Generality Constraint. According to Evans, the Generality Constraint can only be properly met (and hence one can only speak of genuine mastery of the first-person concept) when the subject is capable of conceiving of himself in an impersonal manner as an element of the objective order (1982, chap. 7, particularly 208–210). Clearly, this involves an even more detached perspective on the self than that discussed in the previous paragraph, and one may well baulk at making this a condition on the capacity for genuine place reidentification. Of course, a defender of Peacocke's position does not have to accept Evans's account of how the Generality Constraint is met for first-person thought, but if he does not accept it, it is incumbent on him either to give an alternative account or to explain why it is not applicable at the putatively primitive level under discussion.

What this brings out, I think, is a significant tension in Peacocke's suggestion that a primitive form of the first-person concept is involved in basic spatial reasoning. It seems inappropriate to claim that the constraints and conditions operative in the case of full-fledged first-person thought are operative in this primitive case. But on the other hand, there is a danger of stripping away so many of the trappings of full-fledged first-person thought that it is no longer clear what the force is of claiming that we are dealing with a form of the first-person concept at all. The bottom line of Peacocke's position seems to be that the self has to be explicitly represented for genuine spatial reasoning to take place. It is, to my mind at least, a moot point whether this forces us to conclude that a conceptual grasp of the self has to be present. And certainly the matter will remain undecided until we have a clearer account of spatial reasoning. In the remainder of this essay I would like to make some preliminary moves toward the suggestion that the self can be explicitly grasped in a manner that is not conceptual.

As a first step in this direction, we need suitable criteria for determining, first, whether something is being explicitly represented and, second, whether such an explicit representation is conceptual. A preliminary suggestion on the first issue would be that a creature can only be described as explicitly representing something when, in explaining that creature's behavior, we need to go beyond stimulus–response (S–R) psychology. The sort of explicit representation relevant here comes into play when S–R explanations cease to be applicable. Of course, appeal to mental representations is crucial to S–R psychology (see, e.g., the discussion of the associative-cybernetic model in Dickinson and Balleine 1993), but the type of mental representations I am interested in are those that feature in (proto)intentional accounts of behavior. Clearly, this is not a sufficient condition, but it at least gives us something to work with (cf. Peacocke 1983, chap. 3). On the second issue, that of what qualifies a mental representation as conceptual, I propose that we stick to some form of the Generality Constraint, as discussed earlier. On this criterion, a representation counts as conceptual if it can be combined with any other representations the subject possesses.

Prima facie, it seems that the first of these criteria could be satisfied without the second being satisfied, that is, that we might need to appeal to an explicit representation in a protointentional account of behavior, even though that representation does not support the appropriate form of generalization. If this were the case for the first person, then we would have an explicit but nonconceptual grasp of the self. In the remainder of this essay I would like to discuss a set of experiments carried out by Watson and Ramey (1987) on 3-month-old infants that seem to offer an example of just such a way of grasping the self.

The experiments examine the responses of young infants only 3-months-old to the movements of a mobile suspended above their cribs. The mobile could move in two different ways. In the first, a control situation, it could be rotated electrically by the experimenter (in this case the infant's mother). In the second, the experimental situation, it was set up with a pillow sensitive to pressure in such a way that it would move when the infant moved its head. For a further control group, the mobile was set up not to move at all. The experimental apparatus was set up in the homes of the 48 infants involved, and the infants were exposed to it for 10 minutes a day over 14 consecutive days. The number of pillow activations in each 10-minute period were counted to see if it increased over the 14 days of exposure. Significant increase was found in the experimental group but not in either of the control groups.

The most common way of explaining these experiments is as a form of instrumental conditioning. All that is shown is the gradual development of S–R links between head movements and the movements of the display, so that whenever the infant sees the display, it moves its head. The S–R links develop because the infants enjoy watching the display move. Such an explanation of their behavior need not appeal to any explicit mental representations at all. In this respect the explanation suggests that the experimental behavior is to be explained at the same level as the ecological behavior discussed in the previous section. I do not want to claim that this interpretation is incorrect. What I would like to do, though, is give one reason for thinking that it might not tell the whole story and, on the basis of this, sketch out an alternative interpretation. This alternative interpretation involves attributing to the experimental infants an explicit representation of the self that is nonetheless not conceptual.

The mothers of the experimental infants almost universally reported that their children took great interest and pleasure in the movement of the display. They smiled, cooed, and laughed a lot, fixating intensely on the mobile, with this behavior developing after only a few days' exposure to the apparatus. In contrast, those infants in the first control group, for whom the mobile moved according to a regular pattern, rather than in response to the infants' own movements, showed considerably less interest in the mobile. If, as the S–R account suggests, what drives the reinforcement process is the pleasure taken in watching the mobile move, then it fails to account for the discrepancy between the degrees of pleasure shown by the experimental infants and the first set of control infants. Its prediction would presumably be that both sets of infants should display substantially similar behavior, because they both watch the mobile move and watching the mobile move is an interesting and pleasurable experience—just as for rats, eating food pellets is an interesting and pleasurable experience even when the food pellets arrive without the rat having had to press any levers. But this, of course, is not what happens. The experimental infants are far more interested and amused than the control infants. Why? It is very tempting to suggest that what they take pleasure in is the fact that they have made the mobile move. The source of their pleasure is a power to affect the world that they are discovering in themselves, a capacity to bring about changes in the world. They repeat the action both to confirm the discovery and for the sheer pleasure of it.

By claiming that the infants are taking pleasure in their own agency I am, ipso facto, claiming that they are aware of what they are doing, and therefore aware that they are acting on things that are distinct from them. It seems to follow that they appreciate in a conscious manner the distinction between their own intentions or acts of will and the movements of objects in the world. And this seems to involve an explicit representation of the self. If this line of interpretation is accepted, the first criterion is satisfied. But what about the second? Does this implicate a grasp of self that satisfies the Generality Constraint?

One reason for thinking that it might do would be the thought that the infants' grasp of their causal agency could be generalized via a grasp of the causal properties of other objects, the idea being that what they are discerning in their own case is a special case of ordinary causal interactions in the world. But even if the infants were capable of grasping causal relations between physical objects, this would still not count as an appropriate generalization of their own agency, for two reasons. The first is that the infant's power to affect the world is importantly different from the causal impact of one physical object on another. We talk about agency in the one case and not in the other precisely because the first case has an intentional dimension lacking in the other. So we do not have a generalization of the predicate. The second reason is that we do not have a generalization of the subject either, because the appropriate generalization would have to be one across psychological subjects rather than across physical objects. The Generality Constraint would be satisfied here only if the infants were capable both of generalizing the special sense of agency involved and (relatedly) of grasping the existence of other agents. And it is surely implausible to attribute such sophisticated cognitive abilities to infants at this stage of development.

Now the interpretation I have offered of the infants' behavior may well be resisted, but it will not be resisted because it is in principle impossible. The S–R interpretation could perhaps deal with the apparently recalcitrant features of the behavior, but this would not affect my main point, which is that the coherence (and indeed plausibility) of the interpretation I have put forward suggests that there might be a way of representing the self that is explicit but not conceptual. And if this point is accepted, we have taken the first step to meeting the challenge discussed earlier in this section: the challenge of explaining how the self might be represented in spatial reasoning without it being necessary to ascribe to the subject a grasp of the first-person concept.

Of course, it is one thing to show that the self can be represented in a manner that is explicit but nonconceptual and quite another to show how such a representation can feature in spatial reasoning so as to support the sort of protothoughts that, if Peacocke's argument is accepted, are implicated in conscious place recognition. The second of these tasks has clearly not been done. Considerable work is required here but, by way of conclusion, I offer some brief remarks on the sort of role that this explicit but nonconceptual representation of the self could play in spatial reasoning.

Remember that on Peacocke's account a crucial element of spatial reasoning is "the subject's appreciating that the scene currently presented in his perception is something to which his own spatial relations can vary over time" (1992, 90). This is one of the vital respects in which first-person thought enters the picture. There are various ways in which one can flesh this idea out, depending on how one construes the subject's grasp that he can enter into varying spatial relations to a particular scene. One plausible idea, though, would be that fully grasping this is conditional on realizing that one can intentionally act in a perceptually presented scene—by realizing, for example, that if one decides to return to it from here, one can do so by passing through these intermediate places, or that if there is something there that one wants, one should take this route to obtain it. In this sense, appreciating that the scene currently presented in perception is something to which one's spatial relations can vary over time depends on appreciating how these varying spatial relations afford different possibilities for action. Of course, there is a crucial difference between being able to react in varying ways to one's environment and grasping that there are different possibilities for action open to one. The latter is what I am stressing here, and what is interesting about it is that it seems to implicate the subject's representing himself as an agent. What the subject grasps, on this account, is the close connection between his own intentions and the spatial configuration of the environment. Here, I would tentatively suggest, is where we will find the connection between the primitive nonconceptual mode of representing the self as an agent and the first-person component in spatial reasoning.

4 Conclusion

If this is right, we are considerably closer to an understanding of the notion of a nonconceptual point of view, originally put forward as a way of capturing the minimal requirement on self-conscious thought that it support the right sort of distinction between experience and what it is experience of. We started with the basic coperception of self and environment described in Gibson's ecological account of the structure of perception and built it up by arguing that creatures to which it is legitimate to ascribe a point of view should be capable of conscious place recognition and of representing themselves in an explicit manner. In the final section, following Peacocke, I discussed the connection between these two demands and suggested, *pace* Peacocke, that they could both be accepted without it being necessary to move beyond the nonconceptual level.

Acknowledgments

I have been greatly helped by comments from Bill Brewer, Naomi Eilan, Anthony Marcel, and an anonymous referee.

References

Bermúdez, José Luis. 1994. Peacocke's argument against the autonomy of nonconceptual representational content. *Mind & Language* 9:402–418.

Campbell, J. 1993. The role of physical objects in spatial thinking. In *Spatial Representation: Problems in Philosophy and Psychology*, ed. N. Eilan, R. A. McCarthy, and M. W. Brewer. Oxford: Blackwell.

Cussins, Adrian. 1990. The connectionist construction of concepts. In *The Philosophy of Artificial Intelligence*, ed. Margaret A. Boden. Oxford: Oxford University Press.

Dickinson, Anthony, and Bernard Balleine. 1993. Actions and responses: The dual psychology of behaviour. In *Spatial Representation: Problems in Philosophy and Psychology*, ed. N. Eilan, R. A. McCarthy, and M. W. Brewer. Oxford: Blackwell.

Evans, Gareth. 1982. *The Varieties of Reference*. Oxford: Oxford University Press.

Gibson, J. J. 1979. *The Ecological Approach to Visual Perception*. Boston: Houghton Mifflin.

Lee, D. N., and E. Aronson. 1974. Visual proprioceptive control of standing in human infants. *Perception & Psychophysics* 15:529–532.

Lishman, J. R., and D. N. Lee. 1973. The autonomy of visual kinaesthetics. *Perception* 2:287–294.

Neisser, Ulric. 1976. *Cognition and Reality*. New York: W. H. Freeman.

Neisser, Ulric. 1988. Five kinds of self-knowledge. *Philosophical Psychology* 1:35–59.

Neisser, Ulric. 1991. Two perceptually given aspects of the self and their development. *Developmental Review* 11:197–209.

Peacocke, Christopher. 1983. *Sense and Content*. Oxford: Oxford University Press.

Peacocke, Christopher. 1992. *A Study of Concepts*. Cambridge, MA: MIT Press.

Spelke, E. S. 1990. Principles of object perception. *Cognitive Science* 14:29–56.

Spelke, E. S., and G. Van de Walle. 1993. Perceiving and reasoning about objects: Insights from infants. In *Spatial Representation: Problems in Philosophy and Psychology*, ed. N. Eilan, R. A. McCarthy, and M. W. Brewer. Oxford: Blackwell.

Strawson, P. E. 1959. *Individuals*. London: Methuen.

Strawson, P. E. 1966. *The Bounds of Sense*. London: Methuen.

Watson, John S., and Craig T. Ramey. 1987. Reactions to response-contingent stimulation in early infancy. In *Cognitive Development in Infancy*, ed. J. Oates and S. Sheldon. Hillsdale, NJ: Erlbaum.

3   The Sources of Self-Consciousness

I

In thinking about the sources of self-consciousness we need to separate out two dimensions of the problem. There is, first, a genetic dimension. One might wonder about the origins of the capacity to think full-fledged self-conscious thoughts. That is to say, one might be asking about where this capacity comes from. How does it emerge in the normal course of human development? What are the genetic foundations on which it rests? Are there more primitive types of first-person contents from which full-fledged self-conscious thoughts emerge?

The problem of the sources of self-consciousness has an epistemic dimension as well as a genetic one. From the point of view of ontogeny or phylogeny, when we ask about the sources of self-consciousness we are really asking factual questions about where and when self-consciousness emerges in an individual or in a species. When we ask about the sources of self-consciousness from an epistemic point of view, however, the questions that emerge are of a fundamentally different type. Here we are taking the sources of self-consciousness to be the grounds of self-consciousness. What we want to know are the reasons for which self-conscious judgments

This essay was originally delivered at a meeting of the Aristotelian Society, held in Senate House, University of London, on December 3, 2001. Earlier versions of this essay were delivered at a conference on self-knowledge held at the University of Fribourg in November 2000, at the Institut Jean Nicod in Paris, at the Philosophy Department of the University of Eastern Piedmont at Vercelli in April 2001, and at the University of Glasgow in June 2001. I am grateful to audiences at those occasions for helpful discussion, and to Allan Millar and Brie Gertler for written comments.

and utterances are made. The questions that arise here include the following. How are such judgments justified? In virtue of what do they count as knowledge? In what senses are the different types of self-conscious judgments epistemically privileged? What role do self-consciousness judgments play in the cognitive economy?

My interest in this essay is with the role that the genetic dimension of self-consciousness plays in understanding the epistemology of self-consciousness. I will take as my foil a recent account of some key features of the epistemic dimension of a particular type of self-conscious judgment—the account offered by Christopher Peacocke in his recent book *Being Known* (Peacocke 1999). Working through some of the consequences and implications of Peacocke's account will bring out important ways in which we need to draw on the sources of self-consciousness in the genetic sense for a proper understanding of the sources of self-consciousness in the epistemic sense.

II

Two questions stand at the fore when we think about the epistemic grounds of full-fledged self-conscious judgments. The first question is: What are the grounds on which such judgments are made? The second questions is: In virtue of what can such judgments qualify as knowledge? Clearly, answers to the second question will depend crucially on answers to the first. It is difficult, unless one leans toward the most extreme variety of epistemological externalism, to separate a judgment's status as knowledge from the grounds on which it is made.

Peacocke distinguishes two different types of self-conscious judgments according to their grounds. The first category comprises what he terms *representation-dependent* first-person judgments (I am slightly modifying his terminology and will henceforth use "representation-dependent" to abbreviate "representation-dependent first-person"). These judgments involve taking a first-person representational content at face value and forming a corresponding belief. So, for example, if I am enjoying a visual state with the content that I am in front of the cathedral and, in virtue of that visual state, judge that I am in front of the cathedral, my judgment is representation dependent.

The second category of full-fledged self-conscious judgments are *representation independent*. These judgments are not made by taking a first-person representational content at face value. Here are the examples that Peacocke himself gives:

I am thinking about Pythagoras' theorem.
I see a phone on the table.
I remember attending the birthday party.
I remember that Russell was born in 1872.
I am beginning to dream.
I fear that the motion will not be carried.

The idea that there is a fundamental difference between these two types of judgment is really quite plausible. Judgments in the first category, those that are representation dependent, are derived from corresponding first-person contents in a way that judgments in the second category (those that are representation independent) quite simply are not. When I think about Pythagoras' theorem, for example, the content of my thought is the relation that holds between the lengths of the sides of right-angled triangles. The fact that I am thinking about that relation is not in any sense part of the thought. So, the ensuing judgment that I am thinking about Pythagoras' theorem is *ampliative*. In contrast, when I look at the cathedral in front of me there is a sense in which the fact that I am in front of the cathedral is part of what I see. What is seen is not just the cathedral, but rather the state of affairs of the cathedral standing in certain specifiable spatial relations to *me*. So, the judgment is in some sense an endorsement of the content of my perception.

Both representation-dependent and representation-independent thoughts involve ascribing certain properties to oneself, but the properties are different in the two cases. Judgments that are representation independent are typically psychological self-ascriptions, whereas the properties attributed to oneself in representation-dependent judgments will usually not be psychological. One would expect, therefore, that when these two thoughts qualify as knowledge there will be different accounts of what makes this the case.

According to Peacocke, representation-dependent self-conscious thoughts qualify as knowledge when the following three things hold:

(a) The thinker is taking a first-person representational state at face value.
(b) That first-person representational state is true.
(c) Certain relevant background informational conditions concerning the proper functioning of the faculty generating the state in question are fulfilled.

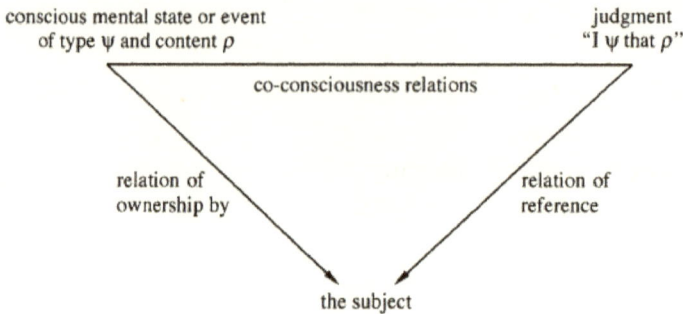

conscious mental state or event   judgment
       of type ψ and content ρ   "I ψ that ρ"

                              co-consciousness relations

          relation of   relation of
          ownership by   reference

                                  the subject

Figure 3.1
Peacocke's delta account of representation-independent judgments. (Fig. 6.2 from Peacocke 1999, p. 279.)

The basic idea here is that I know that the cathedral is there in front of me if I see that there's a cathedral in front of me with all my perceptual systems functioning as they ought to be and that perception leads to my judgment in a suitably noninferential way.

Clearly, no account along these lines can be given for self-conscious judgments that are not representation dependent. There is no way in which taking my occurrent thoughts about Pythagoras' theorem at face value will justify my self-ascriptive judgment that I am thinking about Pythagoras' theorem. For representation-independent judgments Peacocke offers what he calls the delta account. We can best get a grip both on what it is and on why he calls it the delta account by looking at the explanatory diagram he offers (see figure 3.1).

An appropriately formed representation-independent self-ascription will always be a true self-ascription (although not necessarily a true belief).[1] This is because the judgment that, for example, I am thinking about Pythagoras' theorem is co-conscious with my thought about Pythagoras' theorem, and hence the first-person element in the self-ascription will necessarily refer to the very individual thinking the first-order thought. But a belief can be true without counting as knowledge. What makes a representation-independent

1. The distinction between true self-ascriptions and true beliefs emerges when the subject self-ascribes a factive state. There is a sense in which I might truly form the judgment that I remember that the storming of the Bastille took place in 1790, although of course I can't really remember that the storming of the Bastille took place in 1790, given that it took place on July 14, 1789.

self-ascription knowledgeable? Peacocke's answer here is essentially that it is an a priori truth that a representation-independent self-ascription formed in the appropriate way will be true (with respect to its self-ascriptive component—see note 1) because it is an a priori truth that any occurrence of the first person in thought will refer to the thinker of that thought. So, a representation-independent belief formed in the appropriate way will count as knowledge because it is a priori that it is true.[2]

III

The key theoretical difference between representation-dependent judgments and representation-independent judgments is that the former but not the latter involve *taking at face value* a representational content in which the first person features. It is natural to ask how we should understand these first-person contents. We have already seen one example of a representation-dependent judgment—namely, the judgment that I am in front of a cathedral made on the basis of a perception of the cathedral. It is very clear that my perception of the cathedral does have an important first-person dimension. An integral part of what I see when I see the cathedral is that it stands in certain spatial relations to me. But what is the relation between the content of the perceptual state and the content of the self-ascription made on the basis of that perceptual state?

Peacocke himself maintains a studied neutrality here:

We can more generally consider examples in which the thinker's reason for making his judgment "I am F" is his being in some state, other than a belief state, which represents a certain content C as correct. In the class of examples I want to consider, the content C may, but need not, be the same as the content "I am F." Some theorists believe that perceptual states have nonconceptual contents which are distinct in kind from the contents which feature in beliefs. What I have to say is orthogonal to that issue. In the class of examples on which I want to focus, it will be the case that the content C, even if it is distinct from the content "I am F," is still one which stands in an implicational relation to the content "I am F." (1999, 264)

There are, as far as I can see, three possible positions that might be adopted. The first position is that the content C just is the conceptual belief content

2. Again, we need to restrict the truth to the self-ascriptive component. It is not the case that all beliefs that are a priori true qualify as knowledge simply in virtue of being a priori. Thanks to Brie Gertler on this and the preceding footnote.

"I am F"—that is to say, there is a unity of content between the perceptual state and the self-ascription. The second position is that the content C is a first-person nonconceptual content. According to this second position the self is explicitly represented in the content of the justifying perception in a way that underwrites, but somehow falls short of, how the self is represented in the content "I am F." The third position is that content C is a nonconceptual content that has no first-person dimension. The self is not represented explicitly at all.

Maintaining the third option appears to place pressure on the distinction between representation dependence and representation independence. If the self is not represented at all in the justifying perceptual state then it is hard to see how the content "I am F" can be reached by taking the content of that state at face value. It would be much more like a case of representation independence, where the thinker capitalizes on the implicational relation between the justifying perception (e.g., the perception that there is a telephone on the table) and the first-person belief formed on its basis (e.g., "I am looking at a telephone"). It looks, therefore, as if we do not have a choice between the second and third options. If we do not go with the first option then the second option is mandatory.

But can we at least be neutral between the first and second understandings of the relation between justifying perception and first-person belief? Here matters are a little more complicated. According to the first understanding, it will be remembered, there is an identity of content between the target perceptual state and the corresponding self-ascription. That is to say, the self is represented the same way in the original perception and in the self-ascription made on the basis of that perception. If the identity of content thesis is true then the self-ascriptive judgment simply duplicates the content of the original perception. The perceptual content is, roughly, *I am in front of the cathedral*. The self-ascriptive judgment endorses that and is best represented as the propositional attitude of belief being taken to the content *I am in front of the cathedral*. The difference between the self-conscious judgment and the perceptual state on which it is based is simply at the level of force.

The identity of content thesis has had, and continues to have, considerable currency in contemporary philosophy and mind and epistemology. It features most conspicuously in the epistemic theory of perception, according to which perception should be analyzed in terms of the acquisition

of dispositions to believe (Armstrong 1968), but it is also maintained
by philosophers who reject the epistemic theory. John McDowell is a case
in point:

> Suppose someone is presented with an appearance that it is raining. It seems un-
> problematic that if his experience is in a suitable way the upshot of the fact that it
> is raining then the fact itself can make it the case that he knows that it is raining.
> But that seems unproblematic precisely because the content of the appearance is the
> content of the knowledge. (McDowell 1982, 213–214)

The identity of content thesis is a consequence of McDowell's brand of
direct realism—it is because what we believe is what we see that what we
know is available to us through perception.

The identity of content thesis raises an obvious question. What has
happened to the familiar distinction between the content of belief and the
content of perception? If, as many authors (including of course Peacocke
himself) have argued, there is a fundamental difference between the content of perception and the content of belief (Peacocke 1992), then how can
the content of a belief merely duplicate the content of a perception? We are
familiar, for example, with the idea that propositional attitude content is
digital, while perceptual content is analog. Why is this not enough to block
the identity of content thesis?

The simple answer is that the analog/digital distinction does not map
precisely onto the perceptual/doxastic distinction. Many theorists, once
again including Peacocke, have proposed that propositional attitude contents can contain elements that are fundamentally perceptual in form—
what are often termed perceptual-demonstrative modes of presentation
(Peacocke 1983, 1992). The example we are considering seems clearly to
fall into this category. The doxastic *I am in front of the cathedral* is best
viewed as containing the relevant cathedral under a demonstrative mode
of presentation.

But adverting to perceptual-demonstrative contents in this way does
not, I think, address the real worry with the identity of content thesis. In
essence, the problem is not to do with how the cathedral is represented, but
rather with how the self is represented. Whereas there is a certain plausibility in suggesting that there is a single perceptual-demonstrative mode of
presentation of the cathedral that can stand in the content both of perception and of belief, it is hard to see how anything comparable holds for the
representation of the self in perception and perceptually based beliefs. The

self does not feature in perception in anything like the way in which it does in beliefs—even when the beliefs in question are perceptually based.

This conclusion follows, I think, from some basic reflections on the nature of belief. I am taking the content of belief to be an abstract object, something that can be believed by many different people and that can be expressed in a declarative sentence. It must be possible for different people, and indeed the same person at different times, to take different attitudes to the same belief content. Partly this is a matter of it being possible for you to disbelieve something that I believe. Partly it is a matter of it being possible for me to believe something that for you is merely an object of hope—or for me to come to believe that something is the case when previously I simply feared that it might be the case. It's uncontroversial that any plausible general account of the objects of belief must allow this to be the case. And that has certain consequences. Some of them are fairly obvious. It cannot be the case, for example, that I could believe something that it is logically impossible for you to believe. But it also follows, and this is slightly less obvious, that the content of belief must be divorced from the grounds on which one might come to believe that content on any particular occasion. Let's suppose, for example, that I come to the true belief that I am in front of the cathedral because I see it in front of me, while at the same time you come to the erroneous belief that at that very moment I am not in front of the cathedral because you have been told by someone whom you believe to be a good authority on my movements that I am in fact in the museum. There is a single belief-content here that we are evaluating in different ways—namely, the belief-content that I am in front of the cathedral. And if we are to disagree about its truth-value then it cannot be the case that what I believe is tied to, or in any way reflects, the fact that I arrived at the belief on the basis of perception—because if it was then it wouldn't be in conflict with your belief, which you arrived at on the basis of testimony.

But if this is right then it cannot be the case that what I believe is what I see. What I believe, the content of my belief, must be something that is independent of the particular form in which my being in front of the cathedral became manifest to me. As I have stressed, the fact that I am looking at the cathedral is part of what I see—and the self is represented in perception as standing in certain specifiable relations to the cathedral associated with my physical location at the origin of a particular visual array. But then this cannot be the way in which the self is represented in my belief that I am in front of the cathedral. Any such representation of the self would be too specific to feature in a suitably objective belief-content.

IV

So how is the self represented in belief? We can remain neutral on the question of whether the first-person concept should be analyzed as the sense of the first-person pronoun (as suggested, e.g., in Evans 1982) while still noting that there are significant commonalities between how the self is picked out linguistically and how it is represented in belief (and other propositional attitudes). The key to both the first-person pronoun and the first-person concept is the type/token distinction. The first-person pronoun is a linguistic type whose meaning is exhausted by the rule specifying that any appropriately uttered token of that type refers to its utterer. Similarly, the first-person concept is a type that, when tokened in thought, plays a familiarly distinctive functional role for the subject who tokens it. Adequate accounts of both the first-person pronoun and the first-person concept, therefore, will have to operate at two levels. One familiar way of doing this for the first-person pronoun is to define the linguistic meaning (or *character*, as it is sometimes called) of the first-person pronoun as a function from contexts to contents, where contents are functions from possible worlds to the individual of the context (Kaplan 1989, 505–507). One would expect a structurally similar account to hold for the first-person concept, so that the first-person concept is that concept whose tokening generates thoughts with a highly specific and irreducible functional role for the subject who has them. In the case of both pronoun and concept, the account is pitched at the level of the type rather than the token. The meaning of "I" is located at the level of the function from contexts to individuals, rather than at the level of the individuals picked out by particular tokenings of "I." So too is the nature of the first-person concept fixed in a way that is independent of its tokening in particular individuals.

In light of this, the difference between the representation of the self in perception and in thought becomes clear. Frege remarked in "The Thought" that "everyone is presented to himself in a special and primitive way in which he is presented to no one else" (Frege 1918, 12). Appearances suggest that Frege was intending this peculiar perspective to be reflected at the level of thought, and his comments have usually been interpreted as applying to the sense of the first-person pronoun. What I would like to suggest, however, is that Frege's pithy phrase applies quite accurately to the way in which the self is presented in perception, but has no application at all to the way in which the self is represented in the content of belief and other propositional attitudes. There is nothing perspectival about the first-person concept.³

This basic thought can be motivated further by considering the range of representation-dependent thoughts available in other sensory modalities. I can come to the belief that I am near the church because I hear the ringing of the nearby church-bells. My auditory perception has a first-person content, namely, that I am not far from the source of the sound. This is part of the content of perception. It is not something that I infer from what I hear. So, the self must be represented in auditory perception—and yet in a fundamentally different manner from how it is represented in beliefs based on auditory perception. The same holds with even more force for self-conscious beliefs derived from somatic proprioception. Somatic proprioception is a source of first-person contents. Nonetheless, the self does not feature in the content of somatic proprioception in anything like the way it does in the contents of beliefs based on somatic proprioception.

V

Representation-dependent judgments are judgments of the form "I am F" that are made by taking a certain justifying perceptual content C at face value. There is nothing wrong with the idea of a content being taken at face value. It is quite clear that when I form the belief that I am in front of the cathedral on the basis of a perception of the cathedral in front of me I am taking my experience at face value. I am not, for example, making any sort of inference from my perception to the presence of the cathedral. The perception provides an immediate reason for the belief. But the question remains of how best to understand the content that is taken at face value. We have rejected the identity of content thesis, according to which there is no difference in content between the justifying perceptual state and the self-ascriptive belief that is formed on its basis. If the self is

3. For further discussion of the first-person concept and the sense of the first-person pronoun, see Bermúdez 2017.

explicitly represented in perception then it cannot be represented there in the same way as it is in belief. Since we have also rejected the suggestion that there is no representation of the self in the content of the justifying perceptual state, we are forced to accept that representation-dependent judgments are grounded in a form of representation of the self that is essentially nonconceptual. What this means, of course, is that an account is urgently needed of the grounds of representation-dependent first-person judgments. We need an account of the first-person dimension of the target perceptual states.[4]

Let me approach this at a tangent. There is a general issue here about the extent to which perception is fully conceptual. We are familiar with the idea that perception is concept laden—that the content of perception falls, as McDowell often puts it, within the space of reasons (McDowell 1994). We do not see objects in a neutral way, attending simply to their geometric, sensory, and kinematic properties and then, on the basis of that neutral perception, work out how they fit into our conceptual categorization of the world. The concepts are already built into the way in which we perceive the world, although nobody has ever managed to make clear how this works. Nonetheless, to say that perception is concept laden is not to deny that it has a nonconceptual dimension. In a sense it is completely obvious that perception must have a nonconceptual component because otherwise there would be no qualitative difference between the content of

4. This problem arises not only for self-conscious judgments that are representation dependent. It arises also for an important class of representation-independent self-ascriptions. Peacocke's list of representation-independent first-person judgments include autobiographical memories (my self-ascribing the memory of attending the birthday party) and self-ascriptions of perceptions (my self-ascribing the perception of the phone on the table). The second of these is quite clearly derived from a first-person content. What makes it true that I see that the phone is on the table is my occurrent perception of the phone on the table—and, as we've seen at some length with the example of my seeing the cathedral, my occurrent seeing that the phone is on the table is a first-person content. The same holds for the third example—my autobiographical memory of attending the birthday party (assuming, of course, that this memory is episodic). My episodic memory of attending the birthday is a memory of my having attended the birthday party. In both these cases of representation-independent judgment we need to distinguish, just as we did in the representation-dependent case, between the way in which the self is represented in the original perception or memory and the way in which it is represented in the doxastic states formed on the basis of that target state.

perception and the content of propositional attitudes. The critical question is not whether perception has a nonconceptual content, but whether it has a nonconceptual *representational* content—and several authors have argued persuasively that the nonconceptual content of experience is partially (and indeed perhaps completely) representational. These authors, however, have focused primarily on certain limited aspects of the content of perception (see, e.g., Peacocke 1992, chap. 3). They have stressed, for example, how the content of perception is analog rather than digital; how it presents distances in a unit-free manner; and how it supports a fineness of grain that is arguably unavailable to conceptual thought.[5]

However, these three features of the content of perception do not by any means exhaust its nonconceptual representational content. The content of perception includes, I shall suggest, an ontogenetically primitive form of representation of the self. Full-fledged self-consciousness emerges, as I have stressed elsewhere (Bermúdez 1998 and chapters 1 and 2 in this volume), from a foundation of more primitive types of self-awareness—in the propriospecific dimension of exteroceptive perception, in somatic proprioception, in the ability to locate oneself spatially within the world, and in the self-representation implicated in primitive forms of social interaction. These primitive forms of self-consciousness are prior to full-fledged self-consciousness *in the order of development*—and indeed are necessary conditions for the emergence of full-fledged self-consciousness. This genetic story by no means entails, of course, that once full-fledged self-consciousness has been attained, these primitive forms of self-consciousness have any further role to play in the cognitive economy. It could simply be that they just drop out of the picture, rather like some of the basic perceptual expectations that very young infants have about the behavior of distal objects.

Yet, there is a fundamental disanalogy between the perception of distal objects and the perception of the self in this respect. It is plausible to think that young infants parse the perceived array into object-like segments that obey certain basic geometrical and kinematic principles. These have been studied at some length by developmental psychologists. With the acquisition of concepts and language, however, this way of perceiving the world is overridden by the conceptual seeing-as that I have already briefly mentioned. Little if anything remains of the infant perceptual universe in

5. For further discussion and references to debates on the nonconceptual content of perception, see Bermúdez and Cahen 2015.

adult perception. But the perception of the self is not at all like that. The fundamental differences in content between first-person representational states and first-person beliefs based on those states point us toward the persistence of a fundamentally nonconceptual representation of the self in ordinary perception. This provides the key to the way in which perceptual states provide grounds for the representation-dependent first-person judgments that are made by taking them at face value (although not, as we have seen, by duplicating them).

VI

The best account of the nonconceptual representation of the self in visual perception comes, I think, from J. J. Gibson's ecological approach to perception, and I will simply briefly sketch some of the principal respects that he has drawn to our attention in which the self is represented in visual perception (Gibson 1966, 1979).

Gibson stresses certain peculiarities of the phenomenology of the field of vision. Notable among these is the fact that the field of vision is bounded. Vision reveals only a portion of the world to the perceiver at any given time (roughly half in the human case, owing to the frontal position of the eyes). The boundedness of the field of vision is part of what is seen, and the field of vision is bounded in a way quite unlike the way in which spaces are bounded within the field of vision. The self appears in perception as the boundary of the visual field—a moveable boundary that is responsive to the will.

In addition to the boundedness of the visual, the self becomes manifest in visual perception (according to Gibson) because the field of vision contains various body parts that hide, or occlude, the environment. The nose, for example, is distinctively present in just about every visual experience. The cheekbones, and perhaps the eyebrows, also occupy a (slightly less) dominant position in the field of vision. And so too, to a still lesser extent, do the bodily extremities, hands, arms, feet, and legs. These protrude into the field of vision from below in a way that occludes the environment, and yet that differs from how one nonbodily physical object in the field of vision might occlude another. All objects, bodily and nonbodily, can present a range of solid angles in the field of vision (where a solid angle is an angle with its apex at the eye and its base at some perceived object), and the size of those angles varies according to how far the object is from the point of observation. The further away it is, the smaller the angle will be. But the solid angles subtended by occluding body parts cannot be reduced below a certain minimum. Perceived body parts are, according to Gibson, "subjective objects" in the content of visual perception.

These *self-specifying structural invariants* provide only a fraction of the self-specifying information available in visual perception. There are two more important types of self-specifying information.

The mass of constantly changing visual information generated by the subject's motion poses an immense challenge to the perceptual systems. How can the visual experiences generated by motion be decoded so that subjects perceive that they are moving through the world? Gibson's notion of *visual kinesthesis* is his answer to this traditional problem. Whereas many theorists have assumed that motion perception can only be explained by the hypothesis of mechanisms that parse cues in the neutral sensations into information about movement and information about static objects, the crucial idea behind visual kinesthesis is that the patterns of flow in the optic array and the relations between variant and invariant features make available information about the movement of the perceiver, as well as about the environment.

As an example of such a visually kinesthetic invariant, consider that the optical flow in any field of vision starts from a center, which is itself stationary. This stationary center specifies the point that is being approached, when the perceiver is moving. The aiming point of locomotion is at the vanishing point of optical flow. Striking experiments have brought out the significance of visual kinesthesis. In the so-called moving-room experiments, subjects are placed on the solid floors of rooms whose walls and ceilings can be made to glide over a solid and immoveable floor. When experimental subjects are prevented from seeing their feet and the floor is hidden, moving the walls backward and forward on the sagittal plane creates in the subjects the illusory impression that they are moving back and forth. This provides strong support for the thesis that the movement of the perceiver can be detected purely visually, since visual specification of movement seems to be all that is available. When young children are placed in the moving room, they actually sway and lose their balance.

A further important form of self-specifying information is available to be picked up in the field of vision, according to the theory of ecological optics.

This is the result of the direct perception of a class of higher-order invariants that Gibson terms *affordances*. It is in the theory of affordances that we find the most sustained development of the ecological view that the fundamentals of perceptual experience are dictated by the organism's need to navigate and act in its environment, because the animal and the organism are complementary. According to Gibson, the possibilities the environment affords are not learned through experience. Nor are they inferred. They are directly perceived as higher-order invariants. And of course, the perception of affordances is a form of self-perception—or, at least, a way in which self-specifying information is perceived. The whole notion of an affordance is that of environmental information about one's own possibilities for action and reaction.

VII

Gibson's characterization of the phenomenology of visual perception offers important insights into how the self is represented nonconceptually in the content of perception. To return to our earlier discussion of representation-dependent judgments, it is the "ecological self" that features in the content of basic perceptual states and that provides the epistemic grounds for self-conscious judgments made on the basis of those perceptual states. More generally, representation-dependent judgments are grounded in the primitive, nonconceptual representations of the self discussed in more detail in the other chapters in this volume.

This brings us to the second of the two questions identified at the beginning of section II. To understand the epistemology of full-fledged self-conscious judgments it is not enough to understand the grounds on which those judgments are based. We need also to understand why, when those judgments count as knowledge, they should do so.

It will be helpful to begin by turning briefly to how representation-*in*dependent judgments are grounded. These judgments are, in essence, self-ascriptions of mental states, and it follows from the definition of representation-independence that the self-ascriptive component of the representation-independent judgment is not grounded in the content of the state that the subject self-ascribes. A representation-independent judgment is made when a subject makes the transition from φ-ing that p to the self-ascriptive judgment "I am φ-ing that p," but there is nothing in the content p that corresponds to the first-person concept that appears in the self-ascriptive judgment (in obvious contrast to representation-dependent judgments). So how does the subject make the transition? The simple answer is that the transition is available to subjects who have a basic mastery of what might be termed a simple theory of introspection (by analogy with the simple theory of perception and action discussed in Evans 1982 and Campbell 1994). In this case the simple theory of introspection amounts to nothing more than some level of mastery of the a priori link between being aware of a thought and it being the case that one is thinking it—which is, of course, the same a priori link that governs the status as knowledge of the resulting representation-independent judgment (according to Peacocke's delta account).[6] What we see in this case is that the subject's reason for forming the judgment is an appreciation of precisely the factor that qualifies the judgment as knowledge. Let me describe epistemic situations of this type as being *canonically internalist.*

To see how representation-dependent judgments can be just as canonically internalist as representation-independent judgments, we need to explore the relation between representation dependence, representation independence, and the phenomenon that Sydney Shoemaker has described as immunity to error relative to the first-person pronoun. As Shoemaker puts it (with reference to statements rather than judgments):

To say that a statement "a is φ" is subject to error through misidentification relative to the term "a" means that the following is possible: the speaker knows some particular thing to be φ, but makes the mistake of asserting "a is φ" because, and only because, he mistakenly thinks that the thing he knows to be φ is what "a" refers to. (Shoemaker 1984, 7–8)

Immunity to error through misidentification relative to the first-person pronoun (henceforth abbreviated to: immunity to error through misidentification) is a property of judgments that are not based on an act of identification of a particular object as oneself. They are judgments that one has a certain property based on grounds such that knowing that something has that property is *ipso facto* to know that one has that property oneself. It is clear that representation-independent self-ascriptions are immune

6. The simple theory of introspection might also contain such basic principles as that, if one wants to find out whether one believes that p, the best way to proceed is to determine whether p is in fact the case.

to error in this sense.[7] If I form the judgment that I am thinking about Pythagoras' theorem because I am aware of thinking about Pythagoras' theorem then that judgment is not based on an identification of myself as the author of the relevant thought. Rather, knowing that there is a thought about Pythagoras' theorem just is knowing that that thought is a thought that I am having. It is equally clear that representation-dependent thoughts very often share this feature of being immune to error through misidentification. If I form the judgment that I am in front of the cathedral because I see the cathedral in front of me, this is not because I form the belief that someone is in front of the cathedral and then identify that person as myself. Knowing on the basis of perception in this way that someone is in front of the cathedral just is knowing that I myself am in front of the cathedral.

The immunity to error through misidentification of first-person judgments is intimately linked with their status as knowledge, in virtue of the connection between immunity to error through misidentification and the defining property of the first-person concept, namely, that of picking out the thinker of any thought in which it features (in the appropriate way). In a judgment of the form "I am F" that is immune to error through misidentification the only possibility of error is with respect to the predicative component. And hence, provided that the information grounding the predicative component has been acquired in an appropriate manner, one would expect the judgment to count as knowledge. It is natural to conclude, therefore, that an explanation of the immunity to error of first-person judgments will provide the key to explaining their status as knowledge.

Nonetheless, representation-independent and representation-dependent judgments secure their immunity to error through misidentification in fundamentally different ways. In the case of representation-independent judgments the very feature that secures their status as knowledge is what underwrites their immunity to error through misidentification—namely, the a priori link between being aware of a thought and its being the case that one is thinking it. In the case of representation-dependent judgments, on the other hand, immunity to error through misidentification has to be a function of the states on which they are based. Let me offer the following conjecture. Representation-dependent judgments that are immune to error through misidentification are so because they involve taking at face

7. As Peacocke himself points out (Peacocke 1999, 270).

value first-person contents that are themselves immune to error through misidentification. It is easy to see how this works in the case of judgments based on perceptual states, such as the example we have been considering of my forming the belief that I am in front of the cathedral in virtue of seeing the cathedral in front of me. When I see the cathedral in front of me I do not see that the cathedral is in front of someone and then work out that I am that person. Seeing that someone is in front of the cathedral just is seeing that I am in front of the cathedral. And, given this, it is hardly surprising that the resulting judgment is itself immune to error through misidentification. It is plausible to conjecture that a broadly similar account is true of other types of representation-dependent judgments (such as those based on the deliverances of somatic proprioception, for example).[8]

In a sense, however, this merely pushes the problem one step further back. Representation-dependent judgments are immune to error because they are grounded in first-person states that are themselves immune to error through misidentification. But in virtue of what are those first-person states immune to error through misidentification? Immunity to error through misidentification is a formal property of representational states. We need to know what is responsible for it. The answer, in brief (and at least as far as visual perception is concerned), lies in the simple fact that the information about the self provided within the content of visual perception is such that it is manifest to the perceiver that it could not be about any creature except the self. To return to the earlier example, the information that I have about my own spatial position relative to the cathedral could not be information about anyone else's spatial position relative to the cathedral. This is because the body is manifest as the originating point of perception in such a way as to ensure that the self-conscious judgment that I am perceiving the cathedral is immune to error through misidentification.

To get a better understanding of why this is the case we need to revert to the insights into the phenomenology of visual perception gleaned from Gibson. The self is presented in perception as a distinctive and peculiar form of object in virtue of certain features of the content of visual perception. Some of these derive from the fact that the world is presented to the perceiver largely in terms of the affordances it offers. Others arise from the features that led Gibson to describe perceived body parts as subjective

---

8. For further discussion of the immunity to error of judgments based on somatic proprioception, see Evans 1982, Cassam 1995, and Bermúdez 1998.

objects in the field of view—the fact, for example, that body parts can vary in perceived size only within a limited range. The way in which the body appears as the frame and boundary of the visual array is also extremely important. The embodied self is the originating point of perception in a much richer sense than the camera lens is the originating point of a photograph. The way in which the embodied self appears in perception, therefore, reflects the immunity to error of the relevant perceptual content and, by extension, that of the resulting belief content.

None of these features of the content of visual perception are transmitted to the content of self-conscious judgments made on the basis of visual perception, but nonetheless they underwrite the status as knowledge of those self-conscious judgments. They do this because they make it the case that the perceiver's reason for forming the judgment includes an appreciation of precisely those factors that qualifies the judgment as knowledge. The immunity to error of representation-dependent judgments is a function of the fact that the bodily self is the origin of perception. The distinctive way in which the bodily self is presented in visual perception ensures that this is manifest to the perceiver—it is part of what is perceived. This ensures that, to return to the terminology introduced earlier, epistemic situations leading to the formation of representation-dependent judgments are *canonically internalist.*

VIII

By way of conclusion, then, let me return to the general issues with which I began. As mentioned at the beginning of the essay, we can understand the sources of self-consciousness in two different ways—in an epistemic way, as the grounds of self-consciousness, and in a genetic way, as the origins of self-consciousness. What I have tried to argue is that the sources of self-consciousness in the genetic sense are ultimately also the sources of self-consciousness in the epistemic sense. The primitive foundations from which self-consciousness emerges in the course of cognitive development are also the foundation for the epistemic status of full-fledged self-conscious thoughts. My discussion has been restricted to the relatively straightforward example of visual perception and the Gibsonian account of its first-person content. Obviously a fuller development of this general theme will require extending the analysis to other types of first-person content. I hope that I have done enough to make it seem that this is a task worth undertaking.

References

Armstrong, D. M. 1968. *A Materialist Theory of Mind*. London: Routledge.

Bermúdez, J. L. 1998. *The Paradox of Self-Consciousness*. Cambridge, MA: MIT Press.

Bermúdez, J. L. 2017. *Understanding "I": Language and Thought*. Oxford: Oxford University Press.

Bermúdez, J. L., and A. Cahen. 2015. Mental content, nonconceptual. In *Stanford Encyclopedia of Philosophy*. https://plato.stanford.edu/.

Campbell, J. 1994. *Past, Space, and Self*. Cambridge, MA: MIT Press.

Cassam, Q. 1995. Introspection and bodily self-ascription. In *The Body and the Self*, ed. J. Bermúdez, A. J. Marcel, and N. Eilan. Cambridge, MA: MIT Press.

Evans, G. 1982. *Varieties of Reference*. Oxford: Oxford University Press.

Frege, G. 1918/1977. Thoughts. In *Logical Investigations*, ed. P. T. Geach. Oxford: Blackwell.

Gibson, J. J. 1966. *The Senses Considered as Perceptual Systems*. Boston: Houghton Mifflin.

Gibson, J. J. 1979. *The Ecological Approach to Visual Perception*. Boston: Houghton Mifflin.

Kaplan, D. 1989. Demonstratives. In *Themes from Kaplan*, ed. J. Almog, J. Perry, and H. Wettstein. Oxford: Oxford University Press.

McDowell, J. 1982. Criteria, defeasibility and knowledge. *Proceedings of the British Academy* 68:456–479.

McDowell, J. 1994. *Mind and World*. Cambridge, MA: Harvard University Press.

Peacocke, C. 1983. *Sense and Content*. Oxford: Oxford University Press.

Peacocke, C. 1992. *A Study of Concepts*. Cambridge, MA: MIT Press.

Peacocke, C. 1999. *Being Known*. Oxford: Oxford University Press.

Shoemaker, S. 1984. Self-reference and self-awareness. In *Identity, Cause and Mind*. Cambridge: Cambridge University Press.

4 The Elusiveness Thesis, Immunity to Error through Misidentification, and Privileged Access

There has been considerable recent work in the metaphysics and epistemology of self-awareness on what has come to be known as the *elusiveness
thesis* (see, e.g., Shoemaker 1986, 1994; Cassam 1994, 1997; Bermúdez et al.
1995; Bermúdez 1998; Peacocke 1999). According to the elusiveness thesis,
the self cannot be an object of introspective awareness. Alternatively put,
when we find out about our own properties through introspection we are
not acquainted with any object whose properties they are. In this respect,
then, our introspective awareness of ourselves is fundamentally different
from our awareness of ordinary physical objects and other psychological
subjects. This general idea is developed in different ways depending on how
the key notions of *self* and *introspection* are understood.

It is natural to think that this distinctive feature of introspection has
epistemological consequences, and in fact the elusiveness thesis sits easily
with a particular way of thinking about the epistemological issue of privileged access. We clearly have a form of privileged access to our own mental
states. This privileged access is a function of certain ways we have of finding
out about our own mental states, and it is standard to think that it applies
only to introspective ways of finding out about our own mental states.
Pursuing this line of thought, it is hard not to be struck by the thought
that privileged access and the elusiveness thesis might be two sides of the
same coin. Perhaps it is (at least partly) because we do not encounter the
self as an object in introspection that the knowledge of the self that we gain
through introspection is epistemically privileged—the epistemic privilege
derives from the fact that our introspective self-awareness is awareness of
a fundamentally different type from our awareness of ordinary objects and
other psychological subjects.

This idea that there is a close connection between privileged access and the elusiveness thesis will be the subject of this essay. I will not be challenging the general thesis that a significant degree of epistemic privilege attaches to introspective self-awareness—although I shall have some things to say about how that epistemic privilege should be understood. My principal question is whether there are any forms of self-awareness that are epistemically privileged yet nonintrospective. In discussing the general issue of privileged access, philosophers have tended to concentrate on the various types of privileged access that might accrue to introspective awareness of psychological properties (see, e.g., Alston 1971). But there are equally important questions concerning the degree of privileged access accruing to the nonintrospective ways in which we can find out about our physical properties. These nonintrospective forms of self-awareness include proprioceptive bodily awareness and the perception of the self that occurs as an inextricable part of ordinary perceptual awareness. We shall be looking in some detail at the type of privileged access afforded by these nonintrospective modes of self-awareness. We will see that they require a fundamentally different type of explanation from ordinary introspective awareness—a type of explanation in which the elusiveness thesis has no part to play.

Section I surveys different formulations of the elusiveness thesis, focusing on the recent formulation by Sydney Shoemaker linking the elusiveness thesis with the phenomenon of immunity to error through misidentification (relative to the first-person pronoun). In section II, I explore proprioceptive bodily awareness, suggesting that it offers a *prima facie* reason for prising the phenomenon of immunity to error through misidentification apart from the elusiveness thesis. Somatic proprioception offers both a protoperceptual acquaintance with the embodied self and an identification-free source of information about one's bodily properties. Section III looks at the nonintrospective forms of self-awareness that are an inevitable concomitant of exercising the ordinary perceptual systems. Perceptual awareness of the embodied self can give rise to judgments that are immune to error through misidentification and are even more obviously examples of perceptual awareness of the embodied self than somatic proprioception. In section IV we turn to the key question raised by earlier sections. What explains the immunity to error through misidentification of these different types of self-awareness? I shall offer a different explanation for each type.

I

The origins of the elusiveness thesis are usually taken to lie in a famous passage from Hume's *Treatise of Human Nature*:

For my part, when I enter most intimately into what I call myself, I always stumble on some particular perception or other, of heat or cold, light or shade, love or hatred, pain or pleasure. I can never catch *myself* at any time without a perception, and can never observe anything but the perception. When my perceptions are remov'd for any time, as by sound sleep; so long am I insensible of *myself*, and may truly be said not to exist. And were all my perceptions remov'd by death, and cou'd I neither think, nor feel, nor see, nor love, nor hate, after the dissolution of my body, I shou'd be entirely annihilated, nor do I conceive what is farther requisite to make me a perfect non-entity. If anyone upon serious and unprejudic'd reflexion, thinks he has a different notion of *himself*, I must confess I can reason no longer with him. All I can allow him is, that he may be in the right as well as I, and that we are essentially different in this particular. He may, perhaps, perceive something simple and continu'd which he calls *himself*, tho' I am certain there is no such principle in me. (Hume 1739–1740/1978, 252)

The elusiveness thesis, as we find it in Hume, is closely linked with Hume's peculiar form of *irrealism* about the self. The self, as far as Hume is concerned, is nothing over and above a "bundle of perceptions"—and the elusiveness thesis is an important part of his argument for that radical view.

Although the elusiveness thesis is usually credited to Hume, he is not in fact either the only or the earliest major figure in the history of philosophy to have maintained it. We find the elusiveness thesis clearly stated by Descartes who thought that we are never directly acquainted with the thinking "I." This is a direct consequence of his view that the self is a substance—the self is the "thing which thinks," in the famous phrase from the *Meditations*. It is part of Descartes's conception of substance that we are never directly acquainted with substances, only with their properties, as he clearly states in the *Principles*:

However, we cannot initially become aware of a substance merely through its being an existing thing, since this alone does not of itself have any effect on us. We can, however, easily come to know a substance by one of its attributes, in virtue of the common notion that nothingness possesses no attributes, that is to say, no properties or qualities. Thus, if we perceive the presence of some attribute, we can infer that there must also be present an existing thing or substance to which it may be attributed. (Descartes 1984, 210)

So, for Descartes, just as for Hume, all I am directly acquainted with are thoughts. I am not directly acquainted in introspection (or in any other way) with the thinker of those thoughts. Nonetheless, unlike Hume, Descartes does not deny that there is any such thinker. The existence of a thinking self is, for him, guaranteed by the twin metaphysical facts, first, that thoughts are properties and, second, that properties cannot exist unless they are instantiated in something.

There is an interesting difference between Hume and Descartes with respect to the elusiveness thesis. It looks very much from the second part of the quoted passage as if Hume saw the elusiveness thesis as a contingent claim. There is, he seems to be saying, no incoherence in the thought that an introspecting subject might encounter a self lurking among his perceptions ("he may be in the right as well as I"). It is just that, as a matter of fact and, no matter how hard he tries, his attempts to introspect the self have not met with success. This apparent admission of contingency is compatible with Hume's irrealism about the self, provided of course that one takes the nonexistence of a self over and above the bundle of perceptions to be itself a contingent matter. As far as Descartes is concerned, however, the elusiveness thesis holds necessarily rather than contingently. Given that the self is a substance, and given that we cannot enter into any sort of epistemic relation with substances qua substances, it follows as a matter of necessity that we cannot be directly acquainted with the thinking "I."

It is hard, however, not to feel a certain dissatisfaction with the way in which both Descartes and Hume set up the framework that allows them to formulate their respective versions of the elusiveness thesis. The problem arises with the way in which they view the nature of introspective awareness, as if introspection were a matter of scanning the contents of the mind in much the way in which one might scan the contents of a room. Sydney Shoemaker (1986) has provided a formulation of the elusiveness thesis that speaks directly to this concern about the nature of introspective awareness. As Shoemaker understands the elusiveness thesis, it is as much a thesis about the nature of introspection as it is about the nature of the self. One of Shoemaker's targets is the idea that introspection should be understood as a form of perception—the so-called act-object conception of introspection. According to this way of understanding introspection, introspection involves a subject standing in a protoperceptual relation to a mental particular (which might be a thought, a propositional attitude, an emotion, or a sensation). It is something like the act-object conception that lies behind Hume's version of the elusiveness thesis, Hume's claim being in effect that the mental particulars that he encounters when he introspects do not include a self. In Shoemaker's version of the elusiveness thesis, in contrast, the central point is that introspection does not involve protoperceptual awareness of any mental particulars at all—and *a fortiori* no protoperceptual awareness of the self. Perception, as Shoemaker understands it, involves the pickup of what he calls identification information—that is, information that allows the perceiver to pick out one object among a range of objects in virtue of its perceived properties. But there is, he suggests, nothing analogous to such observationally based identification of an object in introspection—neither as applied to mental particulars nor as applied to the self.

Introspection gives rise to judgments that are, to use Shoemaker's own phrase, *immune to error through misidentification relative to the first person pronoun*:

> To say that a statement "a is ϕ" is subject to error through misidentification relative to the term "a" means that the following is possible: the speaker knows some particular thing to be ϕ, but makes the mistake of asserting "a is ϕ" because, and only because, he mistakenly thinks that the thing he knows to be ϕ is what "a" refers to. (Shoemaker 1984, 7–8)

Immunity to error is an epistemological notion relativized to the grounds on which the judgment or statement in question is made. It is a function of the particular form of warrant possessed by a type of judgment or statement, so that, for example, the same sentence can be employed to make two different statements, only one of which is immune to error, if the grounds on which the statement is made on the two occasions of utterance are appropriately different. A useful way of bringing out how the immunity to error through misidentification of a statement or judgment is a function of the grounds for that statement or judgment has been offered by Crispin Wright (1998). As Wright points out, a judgment that is subject to error through misidentification is one whose grounds will survive as grounds for an existential generalization if the misidentification is uncovered. So, suppose that I come to form the judgment "I'm looking scruffy" by seeing a scruffy person on a closed-circuit television display in a shop window and wrongly identifying that person as myself. If I discover the mistake then I must, of course, retract the original judgment—but the grounds on which

I made that judgment will survive as grounds for the existential generalization "Someone is scruffy." What characterizes judgments that are immune
to error through misidentification, however, is that there can be no such
retreat to an existential generalization.

The elusiveness of the self (to introspection) is, for Shoemaker, constitutively linked with the immunity to error of judgments based on introspective self-awareness. The argument is subtle. There is no point, he
thinks, in even considering that the self might be encountered in introspection unless the accessibility of the self could perform some cognitive function, and the self could only be encountered in introspection as
the owner or the bearer of introspectable mental states (rather than what
Hume seems to have been looking for, which is some sort of disembodied entity over and above those mental states). But what cognitive function could be served by the introspectability of the owner of mental states,
other than to allow that owner to be identified? And this is the crux of
the matter, since the whole point of the immunity to error of the deliverances of introspection is that no such identification is needed. Once we
realize that judgments based on introspection are immune to error through
misidentification, the thought that there might be a perceptual encounter with the self in introspection swiftly reveals itself to be incoherent—
simply because there is no gap between knowing that an introspectively
accessible property is instantiated and knowing that it is instantiated
in oneself.[1]

I will be discussing Shoemaker's version of the elusiveness thesis in the
remainder of this essay. It has considerable plausibility. It is hard to see
how one might dispute Shoemaker's claim that introspective awareness
of psychological properties does not involve identification information.
We do not come to the belief that we believe that p by encountering an

1. In fact, Shoemaker has a further argument in support of the elusiveness thesis
(1986, 109). Introspective awareness that, say, the property of believing that p is
instantiated in an observed self would only be sufficient to provide me with knowledge that I myself believe that p if I knew that the observed self was in fact myself.
But how could I do that? Only through the perceived properties of the observed
self. But I could only do this if I already knew that I myself had those perceived
properties—and this knowledge could not, on pain of regress, be derived from introspective observation. So it looks as if introspective observation of the self would be
otiose.

object whose properties allow us to identify it, first, as a belief that p, and then, second, as our own belief that p. The claim as applied to introspective awareness of the self is, if anything, even more obvious.

We can note the obvious relevance to the issue of privileged access of Shoemaker's version of the elusiveness thesis and the correlative conception of introspection. If introspection does not involve any form of observationally based identification, and if (moreover) it does not involve any sort of perceptual or proto-perceptual encounter with the self, then this provides a clear asymmetry between introspection and ordinary perceptual awareness of nonbodily objects—and it is precisely such an asymmetry that it is the burden of the doctrine of privileged access to establish. Privileged access is usually understood in terms of a certain class of beliefs about oneself being immune to a certain type of error, with the type of privileged access being a function of the type of immunity identified—immunity to correction (incorrigibility), immunity to doubt (indubitability), immunity to error (infallibility), immunity to ignorance (self-intimation), and so forth.[2] These types of immunity are invariably discussed with reference to introspective beliefs about one's own psychological states. Shoemaker's version of the elusiveness thesis not only adds a further type of immunity to the list (immunity to error through misidentification), but in fact the type of immunity that it adds arguably has a foundational role to play relative to the other types, in at least the following sense. Any belief that has any of the other types of immunity will be immune to error through misidentification, whereas the converse does not hold—a belief can be immune to error through misidentification without being either incorrigible, indubitable, infallible, or self-intimating. Moreover, it may well be that there are in fact no other types of immunity—that incorrigibility, infallibility, self-intimation, and so on all turn out to be philosophers' fictions. In that case, immunity to error through misidentification would be foundational by default.

All this strongly suggests that the elusiveness thesis holds considerable promise for explaining why there should be any type of privileged access at all. It is hard to see how we could have privileged access to certain types of information about ourselves unless we had ways of acquiring those types of

2. See Alston 1971 for a comprehensive survey of the different types of privileged access.

information that do not lay us open to certain possibilities of error attendant on ordinary perceptual awareness—and the elusiveness thesis seems
to go a considerable way toward explaining why introspective awareness
should be different in this way from ordinary perceptual awareness.[3]

In this essay I shall suggest that the situation is considerably more complex than this attractive picture suggests. One complexity emerges because
somatic proprioception and bodily awareness do provide (or so I shall argue)
a form of protoperceptual acquaintance with the embodied self, while at
the same time being a source of identification-free awareness of one's own
physical properties. So we need to separate out the elusiveness thesis from
the immunity to error through misidentification thesis. The claim about
the self does not follow immediately from the claim about immunity to
error through misidentification.

Further complexity comes from a point that has been almost completely
neglected both in discussions of the elusiveness thesis and in discussions
of privileged access. The elusiveness thesis, as we have discussed it so far, is
a claim about the nature of introspective self-awareness. It says, in effect,
that introspective self-awareness does not involve observation-based identification either of the self or of anything else. The contrast it stresses is
between introspective self-awareness, on the one hand, and ordinary perceptual awareness of physical objects and other psychological subjects, on
the other hand. But even if we accept that this contrast exists, and that
it should be characterized in broadly the terms offered by Shoemaker, a
further question arises. There are ways of finding out about one's physical
and psychological properties that are not introspective (even when introspection is construed broadly, as some authors have suggested, to include
somatic proprioception and bodily awareness). How, if at all, do these fit
into the two-way distinction between introspection and ordinary perceptual awareness? Should they all be construed on the model of ordinary perceptual awareness? Or should some of them be assimilated to introspective
self-awareness? Many philosophers have assumed that when we find out
about ourselves in nonintrospective ways, we are merely applying the same

3. This would not be to reverse Shoemaker's direction of argument. Although he
argues from the phenomenon of immunity to error through misidentification to the
elusiveness thesis, this is perfectly compatible with the thought that the elusiveness
thesis might be an explanation of the immunity to error phenomenon.

methods and techniques of acquiring information that we employ when we find out about the physical properties of ordinary objects in the world or the physical and psychological properties of other embodied subjects. I shall be suggesting that this idea is misplaced—and hence that the elusiveness thesis can at best be only a part of an explanation of privileged access. We have nonintrospective modes of self-awareness that involve forms of privileged access to our own properties.

II

Let me start with somatic proprioception. It has struck several authors that somatic proprioception is a source of information yielding judgments that are immune to error through misidentification (Evans 1982). If, for example, I form the judgment that my arms are folded on the basis of feedback from joint position sense, then there is no sense in which I can be mistaken about whose arms it is that are folded. And if I should find out that the judgment is not in fact warranted (perhaps because the relevant receptors have been artificially stimulated) my grounds for the judgment will not survive as grounds for the existential generalization that someone's arms are folded. Accordingly there has been some discussion of whether somatic proprioception can count as a counterexample to the elusiveness thesis (Ayers 1991; Cassam 1995).

Recall that Shoemaker's version of the elusiveness thesis, like Descartes's version but unlike Hume's, is based on an argument rather than an apparently contingent fact about the contents of the mind. Shoemaker argues, in effect, that there is no point postulating an introspective encounter with the self unless such an encounter serves a cognitive function. Since the only possible cognitive function would be to permit the identification of the states that are being introspected, and since there is no need for such identification (given the immunity to error through misidentification of introspection), the elusiveness thesis follows straightforwardly. The crucial point is that we do not need to be acquainted in introspection with the bearer of our psychological states in order to identify those psychological states as our own. What makes this argument seem so compelling is the fact that it is hard to see what else acquaintance with the self in introspection could achieve besides permitting the identification of the bearer of introspected psychological states.

Clearly, however, no such argument is likely to be effective in the case of somatic proprioception. It is true that the deliverances of somatic proprioception are immune to error through misidentification and, *a fortiori*, that there is no need to be acquainted with the bearer of those states (that is to say, with the embodied self) in order to identify them as one's own.[4] But, in contrast with ordinary psychological self-awareness, there is a range of cognitive functions that can be served by acquaintance with the embodied self. I have discussed these at some length in previous work (Bermúdez 1998; see also chapters 5 through 9 in this volume). Somatic proprioception provides a fundamental way of registering the distinction between self and nonself, and it does this in two basic ways. First, it provides an awareness of the limits of the body, primarily through the sense of touch. Second, it is one of the key ways by which one becomes aware that the body is responsive to one's will. The feedback gained through kinesthesia, joint position sense, and the vestibular system explains how one is aware that the body is responding to motor commands. This yields a way of grasping the body as an object that is responsive to the will. In short, what somatic proprioception offers is an awareness of the body as a spatially extended and bounded physical object that is distinctive in being responsive to the will.

In the case of somatic proprioception, therefore, there is a clear cognitive function to be served by acquaintance with the embodied self, and the elusiveness thesis is correspondingly less plausible. But there is no need to rethink the original proposal that the deliverances of somatic proprioception are immune to error through misidentification. The cognitive functions served by acquaintance with the embodied self in somatic proprioception do not include permitting the identification of proprioperceived states as one's own. The conclusion to draw from this is that the elusiveness thesis comes apart from the thesis about the identification-free nature of awareness of one's own properties. In the case of somatic proprioception the inference from the identification-free nature of the associated self-awareness to the impossibility of acquaintance with the embodied self does not hold.

Nor, of course, does the fact that we are acquainted with the embodied self in somatic proprioception have any implications for the privileged

---

4. There is room for discussion, however, about the precise sense in which they are immune to error through misidentification. See Cassam 1995.

access to our own physical properties that we derive as a function of the identification-free nature of proprioceptive self-awareness. This casts doubt on the earlier suggestion that the elusiveness thesis might play an important role in the explanation of privileged access. I suggested that privileged access might be a function of ways of acquiring information about one's own properties that do not lay us open to certain possibilities of error attendant on ordinary perceptual awareness—and the elusiveness thesis seems to explain why the relevant types of awareness should be different in this way from ordinary perceptual awareness. That suggestion depends, of course, on there being a reciprocal relation between immunity to error through misidentification and the elusiveness thesis, so that no sources of information giving rise to beliefs that are immune to error through misidentification could be described as involving perceptual or protoperceptual acquaintance with the self. But it looks very much as if somatic proprioception is going to be a counterexample, because (as we shall see) a case can be made for assimilating proprioception to perceptual awareness.

Everything depends, of course, on how perceptual awareness is understood. There are ways of understanding perceptual awareness on which it follows straightforwardly that somatic proprioception could not possibly qualify—for example, if perceptual awareness is defined as involving the use of a dedicated sensory organ. We need a characterization as theoretically unladen as possible. Here, as elsewhere in this general area, Sydney Shoemaker has led the way. In his Royce lectures Shoemaker offers a general model of perceptual awareness in terms of the following three constraints (Shoemaker 1994).

The Object Constraint. While sense perception provides one with awareness of facts, this awareness of facts is a function of awareness of the objects involved in these facts in a sense experience distinct from the object of perception.

The Multiple Objects Constraint. "Ordinary modes of perception admit of our perceiving, successively or simultaneously, a multiplicity of different objects, all of which are on a par as nonfactual objects of perception" (Shoemaker 1986, 107).

The Tracking Constraint. Sense perception involves information that allows one to pick out the object of perception through its relational and nonrelational properties. Such information enables the "tracking" of the object over time, and its reidentification from one time to another. (Shoemaker calls this the *Identification Constraint*, but I have renamed it the *Tracking Constraint* to avoid prejudging issues to do with immunity to error through misidentification.)

I have argued at some length elsewhere (Bermúdez 1998, chap. 6) that somatic proprioception can be plausibly be taken to satisfy all three of these constraints, although not, of course, to the same extent as, say, vision.

In brief, the Object Constraint is met because somatic proprioception can provide sensory experiences of, say, limb movement or muscle stretch that yield factual information about the distribution of body parts and that are no less separate from the embodied self than ordinary visual experiences are from the objects they inform us about.[5] The Multiple Objects Constraint is met because the sense of touch is a source of somatic proprioception and can be put to work to yield proprioceptive or exteroceptive information—information about the body or information about nonbodily objects in space. When the sense of touch is being used to yield exteroceptive information it obviously involves the possibility of perceiving a range of different objects, both simultaneously and successively. Even when the attention is fixed firmly on the proprioceptive dimension of tactile awareness, the exteroceptive dimension remains phenomenologically salient in background awareness (Martin 1995). And since it is uncontroversial that deploying the sense of touch exteroceptively permits both the simultaneous and successive perception of a range of distinct objects, it follows that the Multiple Objects Constraint is satisfied in all instances of tactile somatic proprioception, although, of course, in different ways.

In thinking about how the Tracking Constraint might be met, it is worth remembering that one can lose track of one's body over time—or at least of various parts of one's body. This happens, for example, when one absentmindedly walks home on automatic pilot instead of to the shops or taps one's foot in time to a piece of music without noticing. The best reason for describing these as cases where one is losing track of what one's body is doing is the feeling of surprise that comes when one notices what has been going on. What can confuse matters here is a failure to make the distinction

5. Somatic information is a very complex phenomenon and not all its elements involve any form of sensory experience. But some do, which is all that is required for the Object Constraint to be met.

stressed earlier between proprioceptive awareness and the operation of the proprioceptive information systems. In the two examples just given, the proprioceptive information systems are functioning as they must if actions like walking are even to be possible. But this doesn't mean that the subject is keeping track of his body just because those systems are functioning, any more than does the fact that the proprioceptive information systems continue to function while one is asleep. What counts is the lack of the appropriate sort of proprioceptive awareness.

It would be foolish to argue that these three constraints are met in the case of somatic proprioception in anything like the same way in which they are, say, in visual perception. There is a continuum with ordinary visual perception at one end and ordinary psychological introspection at the other, and the question is where somatic proprioception falls on the continuum. My suggestion is simply that it falls somewhat closer to visual perception than to introspection—we might accordingly describe somatic proprioception as a form of protoperceptual awareness. Moreover, it is an obvious consequence of how this conclusion has been established that the embodied self is the object of proprioceptive protoperceptual awareness. This means, to return to the main thread of the argument, that our earlier suggestion about how privileged access might be explained must be rejected in the case of somatic proprioception. Somatic proprioception is a source of information for judgments that are immune to error through misidentification, but the explanation for this cannot be that somatic proprioception does not involve any form of perceptual acquaintance with the embodied self.

It is starting to look as if we are going to require different explanations of privileged access. Even if the explanation in terms of the elusiveness thesis will suffice for ordinary psychological introspection, it will clearly not do for somatic proprioception. We will return to these issues in section IV. In the next section, I will turn to other forms of self-awareness that bear a striking resemblance to those features of somatic proprioception that we have been stressing in this section. Namely, they provide information that is immune to error through misidentification, and hence a degree of privileged access, while involving perceptual awareness of the embodied self—and in fact a far more unequivocal example of perceptual awareness of the embodied self than occurs in somatic proprioception.

III

Let us say that through introspection and somatic proprioception we have certain ways of finding out about ourselves, and that the properties we can find out about through introspection include both physical and psychological properties. Two further points should be clear. The first is that there is a range of further ways of finding out about our physical and psychological properties. We can find out about our physical and psychological properties by exercising any of the five senses. We can also, of course, rely on testimony or memory. The second is that this range of ways of finding out about ourselves can be divided quite naturally into two categories, according to whether or not they involve anything that might be described as acquaintance with the embodied self. Suppose that I am trying to find out how long my hair is. I might just take a look in the mirror. Alternatively I might search my memory banks to find out whether I have recently had a haircut. The first of these ways of finding out involves precisely the sort of encounter with the embodied self that, according to the elusiveness thesis, is not possible in introspection. For the purposes of this essay I shall assume that the five world-directed senses exhaust the direct but nonintrospective ways of finding out about our physical and psychological properties, and that testimony and memory are canonical examples of indirect, nonintrospective modes of self-awareness.

We can, therefore, identify four fundamentally different types of self-awareness—namely, introspective self-awareness, proprioceptive self-awareness, direct nonintrospective self-awareness, and indirect nonintrospective self-awareness. Many philosophers have assumed that when we find out about ourselves in the third and fourth of these ways we are merely applying the same methods and techniques of acquiring information that we employ when we find out about the physical properties of ordinary objects in the world or the physical and psychological properties of other embodied subjects. The attractiveness of this idea in broad terms is easy to appreciate when we are dealing with forms of self-awareness that are nonintrospective and indirect. It is hard to see why there should be any difference between how I use testimony to find out about myself and how I use it to find out about anyone else. The idea also has a *prima facie* appeal when it comes to perceptual self-awareness, particularly when one considers the examples standardly given to illustrate the distinction between that and introspective self-awareness. These examples usually involve the use of mirrors or some other more or less nonstandard perceptual situation in which one observes someone performing some action or having a certain property and then identifies that person as oneself. In cases like these an act of recognition always takes place and there is a correlative possibility of misidentification.

Wittgenstein's distinction between uses of "I" as subject and uses of "I" as object in the *Blue Book* offers a good illustration of the temptation to map the distinction between introspective and nonintrospective self-awareness on to the distinction between identification-free and identification-involving judgments. Wittgenstein identifies two different types of first-person judgment, corresponding to two different forms of self-awareness.

> There are two different cases in the use of the word 'I' (or 'my') which I might call 'the use as object' and 'the use as subject'. Examples of the first kind of use are these: 'My arm is broken', 'I have grown six inches', 'I have a bump on my forehead', 'The wind blows my hair about'. Examples of the second kind are: '*I* see so-and-so', '*I* try to lift my arm', '*I* think it will rain', '*I* have a toothache'. (Wittgenstein 1958, 66–67)

Judgments of the sort that would be verbally expressed by Wittgenstein's "use as subject" of the first-person pronoun are based on introspective self-awareness, while judgments expressible through the "use as object" will be based on nonintrospective self-awareness (whether direct or indirect). As we can see in the continuation of the passage, Wittgenstein thinks what distinguishes the use as subject from the use as object is the fact that the form of self-awareness grounding the use as subject is identification-free. The passage continues:

> One can point to the difference between these two categories by saying: The cases of the first category involve the recognition of a particular person, and there is in these cases the possibility of an error, or as I should rather put it: The possibility of an error has been provided for. ... It is possible that, say in an accident, I should feel a pain in my arm, see a broken arm at my side, and think it is mine when really it is my neighbor's. And I could, looking into a mirror, mistake a bump on his forehead for one on mine. On the other hand, there is no question of recognizing a person when I say I have toothache. To ask 'are you sure that it's you who have pains?' would be nonsensical. (Wittgenstein 1958, 67)

In this passage, identification-free self-awareness seems to be confined to introspective awareness of one's psychological properties, implying that any nonintrospective form of self-awareness will involve some sort of observation-based identification of a particular person as oneself. And in fact, this conclusion appears to have been tacitly accepted even by those who challenge the premise that identification-free self-awareness is confined to the domain of the psychological. When Gareth Evans suggested that we can, through somatic proprioception, have identification-free awareness of our physical properties (e.g., Evans 1982), he challenged the alleged entailment from immunity to error through misidentification to introspective awareness of the psychological. But Evans seems not to have challenged the alleged entailment from nonintrospective perceptual awareness to susceptibility to error through misidentification.

Yet this second alleged entailment cannot be accepted. Various central categories of nonintrospective direct self-awareness neither depend on observation-based identification nor are susceptible to error through misidentification.[6] I might, for example, see where I am relative to a particular landmark in front of me and, on that basis, come to form a judgment such as "I am in front of the department store." It is clear that in forming this judgment I do not identify myself as the person who is in front of the department store. Coming to find out in this way through perception that someone is in front of the department store just is coming to find out that I myself am in front of the department store. Nor is it possible for me to be mistaken about who it is who is in front of the department store. My judgment is immune to error through misidentification relative to the first-person pronoun. Of course, it is possible to imagine cases where I do form the judgment "I am in front of the department store" on the basis of ordinary perceptual awareness and yet that are not immune to error through misidentification. I might, for example, catch a glimpse in a shop window of a person with the department store behind him and then work out that that person is, in fact, me. But these sorts of cases can hardly be taken as standard.

Similar points hold for cases in which one becomes aware of one's locomotive properties through ordinary perceptual awareness. It is clear that ordinary visual perception can yield not only information about whether

6. It should be stressed that I am talking about immunity to error relative to the first-person pronoun. It is not news that perceptual awareness can be a source of judgments that are immune to error relative to, say, the demonstrative pronoun.

one is moving or at rest, but also a fairly accurate indication of one's speed and trajectory. This type of awareness of one's physical properties is identification free and immune to error through misidentification relative to the first-person pronoun. I do not normally first discover that someone is moving at a certain speed in a certain direction and then work out that that person is myself—nor is it possible for me to be mistaken about who it is moving at that speed in that direction.

This point needs handling with some delicacy. Someone might object that this type of kinesthetic information does seem prone to errors of misidentification. To take what should be a familiar case, if I am sitting in a train and the train next to mine starts moving then I may well gain the false impression that I myself am moving. Why is this not a case in which I am subject to error through misidentification, given that I mistakenly identify myself as moving when I am not moving? To appreciate what is going on here, it is helpful to recall Wright's reminder that the grounds for a judgment that is subject to error through misidentification will survive as grounds for a corresponding existential generalization if the identification turns out to be mistaken. Nothing like this occurs in the train case. When I discover that my train is in fact stationary, I cannot then retreat to the claim "Someone is moving, even if I am not."[7] The visual information on which I based my judgment provided an illusion of movement, and when my judgment is defeated so too is the judgment that there is any movement at all.

Although I have been discussing visual perception exclusively, these types of nonintrospective self-awareness also occur in other sensory modalities. As Gareth Evans pointed out, for example, audition is a powerful source of information about one's location and is also one of the cues we employ to keep track of our movement. But vision is, of course, dominant and has been the most closely studied as a source of self-awareness (particularly by psychologists in the Gibsonian tradition, to be discussed further in section IV).

The important point, for present purposes, is that these cases of direct nonintrospective self-awareness provide further examples of how the particular type of privileged access associated with judgments that are immune to error through misidentification comes apart from the elusiveness

7. People traveling in the other train are clearly not to the point here.

thesis. All the judgments we have considered in this section are obviously immune to error through misidentification and equally obviously involve a direct perceptual acquaintance with the embodied self. On the scale running from psychological introspection at one end and ordinary perceptual awareness at the other, they fall somewhere between somatic proprioception and ordinary perceptual awareness. They provide, then, even clearer evidence that the elusiveness thesis cannot provide a satisfying explanation of the privileged access associated with immunity to error through misidentification.

IV

We have seen that there are (at least) three different types of self-awareness possessing the privileged access characterized by immunity to error through misidentification. If one concentrates on the most obvious and familiar of these types—namely introspection of one's own psychological properties—then it is natural to think that privileged access is a function of the fact that the type of self-awareness involved is not in any way perceptual. This nonperceptual nature of introspective self-awareness is closely linked with the fact that introspection does not involve any sort of encounter with the self as the bearer of these psychological properties, and so one might think that there is a plausible line of explanation running from the elusiveness thesis via the nonperceptual nature of introspective self-awareness to the privileged access associated with the immunity to error through misidentification of introspectively derived psychological self-ascriptions. The discussion in the previous two sections, however, shows that even if this line of explanation works for introspective judgments, there are important classes of epistemically privileged judgments about one's physical and psychological properties on which it can get no purchase. We need to look further for a full understanding of the type of privileged access associated with immunity to error through misidentification—and different sources of information leading to judgments that are immune to error through misidentification will work in different ways to afford different types of privileged access.

Even in the case of psychological self-ascriptions one might wonder whether the proposed explanation could be fully satisfying. The fact that there is no introspective encounter with the bearer of psychological

properties is not a full explanation of the nonperceptual nature of introspective self-awareness and hence, *a fortiori*, not of the privileged access
yielded by such self-awareness. We might flesh out the sense in which psychological self-ascriptions based on introspective self-awareness are nonperceptual in the following way. A subject making such a self-ascriptive
judgment moves from ϕ-ing that p to the self-ascriptive judgment "I am
ϕ-ing that p." This transition is based on an awareness of ϕ-ing that p but
not on an awareness of himself ϕ-ing that p. The elusiveness thesis explains
only a part of this. It explains why there is no awareness of himself ϕ-ing
that p, but it does not explain how a subject can form the judgment that he
is ϕ-ing that p in the absence of such an awareness.

So how does the subject make the transition? The simple answer
(explored at greater length in chapter 3 above) is that the transition is available to subjects who have a basic mastery of what might be termed a simple
theory of introspection (by analogy with the simple theory of perception
and action discussed in Evans 1982 and Campbell 1994). In this case, the
simple theory of introspection amounts to nothing more than some level
of mastery of the *a priori* link between being introspectively aware of a
thought and it being the case that one is thinking it—which is, of course,
an appreciation of the fact that psychological self-ascriptions are identification free.[8]

Can we use a similar account to explain self-ascriptions based on somatic
proprioception? The most obvious difference between proprioceptively
based judgments about one's physical properties and introspectively based
judgments about one's psychological properties is that it is not even a matter of natural necessity that one can only become aware of one's own bodily
properties through somatic proprioception. It is perfectly compatible with
the existing laws of nature that one might be hooked up to someone else
in such a way that one receives proprioceptive input from that person's
body as well as from one's own and hence actually needs to identify which
body a given proprioceptive input is coming from. This possibility does not

8. As Peacocke has brought out in his recent work on these matters, this is the same
a priori link that governs the status of the judgment as knowledge. What we see in
this case is that the subject's reason for forming the judgment is an appreciation of
precisely the factor that qualifies the judgment as knowledge. For further discussion
of Peacocke's account of self-ascriptive judgments, see Bermúdez 2001, included as
chapter 3 in this volume.

cast doubt on the immunity to error through misidentification of somatic proprioception, given that, as things are, we are not wired up to other bodies and have no reason to think we might be. In fact, it is really the lack of any grounds for thinking that we might be wired up to other bodies that secures immunity to error through misidentification. That is what makes it inconceivable to ask whose body a given input is coming from, and what prevents the grounds for a defeated proprioceptively based self-ascription surviving as the grounds for an existential generalization. Nonetheless, the fact that there is such a possibility does show that this immunity is at best *de facto* rather than logical, to employ Shoemaker's distinction.[9] And, if the immunity to error is merely *de facto* then there can be no *a priori* link between being proprioceptively aware of some bodily property and that property being a property of one's own body. Nonetheless, this is compatible with there being a simple theory of proprioception based on the *de facto* link between ownership and the objects of proprioception. One would expect this simple theory to be more complicated than that implicated in ordinary psychological introspection, given the points made earlier about the role of proprioception in underwriting an awareness of one's body as a bounded physical object uniquely responsive to the will.[10]

Things get more complicated, however, when we turn to judgments based on the perception-based forms of self-awareness discussed in the previous section. We need a completely different account of the immunity to error through misidentification of these judgments. The proposal I

9. See Cassam 1995 for further discussion. One might wonder, of course, whether anything could be immune to error through misidentification in a logical sense. Could I not be wired up to someone else's brain in such a way that introspection would be a source of information about her thoughts as well as my own? Everything depends on how the ownership of thoughts is determined, and there are two conflicting pressures to accommodate. On the one hand, we often speak as if introspecting a thought is sufficient for that thought to be one's own—in which case the rewiring hypothesis would merely result in an expansion of one's thinking repertoire. But, on the other hand, we usually take it that a thought can only have one owner—in which case the rewiring hypothesis could only be interpreted as my introspecting someone else's thoughts. My inclination would be to think that the first of these outweighs the second.

10. For a different (and I now think more plausible) view of what grounds the immunity to error through misidentification of judgments based on somatic proprioception, see particularly chapter 8 in this volume.

will develop in the remainder of this essay is that their immunity to error through misidentification is a function of the distinctive way in which the self is represented in the content of perception. I will develop this proposal for visual perception, since vision is the dominant modality and has received the most detailed study. It will be recalled from the previous section that two types of visually grounded judgments are immune to error through misidentification in the required sense. The first type includes perceptually based judgments about one's own location, such as "I am in front of the cathedral." The second type includes judgments about the nature and direction of one's movement such as "I am veering toward the central reservation" or "I am walking toward the door."

In discussing these two types of judgment I will be leaning in particular on the account of vision developed by the perceptual psychologist J. J. Gibson (particularly in Gibson 1966 and 1979). It is in Gibson's work that we find the most developed account of how the embodied self features in the content of perception as a distinctive object. I shall be arguing that those features of the content of perception to which Gibson draws our attention play a crucial role in underwriting the immunity to error through misidentification of perceptually grounded first-person judgments.

Let me start, though, by getting clear on the nature of the problem. What exactly are we looking for in an account of the immunity to error through misidentification of the relevant class of judgments? Our earlier discussion of introspection and somatic proprioception provides a clue. What we sought there was an account of what warrants the immediate transition from one's awareness of ϕ-ing to the judgment that one is oneself ϕ-ing. Judgments that are immune to error through misidentification are identification free in an epistemic sense. That is, the warrant for them does not depend on the warrant one might have for identifying a particular person as oneself. Nonetheless, there must be some warrant for what one might term the self-specifying aspect of the judgment. In the case of proprioceptive and introspective judgments, the warrant comes from mastery of the link (*a priori* in the case of introspection and *de facto* in the case of proprioception) between being aware of a particular property and that property being one's own. These links exist because both introspection and proprioception are modes of acquiring information that yield information only about one's own properties. Clearly, there are no such links in the case of perceptual awareness, since the bodily self is presented in perception as one of a range of physical objects. So what provides the warrant for the self-specifying aspect of the judgment?

The answer lies, I claim, in the distinctive way in which the embodied self appears in the content of visual perception. In the case of self-locating beliefs, the embodied self is fixed as a distinctive object at the origin of the field of view in such a way that perceptually derived information about the position of objects in the world is explicitly relational. The self-specifying aspect of a perceptually based self-locating judgment is warranted because it is grounded in what is given explicitly in the content of perception— and the immunity to error through misidentification derives from the fact that this relational information yielded by vision could not be information about the position of anyone but oneself. The same holds for perceptually based judgments about one's movement. It is part of the content of perception that one is moving—one can normally tell with considerable accuracy the difference between moving relative to the environment and having the environment move relative to oneself. Again the information is explicitly relational—and relational in a way such that it could not possibly be information about anyone else's movement.

It is important to realize that the embodied self is the originating point of perception in a much richer sense than simply being the geometrical origin of the field of view. This is so in two respects that Gibson has drawn to our attention. The first is that the embodied self is directly perceived as the boundary of the field of view. The field of view is oval, bounded by the shape of the head. The head serves to block out roughly half of the surrounding environment, but it does this in a way rather different from the way one nonbodily object blocks out another. The boundaries are vague and indefinite. They define the point of observation in a way that cannot in principle be shared by anyone else. Those facial features that occupy permanent structural positions within the field of view enhance this perspectival uniqueness. The nose, for example, is almost always present in visual experience and serves itself to mark an important boundary within the field of view. The nose is the leftmost thing that can be seen by the right eye and the rightmost thing that can be seen by the left eye. Moreover, of all the edges that the observer can see, the nose sweeps across the field of view when the observer moves his head at a faster rate than any other perceived surface. For many of us the eyebrows and cheekbones also occupy a permanent place framing the perceived environment. The second point that Gibson stresses is that even those body parts that do not occupy fixed positions in the field of view are nonetheless perceived in a manner quite unlike the way in which nonbodily physical objects are perceived. The bodily extremities protrude into the field of vision from below in a way that occludes the environment, and yet that differs from the way in which one nonbodily physical object in the field of vision might occlude another. A solid angle is an angle with its base at some perceived object and its apex at the eye. Every object is capable of presenting a range of solid angles, depending on its size and distance from the perceiver. The farther away the object, and/or the smaller it is, the smaller the solid angle. But the solid angles subtended by occluding body parts cannot be reduced below a certain minimum—the minimum corresponding to the maximum distance the body part in question can travel from the point of observation. Perceived body parts are, in Gibson's provocative phrase, "subjective objects" in the content of visual perception.

We see, then, that the self is presented in perception as an object of a distinctive and peculiar type in virtue of certain features of the content of visual perception. Some of these arise from the features that lead Gibson to describe perceived body parts as subjective objects in the field of view—the fact, for example, that body parts can vary in perceived size only within a limited range. The way in which the body appears as the frame and boundary of the visual array is also extremely important. All of these features serve to create, for each of us, a distinctive and unique visual perspective on the world. It is the fact that self-locating judgments are made on the basis of information derived from such a unique visual perspective that explains their immunity to error through misidentification. The uniqueness of the visual perspective on the world does not just make it the case that one's perceptually derived information about where one is relative to objects in the perceived environment could not possibly be about anyone but oneself. More importantly, the uniqueness of the visual perspective is itself directly perceived in virtue of those features of the environment we have been discussing and so, by extension, it is visibly manifest to the perceiver that the information about the self gained through vision could not be about any creature except the self. And it is this that warrants the self-specifying aspect of perceptually based judgments that are immune to error through misidentification.

These features that make up the uniqueness of the visual perspective all play a part in underwriting both types of judgment identified in the previous section—judgments about one's own location relative to perceived objects around one and judgments about one's own movement relative to the perceived environment. For the second class of judgments, further aspects of the self-specifying information available in visual perception also come into play. Once again, Gibson's analysis of vision proves helpful. One of Gibson's major contributions to the study of vision is the proposal to reconstrue the visual field as a constantly moving and constantly reconfiguring set of illuminated surfaces and concomitant solid visual angles, rather than in terms of empty space containing bounded objects (figures on a ground). We do not, he thinks, ever see empty space surrounding discrete objects. What we see is a complex and gapless structure of surfaces. Some of these surfaces are surfaces of objects, while others are not (the various surfaces in the sky, for example). To each surface there corresponds a solid visual angle with its base at the face of the visible surface and its apex at the point of observation. We can, for simplicity's sake, think of these solid angles as cones (recalling Euclid's visual cones), although, of course, their shape will vary with the visible outline of the surface in question. As the observer moves through the environment the solid angles change, as one surface moves in front of another (relative to the perceiver) or as the observer approaches or moves away from the surface. This is what Gibson terms optic flow.

The particular pattern of changes in the optic flow specifies the perceiver's trajectory through the environment. What allows the perceiver to extract a meaningful indication of his trajectory from the changing structure of the optic flow is that there is an underlying invariant structure to the optic flow. For present purposes, the crucial point is that the optic flow contains a stationary point determined by the movement of the observer. The optical flow in any field of vision starts from a center that is itself stationary, and this stationary center specifies the point that is being approached, when the perceiver is moving. The aiming point of locomotion is at the vanishing point of optical flow. This means that the entire structure of the field of view is determined by the direction of the perceiver's movement. And this creates an effect that is an almost exact counterpart of the effect created by the uniqueness of the visual perspective. The field of view is centered on the observer in the ways discussed earlier (and also in the sense that the point of observation marks the apex of all the solid angles in the field of view). But it is also centered on the aiming point of locomotion, for that is where the movement of the optic flow begins. This is what underwrites the self-specifying aspect of judgments about one's own movement. Once again, it is manifest to the perceiver that visually derived information about movement relative to the perceived environment could not be information about anyone else's movement relative to the perceived environment—for the very structure of the optic array is given in terms of the perceiver's own direction of movement.

V

This essay began by proposing an attractively simple picture of the relation between the elusiveness thesis, immunity to error through misidentification and privileged access. The phenomenon of immunity to error through misidentification relative to the first-person pronoun is characteristic of the most fundamental sources of information providing privileged access to our own psychological and physical properties. Moreover, it seems to be more basic than the other proposed forms of privileged access, in the sense that it is presupposed by them but does not presuppose them. When one concentrates on introspective access to one's own psychological properties, it is natural to think that immunity to error through misidentification is a function of the fact that the self cannot be an object of introspective awareness; that is, the elusiveness thesis seems to explain why introspection does not involve possibilities of error attendant upon ordinary perceptual awareness.

The burden of this essay, however, has been to show that this cannot be the whole story. The phenomenon of immunity to error through misidentification relative to the first-person pronoun extends far more widely than introspective awareness of our own psychological properties. Judgments that are immune to error through misidentification relative to the first-person pronoun can be made on the basis of somatic proprioception, as well as on the basis of the self-awareness provided in and through ordinary perceptual awareness. Here the elusiveness thesis does not apply. A different explanation is required, therefore, for the warrant attaching to judgments based on these sources of information—and, in particular, for the self-specifying aspect of those judgments corresponding to the immunity to error through misidentification of the information source on which they are based. Proposals for developing such accounts were offered in section IV. The upshot of the discussion is that, although immunity to error through misidentification is indeed an important type of privileged access, it does itself require explanation, and, moreover, there will be different explanations for the different sources of information at stake. The domain of privileged access is both wider and more complex than it is often taken to be.

References

Ayers, M. 1991. *Locke: Epistemology and Ontology*. London: Routledge.

Alston, W. 1971. Varieties of privileged access. *American Philosophical Quarterly* 8:223–241.

Bermúdez, J. L. 1998. *The Paradox of Self-Consciousness*. Cambridge, MA: MIT Press.

Bermúdez, J. L. 2001. Sources of self-consciousness. *Proceedings of the Aristotelian Society* 102:87–107.

Bermúdez, J. L., A. J. Marcel, and N. Eilan, eds. 1995. *The Body and the Self*. Cambridge, MA: MIT Press.

Campbell, J. 1994. *Past, Space and Self*. Cambridge: Cambridge University Press.

Cassam, Q., ed. 1994. *Self-Knowledge*. Oxford: Oxford University Press.

Cassam, Q. 1995. Introspection and bodily self-ascription. In *The Body and the Self*, ed. J. L. Bermúdez, A. J. Marcel, and N. Eilan. Cambridge, MA: MIT Press.

Cassam, Q. 1997. *Self and World*. Oxford: Clarendon Press.

Descartes, R. 1984. *The Philosophical Writings of Descartes*, vol. 1. Ed. J. Cottingham, R. Stoothoff, and D. Murdoch. Cambridge: Cambridge University Press.

Evans, G. 1982. *Varieties of Reference*. Oxford: Oxford University Press.

Gibson, J. J. 1966. *The Senses Considered as Perceptual Systems*. Boston: Houghton Mifflin.

Gibson, J. J. 1979. *The Ecological Approach to Visual Perception*. Boston: Houghton Mifflin.

Hume, D. 1978. *A Treatise of Human Nature*, ed. L. A. Selby-Bigger, rev. P. H. Nidditch. Oxford: Clarendon Press. Originally published 1739–1740.

Martin, M. 1995. Bodily awareness: A sense of ownership. In *The Body and the Self*, ed. J. L. Bermúdez, A. J. Marcel, and N. Eilan. Cambridge, MA: MIT Press.

Peacocke, C. 1999. *Being Known*. Oxford: Oxford University Press.

Shoemaker, S. 1984. Self-reference and self-awareness. In *Identity, Cause and Mind*. Cambridge: Cambridge University Press.

Shoemaker, S. 1986. Introspection and the self. *Midwest Studies in Philosophy* 10. Reprinted in Shoemaker 1996.

Shoemaker, S. 1994. Self-knowledge and "inner sense." *Philosophy and Phenomenological Research* 54:249–314. Reprinted in Shoemaker 1996.

Shoemaker, S. 1996. *The First-Person Perspective and Other Essays*. Cambridge: Cambridge University Press.

Wittgenstein, L. 1958. *The Blue and Brown Books*. Oxford: Blackwell.

Wright, C. 1998. Self-knowledge: The Wittgensteinian legacy. In *Knowing Our Own Mind*, ed. C. Wright, B. Smith, and C. Macdonald. Oxford: Oxford University Press.

5 The Phenomenology of Bodily Awareness

Introduction

As embodied subjects, we are aware of our bodies in distinctive ways.[1] One source of this distinctiveness is that we have ways of finding out about our own bodies that we do not have about any other physical objects in the world. There are distinctive information channels that allow us directly to monitor both the body's homeostatic states and its spatial properties. Some of these information channels are conscious and others unconscious. They all contribute, however, to a distinctive type of experience, namely the experience of oneself as an embodied agent. It is this distinctive type of experience that I call the *phenomenology of bodily awareness*. The phenomenology of bodily awareness has an important role to play in self-consciousness. It is, moreover, of critical importance in generating and controlling action.

Bodily awareness is a complex phenomenon that has received attention from a number of different theoretical and experimental approaches. It of course has intricate and highly developed physical underpinnings that are relatively well understood. Physiologists and neurophysiologists have devoted considerable attention to understanding the mechanisms of *proprioception* (awareness of limb position and bodily configuration) and *somatosensation* (bodily sensation).[2] We have a good understanding of how bodily sensations originate in specialized receptors distributed across the

1. This essay has been greatly improved by comments from David Smith, Amie Thomasson, and an anonymous reviewer for Oxford University Press. A much shorter version of the central sections was published as Bermúdez 2004.

2. For a very helpful introduction, see part 3 of Roberts 2002.

surface of the skin and within the deep tissues. Some of these receptors are sensitive to skin and body temperature. Others are pain detectors (*nociceptors*). There are receptors specialized for mechanic stimuli of various kinds, such as pressure and vibration. Information about muscle stretch comes from muscle spindles. Other receptors monitor stresses and forces at the joints and in the tendons. Information from all of these receptors and nerve endings is carried by the spinal cord to the brain along three different pathways. One pathway carries information stemming from *discriminative touch* (which is a label for a complex set of tactile ways of finding out about the shape and texture of physical objects).[3] Another carries information about pain and temperature. The third carries proprioceptive information. Each of these pathways ends up at a different brain area. The discriminative touch pathway travels to the cerebral cortex, while the proprioceptive pathway terminates in the cerebellum. The properties of these brain areas have been well studied. We know, for example, that tactile information is processed in the somatosensory cortex, which is located in the parietal lobe. The somatosensory cortex is *somatotopically* organized, with specific regions representing specific parts of the body. The cortical space assigned to information from each bodily region is a function of the fineness of tactile discrimination within that region (which is itself a function of the number of receptors there). Neuropsychologists, neuroimagers, and computational neuroscientists have made considerable progress in understanding how somatosensory and proprioceptive information is processed in the brain and how that processing can be disturbed by brain injury.

Explanations of the physiological underpinnings of bodily awareness can at best form only part of an understanding of the distinctiveness of the experience of embodiment—of what I earlier termed the phenomenology of bodily awareness. The gap between an understanding of the mechanisms underlying experience and the distinctive character of that experience has been much stressed in contemporary philosophy—many would think excessively so. Moving beyond physiology, bodily awareness has been approached from a number of perspectives. From the scientific point of view, much light has emerged from the study of patients with various forms

3. See Hsiao et al. 2002 for a useful tutorial on the neural basis of discriminative touch.

of disorders of bodily awareness, such as *deafferentation* (where patients lose the ability to feel peripheral sensations) and *autotopagnosia* (where patients lose the ability to recognize and point to body parts). The verbal reports from patients suffering from neuropathies such as these can be very instructive in plotting the phenomenology of normal bodily awareness, precisely because of the insight they provide into what bodily awareness is like when certain central elements of normal bodily awareness are absent or distorted. So too can experimental exploration of the implications of abnormal bodily awareness for different types of motor behavior and deliberative action. As we will see further below, attention to the neuropathological data allows us to make considerable progress toward a taxonomy of the different components of bodily awareness.

From a philosophical point of view, there has been a resurgence of interest in the phenomenon of bodily awareness within the analytic tradition.[4] In many ways this is an extension of analytical philosophers' preoccupation with pain as a paradigmatic mental state. It is natural to compare and contrast the metaphysics and epistemology of pain with, say, the metaphysics and epistemology of bodily awareness. Many of the issues that arise mesh naturally with established concerns within the analytic tradition. So, for example, philosophers have explored whether the information about the body yielded by the various mechanisms of bodily awareness has the same type of *privileged* status that many theorists grant to the information about our own mental states that we derive from introspection. There are, moreover, long-standing debates about the role of bodily continuity in personal identity to which one might expect thinking about bodily awareness to be highly relevant. Many philosophers, beginning with Locke, have argued that psychological continuity (in the form of memories and other diachronic mental states) is what really matters for personal identity, so that bodily continuity is neither necessary nor sufficient for securing personal identity. The plausibility of this line of argument is likely to

---

4. Early work includes Armstrong 1962, which is a book-length treatment of bodily sensation, and Anscombe's short paper of the same year on sensations of position (Anscombe 1962), which proved very influential. Brian O'Shaughnessy's two-volume *The Will* (O'Shaughnessy 1980) marked the beginning of more recent work in this area. For a representative sample, see the philosophical essays in Bermúdez et al. 1995, together with Cassam 1997 and Bermúdez 1998, as well as chapters 6 through 9 in this volume.

rest, at least partially, on the centrality that one accords to awareness of one's own body in underwriting one's sense of self. More generally, just as analytical philosophers have moved toward recognition that the mind is embedded within a social and physical context, and hence that we have to take social and environmental factors into account in thinking about the nature and content of mental states, so too are they coming to realize that we have to consider cognition and self-consciousness within an embodied context.

However, despite this resurgence of interest within the analytical tradition, the experiential dimension of bodily awareness has been most extensively explored within the phenomenological tradition.[5] The most comprehensive treatment is to be found in part 1 of Merleau-Ponty's *Phenomenology of Perception* (Merleau-Ponty 1962). One particularly interesting feature of Merleau-Ponty's work in this area is how deeply informed it is by a detailed knowledge of current research in neuropsychology and neurophysiology at the time he was writing. Although the scientific study of bodily awareness has made huge advances since he was writing in the 1940s, the interface that he opened up between our understanding of experience, on the one hand, and our understanding of the mechanisms underlying that experience continues to be vitally important. And it remains the case that no subsequent author has explored this interface with anything like Merleau-Ponty's depth and insight.

The problem that I will be addressing in this essay can be understood in terms of two of the different strands that we find in Merleau-Ponty's rich exploration of the phenomenology of bodily awareness. From a phenomenological point of view, Merleau-Ponty explores in very insightful ways our distinctive ways of finding out about, and acting through, our bodies—the ways in which, as he puts it, "the body is the vehicle of being-in-the-world" (1962, 82). His project here is phenomenological in the nontechnical sense of the word. That is to say, he is concerned with characterizing agency and bodily awareness from the perspective of the experiencing subject. The distinction between first-person and third-person perspectives is useful at this point. Merleau-Ponty does not present matters quite in these terms, but it

5. My talking of the analytical and phenomenological traditions as distinct should be understood in purely sociological terms. As should become clear, my interest in this essay is with issues that arise at the intersection of cognitive science, phenomenology, and analytical philosophy of mind.

is one component of how he understands the distinction between the *for-itself* and the *in-itself*—a distinction that goes back at least as far as Hegel's *Phenomenology of Spirit*, although Merleau-Ponty's usage is no doubt more closely tied to Sartre's use of the distinction in *Being and Nothingness*. From a first-person perspective, we experience the body *qua* for-itself, via the ways that it structures and gives meaning to our engagements with the physical world. From a third-person perspective, in contrast, we treat the body *qua* in-itself, as a complex of muscles, bones, and nerves that enters into causal interactions with other objects and that can in principle be studied and understood as one object among others, albeit a distinctive and highly complex object.[6]

The general contours of the distinction that Merleau-Ponty is making between the in-itself and the for-itself should be congenial to many theorists working within analytical philosophy of mind, although they would probably have some difficulty with how it is formulated. The basic idea that we cannot understand human agency in the same way that we understand causal interactions between nonanimate physical objects has been widely canvassed within the analytical tradition. One obvious point of contact is with theorists writing in the Wittgensteinian tradition, particularly those such as Anscombe, Taylor, and Kenny who argued that the reasons for which people act should not be understood in causal terms.[7] But there are points of contact with theorists who accept that reasons can be causes. The distinction that some have tried to make between agent causation and event causation is somewhat in the spirit of Merleau-Ponty's distinction.[8] So too is the approach of Davidson's anomalous monism, which is based on

6. Merleau-Ponty emphatically distinguishes himself from those who construe the in-itself/for-itself distinction in terms of a distinction between the physiological, on the one hand, and pure consciousness, on the other. As emerges clearly in his discussion of the patient Schneider (see further below), Merleau-Ponty understands the for-itself in terms of what he calls motor intentionality, a complex theoretical notion that is intended to overcome standard construals of the gap between the realm of the physiological and the realm of consciousness. As he cautions the reader (1962, 124), "As long as the body is defined in terms of existence in-itself, it functions uniformly like a mechanism, and as long as the mind is defined in terms of pure existence for-itself, it knows only objects arrayed before it."

7. See, e.g., Anscombe 1957, Taylor 1964, and Kenny 1963.

8. For agent causation see Chisholm 1976 and O'Connor 2000.

a sharp distinction between the law-governed domain of the physical and the norm-governed realm of the psychological.[9]

There are two aspects of Merleau-Ponty's approach to agency and bodily experience, however, that analytical philosophers are likely to find unpalatable. The first is its susceptibility to an interpretation that draws strong metaphysical conclusions from the phenomenological distinction between the for-itself and the in-itself. Merleau-Ponty frequently writes as if the experienced body in some sense stands outside the physical world. He draws a distinction between the phenomenal body and the objective body that can be interpreted in a manner incompatible with any ontological position that, in the last analysis, treats the body as simply a highly developed biochemical object that stands apart from other objects in the world only in virtue of its complexity and organization.[10] It is unclear, to this reader at least, where Merleau-Ponty draws the line between phenomenology and ontology in *Phenomenology of Perception*, but he often writes in a distinctly idealist vein, saying for example that "the constitution of our body as object" is a "crucial moment in the genesis of the objective world." This dimension of his thinking might seem to place the experienced body outside the physical world in a way that is incompatible with even the weakest form of philosophical naturalism.

Even if we do not take Merleau-Ponty to be committed to such a drastic ontological position, and instead see him as primarily exploring a distinction between two ways of experiencing the body,[11] he develops his views in a way that has significant repercussions for how we think about explanation—repercussions that philosophers of mind in the analytic tradition are unlikely to find congenial. As we will see in more detail in the next section, Merleau-Ponty is more than happy to draw the conclusion that the explanatory power of scientific investigation is severely constrained by the

9. See the essays in Davidson 1980, particularly "Mental Events" and "Philosophy as Psychology."

10. There are, of course, a number of philosophers who reject philosophical naturalism, particularly with respect to the qualitative features of experience. But no one (to the best of my knowledge) has ever suggested that this rejection should have any consequences for how we think about the ontology of the body.

11. For a clear interpretation of Merleau-Ponty along these lines, see Priest 1998, chap. 4.

distinction between the phenomenal body and the objective body (which is a special case of his overall distinction between the phenomenal world and the objective world).[12] The phenomenal body, Merleau-Ponty thinks, cannot be elucidated scientifically. Science can only inform us about the objective body.

The aim of this essay is to offer a way of doing justice to the phenomenological insights of Merleau-Ponty's thinking about bodily awareness and its role in agency without following him in the limitations he places on the explanatory power of the scientific study of the body. I shall discuss one central feature of bodily awareness in a way that tries to respect the points that Merleau-Ponty stressed about the distinctive phenomenology of the experienced body. This feature is what Merleau-Ponty terms the "spatiality" of the body, which he discusses in the lengthy third chapter of part 1 of *Phenomenology of Perception*, "The Spatiality of One's Own Body and Motility." There are, I shall argue, some very fundamental differences between how we experience the spatiality of our own bodies and how we experience the spatiality of nonbodily physical objects. Bodily space, I shall argue, is represented in a fundamentally different way from the space within which we perceive and act on nonbodily physical objects. I will stress that we need to understand the spatiality of bodily awareness in terms of a non-Cartesian frame of reference, in contrast to the Cartesian frames of reference that structure our perception of, and interactions with, nonbodily physical objects. This basic distinction between two different types of frame of reference goes a long way, I shall suggest, toward accommodating what Merleau-Ponty correctly sees as the distinctiveness of the spatiality of our own bodies. And yet it is, of course, a distinction between two ways of representing space, rather than between two types of space—a distinction at the level of Fregean sense rather than Fregean reference. The fact that we experience our own bodies in terms of a non-Cartesian reference frame

12. Merleau-Ponty's views on the relation between the phenomenal world and the objective world are instructively summarized in the following passage from Dillon (1988): "the objective world is an ideal variant of the phenomenal world. It is an end posited by thought troubled by its own partiality. It is the name for a universal validity that once was conceived through the symbols of divinity and now is conceived through the optimistic projections of science. Objectivity is a responsibility we assume; to take it as a character of the real is to collapse time, ignore ambiguity, and presume a vantage that does not exist."

is perfectly compatible with our bodies being ontologically on a par with objects that we experience in terms of a Cartesian reference frame. Moreover, and this is the key methodological point, there is nothing about this distinction between two different frames of reference that stands in the way of our taking a third-person perspective on how bodily awareness feeds into and controls motor behavior and intentional action. I shall make good on this claim in the final section by illustrating how this approach to the experienced spatiality of somatic proprioception can be integrated with contemporary work on the psychology of motor control.

1   Merleau-Ponty on Bodily Awareness and the Body

The general tenor of Merleau-Ponty's thinking about our experience as embodied agents is given by his concise comment that "The outline of my body is a frontier which ordinary spatial relations to do not cross" (Merleau-Ponty 1962, 98). There is, he claims, a very fundamental discontinuity between the experienced spatiality of the physical world and the experienced spatiality of the body—more precisely, of the lived body, of the body as we might experience it from the inside. The body is not an object—or, more precisely, the lived body, the experienced body, cannot be understood as an object on a par with other objects in the external world.

In presenting Merleau-Ponty's analysis of the phenomenology of bodily experience, I will focus on his discussion of the patient Schneider in the long chapter entitled "The Spatiality of One's Own Body and Motility." He is discussing a patient suffering from what he terms *psychic blindness*—the essence of the disorder being an inability to carry out what he (Merleau-Ponty) calls abstract movements, such as moving his arms and legs to order, naming and pointing to body parts, when his eyes are shut. He points out that there are certain movements that this patient is perfectly capable of making. Some of these are what we might call body-relative reactions. Here is an example.

A patient of the kind discussed above, when stung by a mosquito, does not need to look for the place where he has been stung. He finds it straight away, because for him there is no question of locating it in relation to axes of coordinates in objective space, but of reaching with his phenomenal hand a certain painful spot on his phenomenal body, and because between the hand as a scratching potentiality and the place stung as a spot to be scratched a directly experienced relationship is presented in the natural system of one's own body. (Merleau-Ponty 1962, 105–106)

Here the distinction between the epistemological and the metaphysical strands in Merleau-Ponty's thinking comes across very clearly. The epistemological point that he makes about the experience of localizing a sensation on the body seems exactly right. When one performs a simple body-relative action such as scratching a mosquito sting there is indeed no question of locating the sting on some sort of objective coordinate system, working out where one's hand is on the same coordinate system, and then plotting a path between the two locations. The locations of both hand and sting are given in body-relative space (and I shall have more to say later about how this should be understood).

Merleau-Ponty uses these points about the phenomenology of bodily awareness to draw an explicit distinction between "objective space" and "the natural system of one's own body." The following passage is instructive:

The whole operation takes place in the domain of the phenomenal; it does not run through the objective world, and only the spectator, who lends his objective representation of the living body to the acting subject, can believe that the sting is perceived, that the hand moves in objective space, and consequently find it odd that the same subject can fail in experiments requiring him to point things out. (Merleau-Ponty 1962, 106)

These basic ideas then get generalized into a global distinction between the phenomenal body and the objective body. A few lines further on he writes: "It is never our objective body that we move, but our phenomenal body, and there is no mystery in that, since our body, as the potentiality of this or that part of the world, surges toward objects to be grasped and perceives them" (Merleau-Ponty 1962, 106). The distinction between the phenomenal body and the objective body plays an important role in *Phenomenology of Perception*. The phenomenal body is supposed to play a foundational role in the very constitution of the objective world. Here is a representative passage:

The body is not one more among external objects. It is neither tangible nor visible in so far as it is that which sees and touches. The body, therefore, is not one more among external objects, with the peculiarity of always being there. If it is permanent, the permanence is absolute and is the ground for the relative permanence of disappearing objects, real objects. The presence and absence of external objects are only variations within a field of primordial presence, a perceptual domain over which my body exercises power. Not only is the permanence of my body not a particular case of the permanence of external objects in the world, but the second cannot be understood except through the first: not only is the perspective of my body not a particular case of that of objects, but furthermore the presentation of objects in perspective cannot be understood except through the resistance of my body to all variations in perspective. (Merleau-Ponty 1962, 92)

I am not a Merleau-Ponty scholar, and I do not want to make any strong claims about what is going on here. What I would like to stress, however, is a conditional claim, namely, that *if* we accept Merleau-Ponty's distinction between the phenomenal body and the objective body at face value, then it looks as if there will be very little scope for scientific study of the interesting and important aspects of bodily experience. Science, whether cognitive science, empirical psychology, or neurophysiology, can only inform us about the objective body. It can have nothing to say about the phenomenal body.

It would seem that Merleau-Ponty himself accepted this implication of the distinction between the phenomenal body and the objective body. That the distinction imposes limits on what we can learn from physiology and psychology is clearly stated in the first two chapters of part 1. In chapter 1, "The Body as Object and Mechanistic Physiology," Merleau-Ponty argues with some power that the physiological study of the body intrinsically involves an objectification of something that is fundamentally nonobjective. To study the physiology of the body is to treat the *for-itself* as an *in-itself*—to try to reduce the distinctive functioning of the body to mechanical causation of the type that governs interactions between nonbodily physical objects. As Merleau-Ponty brings out in discussing the phenomena of *phantom limb* and *anosognosia* (a patient's refusal to accept the reality of his or her illness and deficits), the physiological treatment of neuropsychological disorders imposes upon us the burden of explaining how "the psychic determining factors and the physiological conditions gear into each other" (77)—an explanatory burden that he thinks it impossible to discharge. If we are to understand the phenomenology of bodily awareness, Merleau-Ponty concludes, there is little to be gained from studying the physiology of the body.

In chapter 2, "The Experience of the Body and Classical Psychology," Merleau-Ponty takes a related but somewhat different tack. Although classical psychology, no less than classical physiology, is committed to treating the body as objective, he argues that it itself points us toward the inadequacy of the objectifying perspective. It is a little unclear what he means by "classical psychology," but the points he wants to extract are clear enough. Within psychology we find descriptions of the body and of the role of the body in action that are, he thinks, simply incompatible with the idea that the body is just an object in the world among other objects. As far as this essay is concerned, one particularly interesting example Merleau-Ponty gives is the contrast drawn by "classical psychology" between ordinary perception of the movement of extrabodily physical objects and kinesthetic perception of bodily movement. Kinesthetic perception of bodily movement is global, he suggests, while our perception of the movement of ordinary objects is successive. Whereas we simply feel the body move, we perceive the movement of nonbodily objects by comparing their different positions at different times. The contrast is crude, according to Merleau-Ponty, but contains a germ of truth:

What they were expressing, badly it is true, by "kinaesthetic sensation" was the originality of the movements which I perform with my body: they directly anticipate the final situation, for my intention initiates a movement through space merely to obtain the objective initially given at the starting-point; there is as it were a germ of a movement which only secondarily develops into an objective movement. I move external objects with the aid of my body, which takes hold of them in one place and shifts them to another. But my body itself I move directly, I do not find it at one point of objective space and transfer it to another. I have no need to look for it, it is already with me. (1962, 94)

Nonetheless, Merleau-Ponty thinks, psychologists have failed to carry through their insights into the phenomenology of our experience of our own bodies. And what this means, of course, is that we can learn relatively little about the phenomenology of the body from empirical psychology—all we can learn, really, is the inadequacy of the objectifying approach of psychologists.

This pessimism about the possibility of learning from physiology and psychology might seem to be in tension with Merleau-Ponty's interdisciplinary focus, and his constant appeal to neuropsychological case studies. However, the appearance is deceptive. What Merleau-Ponty is objecting to is the idea that we can understand the phenomenology of bodily awareness by studying the mechanisms that make the associated experiences possible—or, to put it in different terms, that we can study a first-person phenomenon through physiological and psychological mechanisms that are only susceptible to a third-person approach. But this is not in any sense incompatible with the thought that we can learn about the first-person phenomenon of bodily awareness by looking at the behavior of subjects in whom those mechanisms are not functioning properly—and indeed at how those subjects describe their experience of the world. It is mechanistic explanation of bodily awareness that Merleau-Ponty opposes, rather than scientific investigation per se.

Nonetheless, although Merleau-Ponty's position is perfectly consistent, one can certainly wonder whether it is desirable. The price is high. It is difficult when reading Merleau-Ponty not to be convinced in very general terms that there must be some sort of distinction between two ways of thinking about the body—between those two approaches that he connects with the distinction between the *for-itself* and the *in-itself*. But should we follow him in concluding that there can be no dialogue between these two approaches; that there is nothing to be learned about the body *qua* for-itself by exploring the body *qua* in-itself? It is natural to wonder whether there might not be a way of doing justice to at least some of those features of bodily awareness that led Merleau-Ponty to make such a sharp distinction between the for-itself and the in-itself within a theoretical perspective that treats the body as ontologically on a par with nonbodily objects.

3 Types and Levels of Bodily Awareness

Let us look again at the crucial passage where Merleau-Ponty first begins to draw metaphysical conclusions from the phenomenology of bodily awareness.

The whole operation takes place in the domain of the phenomenal; it does not run through the objective world, and only the spectator, who lends his objective representation of the living body to the acting subject, can believe that the sting is perceived, that the hand moves in objective space, and consequently find it odd that the same subject can fail in experiments requiring him to point things out. (Merleau-Ponty 1962, 106)

The crucial claims here are both negative. The first is the denial that we should view Schneider's awareness of his own body as awareness of an object (viz. the objective body), while the second is the denial that we should view Schneider's reaching behavior as taking place in objective space. Only thus,

Merleau-Ponty appears to be arguing, can we make sense of Schneider's simultaneous ability to respond to stimuli on his own body and inability to point on command to locations on his own body.

This argument is not, as it stands, very persuasive. It seems plausible that a number of different information systems and neural circuits are involved in our awareness of our own bodies, and one would expect it to be occasionally the case that some of these systems and circuits are damaged while others are preserved. Indeed theorists concerned to distinguish various types of neural system frequently place considerable weight on the *dissociations* between different abilities and skills revealed by differential preservation in neuropathologies.[13] From this perspective, the points that Merleau-Ponty notes are far better viewed as evidence for a distinction between two different ways of processing information about the body than as evidence for an ontological distinction between the objective body and the phenomenal body. To put the point in terms employed earlier, we can locate the distinction at the level of sense rather than the level of reference.

Of course, adopting this strategy only makes sense within the context of a general taxonomy of different types of bodily awareness—a taxonomy motivated by reflection on a wider range of cases and factors than those that are at issue here. In the remainder of this section, I will make some remarks in this direction before returning to Merleau-Ponty's analysis of Schneider.

We can begin with a general distinction between high-level and low-level representations of the body. High-level representations of the body feed directly into central cognitive/affective processes, while low-level representations of the body feed directly into action. The distinction here is *not* between personal and subpersonal or between conscious and unconscious. Both low-level and high-level representations of the body function at the personal level and are usually conscious. The distinction will become clearer, however, with some examples.

Within the general category of high-level representations of the body, we can distinguish at least four types of representation or bodies of information:

Conceptual representations of the body (the set of beliefs we all have about the structure and nature of our body: how the body fits together, the functions

13. See Shallice 1988 for an influential textbook promoting this approach.

of particular body parts, their approximate locations, and the sort of things that can go wrong with them).

Semantic knowledge of the names of body-parts (knowledge that interfaces with nonsemantic ways of identifying events in the body to allow us to give verbal reports of what is going on in our bodies).

Affective representations of the body (representations of the body associated with emotional responses to the body).

Homeostatic representations of the body (representations of the body relative to basic criteria of self-regulation and self-preservation).

Conceptual representations of the body are the least interesting, both philosophically and scientifically. There seems little reason to think that such conceptual representations will be any different in kind from the set of commonsense beliefs that we all have about the physical and social world. Homeostatic bodily representations present a number of interesting issues, but these are best considered in the context of the lower-level mechanisms that give rise to them. From the point of view of bodily awareness, it is more interesting to consider how the body is represented in the mechanisms that give rise to the experience of pain than it is to consider the judgment that one is in pain.

The remaining two types of higher-level representation are more interesting. There are identifiable pathologies specific to both semantic and affective representations of the body. The pathologies associated with affective representations of the body are familiar. Bulimia and anorexia are good examples—forms of emotional response based on distorted representations of the body. Patients with *autotopagnosia* have difficulty in naming body parts or pointing to body parts identified by name or by the application of some stimulus, either on their own bodies or on a schematic diagram of the body. The problems here are not *purely* semantic. Semantic representation of the body is not simply a matter of knowing the names of body parts. Although superficially similar deficits can be found in some aphasic patients (Semenza and Goodglass 1985), autotopagnosic patients do not have a localized word-category deficit. They lack a particular way of representing bodily locations, as we see from the fact that the problem carries across to pointing to body parts identified by the application of a stimulus.

Turning to lower-level representations of the body, here too we find a range of phenomena and associated information channels that need to be distinguished. The first is information about the structure and limits of the body. This type of body-relative information has a number of distinctive pathologies. The best-known example is the phenomenon of phantom limb found in many patients with amputated limbs, as well as some with *amelia*, the congenital absence of limbs (Melzack 1992). This first category of body-relative information performs two tasks. First, it is responsible for the felt location of sensations. Sensations are referred to specific body parts in virtue of a body of information about the structure of the body. Second, the same body of information informs the motor system about the body parts that are available to be employed in action.

This type of body-relative information should be distinguished from semantic representations of the body. In deafferented patients these types of information are dissociated in both directions. Deafferented patients have lost peripheral sensations in certain parts of the body. Jacques Paillard's patient GL suffers from almost complete deafferentation from the mouth down, although she retains some sensitivity to thermal stimuli. If a thermal stimulus is delivered to a point on her arm that she is prevented from seeing, then, although she is unable to point to the location of the stimulus on her body, she is able to identify the location verbally and on a schematic body diagram. In my terms, she possesses semantic information without body-relative information. The dissociation also holds in the opposite direction. Another of Paillard's patients had a parietal lesion that resulted in central deafferentation of the forearm. Although she could not verbally identify and report on a tactile stimulus delivered to her deafferented hand in a blindfolded condition, she was able to point to the location of the stimulus (Paillard et al. 1983).[14] Here we have body-relative information without semantic information.

14. Unlike the very similar and well-documented phenomenon of blindsight (Weiskrantz 1986) there was no need to apply a forced-choice paradigm. The dissociation here may well be between an action-based representation of the body and an objective representation of the body (cf. Cole and Paillard 1995). An action-based representation of the body represents body location in a way that feeds directly into action, whether that action is body directed or world directed. It is this that is lost in GL, but preserved in the patient with the deafferented forearm. In what I am calling an objective representation of the body, on the other hand, the body does not feature purely as a potentiality for action, but rather as a physical object whose parts stand in certain determinate relations to each other.

There is a second type of lower-level representation of the body. This is a moment-to-moment representation of the spatial position of the various parts of the body. This moment-to-moment representation of bodily position is essential for the initiation and control of action, and needs to be constantly updated by feedback from moving limbs. This representation has been called the *short-term body-image* by Brian O'Shaughnessy (O'Shaughnessy 1995), but the name is misleading, suggesting that there is a single way in which the disposition of body parts is represented, whereas in fact the spatial location of any given body part can be coded in three different and independent ways.

The first type of coding is relative to objects in the distal environment. Consider a simple action, like reaching one's hand out for an object. The success of this action depends on an accurate computation of the trajectory from the initial position of the hand to the position of the relevant object.[15] This requires the position of the hand and the position of the object to be computed relative to the same frame of reference. I shall call this *object-relative spatial coding*. It is most likely that object-relative spatial coding takes place on an egocentric frame of reference—that is to say, a frame of reference whose origin is some body part. The reason for calling this type of coding object-relative is that it deals primarily with the spatial relations between body parts and objects in the distal environment.

But many actions are directed toward the body rather than to objects independent of the body. Some of these actions are voluntary, as when I clasp my head in my hands in horror. Some are involuntary, as when I scratch an itch. Many more are somewhere between the two, as when I cross my legs or rub my eyes. Clearly, the possibility of any of these sorts of action rests on information about the location of the body parts in question relative to each other. We can call this sort of information *body-internal spatial coding*. It is information about the moment-by-moment position of body parts relative to each other.

Body-internal spatial coding is required, not just for body-directed action, but also for many types of action directed toward objects in the distal environment. Psychological studies of action often concentrate on very simple actions, such as grasping objects with one hand. But the vast majority of actions require the coordination of several body parts. When I play

---

15. This will be discussed further in the final section.

volleyball, for example, I need to know not just where each of my hands is relative to the ball as it comes over the net, but also where each of my hands is relative to the other hand. Both body-internal and object-relative spatial coding is required.

A third type of information about the moment-to-moment disposition of the body is just as important for the initiation and control of action as the first two. This is information about the orientation of the body as a whole in objective space, primarily involving information about the orientation of the body with respect to supporting surfaces and to the gravitational field. This information comes from the calibration of information from a number of sources. The three principal sources of orientational information are vision, the vestibular system in the inner ear, and the proprioceptive/kinesthetic system (at least two of which must be properly functioning for orientational information to be accurate). I shall call this *orientational coding.*

If the taxonomy I have offered is correct then there seem to be the following principal types of information about the body:

High-level

- Beliefs about the structure and nature of body parts
- Semantic localization (enabling verbal report)
- Affective representations of the body

Low-level

- Representation of the structure and limits of body (enabling localization of sensation and specifying range of body parts available for action)
- Representation of the moment-to-moment disposition of body parts

    —Objective-relative spatial coding

    —Body-internal spatial coding

    —Orientational spatial coding

Let us return, then, to Schneider. What Merleau-Ponty finds so striking in Schneider is his inability to point on command to locations on his own body, when this is taken in the context of his residual abilities to respond to stimuli on his body by grasping and other body-directed behaviors. The following passage contains a very clear statement of the reasoning that leads him to the conclusion that we cannot understand the distinction between pointing and grasping in physiological terms.

If the grasping action or the concrete movement is guaranteed by some factual connection between each point on the skin and the motor muscles that guide the hand, it is difficult to see why the same nerve circuit communicating a scarcely different movement to the same muscles should not guarantee the gesture of *Zeigen* [pointing] as it does the movement of *Greifen* [grasping]. Between the mosquito which pricks the skin and the ruler which the doctor presses on the same spot, the physical difference is not great enough to explain why the grasping movement is possible, but the act of pointing impossible. The two 'stimuli' are really distinguishable only if we take into account their affective value or biological meaning, and the two responses cease to merge into one another only if we consider the *Zeigen* and the *Greifen* as two ways of relating to the object and two types of being in the world. But this is precisely what cannot be done once we have reduced the living body to the condition of an object. (1962, 123)

Without denying the insights that emerge from the existential analysis to which Merleau-Ponty subsequently turns, the argument here is far from persuasive. Merleau-Ponty may well be right that there is little physical difference between the mosquito bite and the touch of a ruler (although this is far from obvious), but this is the wrong place to look for an explanation of why one type of movement is possible but not the other. It seems far more plausible, particularly in the light of the taxonomy above, to seek an explanation in terms of the different representations of the body that the two types of movement respectively involve. So, for example, we might wonder whether Schneider's difficulty in pointing is not, at least in part, best identified as a deficit in high-level bodily representations—as a problem in the mechanisms that underwrite explicit localization. It might also be the case that there are two fundamentally different forms of coding of moment-to-moment body parts in play in the two movements. Sensations such as mosquito bites are experienced within the boundaries of the body, in such a way that the movement of scratching the bite requires body-relative spatial coding, as opposed to the touch of a ruler which might be thought to require object-relative spatial coding. This would mean that pointing, unlike grasping, would require calibration of different forms of information about the location of body parts.[16]

The point here is not that we should interpret Schneider's pathology in one or both of these ways. Rather, the claim is that careful distinctions between different types and levels of information about the body offer a

16. There are interesting parallels between Schneider and Jacques Paillard's patient with the deafferented forearm discussed earlier.

greater number of potential resources for understanding what is going on in Schneider's curious pattern of body-related motor behavior than Merleau-Ponty considers. In place of the simple distinction between the objective body and the phenomenal body, it makes sense to consider more complex distinctions between various ways of representing the objective body. Quite apart from avoiding metaphysical difficulties with Merleau-Ponty's notion of the phenomenal body, this approach is likely to give a more nuanced way of tackling the phenomenology of bodily awareness.

4 The Spatiality of Bodily Awareness

It remains the case, however, that the finer-grained analysis of different types of information about the body proposed in the previous section does not yet do justice to Merleau-Ponty's deeper motivation for the distinction between the phenomenal body and the objective body—namely his insistence that the spatiality of the body is fundamentally different from the spatiality of the objective world. I turn to this claim in this section, where I offer a way of thinking about how we represent bodily space that distinguishes it sharply from our representation of "body-external" space.

Almost all existing discussions of the spatiality of proprioception have presupposed that exteroceptive perception, proprioception, and the intentions controlling basic bodily actions must all have spatial contents coded on comparable frames of reference (where a frame of reference allows locations to be identified relative to axes centered on an object). This is an obvious assumption, since action requires integrating motor intentions and commands with perceptual information and proprioceptive information. Since the spatial locations of perceived objects and objects featuring in the contents of intentions are given relative to axes whose origin lies in the body—in an *egocentric frame of reference*—it is natural to suggest that the axes that determine particular proprioceptive frames of reference are centered on particular body parts, just as are the axes determining the frames of reference for perceptual content and basic intentions. The picture that emerges, therefore, is of a number of different representations of space, within each of which we find representations both of bodily and of non-bodily location. So, for example, we might imagine reaching behavior to be controlled by an egocentric frame of reference centered at some location on the hand—a frame of reference relative to which both bodily location (such as the mosquito bite on my arm) and nonbodily location (such as the cup on the table) can be identified.[17]

Despite its appealing economy, however, this account is ultimately unacceptable, because of a fundamental disanalogy between the *bodily space* of proprioception and the egocentric space of perception and action. In the case of vision or exteroceptive touch there is a perceptual field bounded in a way that determines a particular point as its origin. Since the visual field is essentially the solid angle of light picked up by the visual system the origin of the visual field is the apex of that solid angle. Similarly, the origin of the frame of reference for exploratory touch could be a point in the center of the palm of the relevant hand. But our awareness of our own bodies is not like this at all. It is not clear what possible reason there could be for offering one part of the body as the origin of the proprioceptive frame of reference.

There are certain spatial notions that are not applicable to somatic proprioception. For any two objects that are visually perceived, it makes obvious sense to ask both of the following questions:

(a) Which of these two objects is further away?
(b) Do these objects lie in the same direction?

The possibility of asking and answering these questions is closely bound up with the fact that visual perception has an origin-based frame of reference. Question (a) basically asks whether a line between the origin and one object would be longer or shorter than a corresponding line between the origin and the other object. Question (b) is just the question whether, if a line were drawn from the origin to the object that is furthest away, it would pass through the nearer object.

Neither question makes sense with respect to proprioception. One cannot ask whether this proprioceptively detected hand movement is farther away than this itch, nor whether this pain is in the same direction as that pain. What I am really asking when I ask which of two objects is farther away is which of the two objects is farther away from me, and a similar tacit self-reference is included when I ask whether two objects are in the same direction. But through somatic proprioception one learns about events taking place within the confines of the body, and there is no privileged part

17. The remainder of this section draws on Bermúdez 1998, chap. 6.

of the body that counts as *me* for the purpose of discussing the spatial rela-tions they bear to each other.

To get a firmer grip on the distinctiveness of the frame of reference of bodily awareness one need only contrast the bodily experience of normal subjects with that of completely deafferented subjects, such as Jonathan Cole's patient IW. The moment-to-moment information about their bod-ies that deafferented patients possess is almost exclusively derived from vision. Their awareness of their own body is continuous with their experi-ence of the extrabodily world. They are aware of their bodies only from the same third-person person perspective that they have on nonbodily physical objects. The frame of reference for their bodily awareness does indeed have an origin—the eyes—and for this reason both of the two questions men-tioned make perfect sense. But this is not at all the way in which we experi-ence our bodies *from a first-person perspective*.

The conclusion to draw from this is that the spatial content of bodily awareness cannot be specified within a Cartesian frame of reference that takes the form of axes centered on an origin. But then how is it to be specified?

We can start from the basic thought that an account of the spatiality of bodily awareness must provide criteria for sameness of place. In the case of somatic proprioception this means criteria for sameness of bodily location. But there are several different types of criteria for sameness of bodily loca-tion. Consider the following two situations:

i.   I have a pain at a point in my right ankle when I am standing up and my right foot is resting on the ground in front of me.
ii. I have a pain at the same point in my ankle when I am sitting down and my right foot is resting on my left knee.

According to one set of criteria the pain is in the same bodily location in (i) and (ii)—that is to say, it is at a given point in my right ankle. According to another set of criteria, however, the pain is in different bodily locations in (i) and (ii), because my ankle has moved relative to other body parts. Let me term these *A-location* and *B-location*, respectively. Note, moreover, that B-location is independent of the actual location of the pain in "objective space." The B-location of the pain in (ii) would be the same if I happened to be sitting in the same posture five feet to the left.

Both A-location and B-location need to be specified relative to a frame of reference. In thinking about this we need to bear in mind that the human body has both moveable and (relatively) immoveable body parts. On a large scale the human body can be viewed as an immoveable torso to which are appended moveable limbs—the head, arms, and legs. Within the moveable limbs there are small-scale body parts that can be directly moved in response to the will (such as the fingers, the toes, and the lower jaw) and others that cannot (such as the base of the skull). A joint is a body part that affords the possibility of moving a further body part, such as the neck, the elbow, or the ankle. In the human body, the relatively immoveable torso is linked by joints to five moveable limbs (the head, two legs, and two arms), each of which is further segmented by means of further joints. These joints provide the fixed points in terms of which the particular A-location and B-location of individual body parts at a time can be given.

A particular bodily A-location is given relative to the joints that bound the body part within which it is located. A particular point in the forearm is specified relative to the elbow and the wrist. It will be the point that lies on the surface of the skin at such-and-such a distance and direction from the wrist and such-and-such a distance and direction from the elbow. This mode of determining A-location secures the defining feature of A-location, which is that a given point within a given body part will have the same A-location irrespective of how the body as a whole moves, or of how the relevant body part moves relative to other body parts. The A-location of a given point within a given body part will remain constant in both those movements, because neither of those movements will bring about any changes in its distance and direction from the relevant joints.

The general model for identifying B-locations is as follows. A particular constant A-location is determined relative to the joints that bound the body part within which it falls. That A-location will either fall within the (relatively) immoveable torso or it will fall within a moveable limb. If it falls within the (relatively) immoveable torso then its B-location will also be fixed relative to the joints that bound the torso (neck, shoulders, and leg sockets)—that is to say, A-location and B-location will coincide. If, however, that A-location falls within a moveable limb, then its B-location will be fixed recursively relative to the joints that lie between it and the immoveable torso. The B-location will be specified in terms of the angles of the joints that lie between it and the immoveable torso. Some of these joint angles will be rotational (as with the elbow joint, for example). Others will be translational (as with the middle finger joint).

The way of specifying A-location and B-location seems to capture certain important elements in the phenomenology of bodily awareness.

• We do not experience peripheral body parts in isolation, but rather as attached to other body parts. Part of what it is to experience my hand as being located at a certain place is to experience that disposition of arm-segments in virtue of which it is at that place.
• It is part of the phenomenology of bodily awareness that sensations are always experienced within the limits of the body. This is exactly what one would expect given the coding in terms of A-location and B-location. There are no points in (nonpathological) body-space that do not fall within the body.
• Although B-location is specified recursively in terms of the series of joint angles between a given A-location and the immovable torso, the torso does not function as the origin of a Cartesian frame of reference.

To return, then, to Merleau-Ponty, my proposal is that a due recognition of the distinctive frame of reference relative to which proprioception and somatosensations are located can do justice to many of his insights about the phenomenology of bodily awareness. Moreover, and this is the important point when it comes to skepticism about Merleau-Ponty's distinction between the objective body and the phenomenal body, the distinctiveness of bodily awareness is being accommodated at the level of sense rather than at the level of reference—that is, in terms of how we represent the body. There is no temptation to postulate a phenomenal body that stands apart from the objective body. The fact that we experience our own bodies in terms of a non-Cartesian reference frame does not in any sense rule out our bodies being ontologically on a par with objects that we experience in terms of Cartesian reference frame. Nor does it preclude our studying bodily experience from the third-person, scientific perspective. Indeed, as I shall try to bring out in the next section, properly understanding the reference frame governing bodily awareness offers a fruitful framework for the scientific study of bodily awareness.

5   The Spatiality of Bodily Awareness and the Control of Action

The previous section offered a way of thinking about the spatiality of bodily awareness as fundamentally different from the spatial content of vision and other forms of exteroceptive awareness. One obvious question this raises is how proprioceptive content features in the control of action, given that action requires the contribution and integration of proprioceptive and exteroceptive awareness. What I will try to do in this final section is explain how the account I have offered of the spatial content of somatic proprioception fits in with some influential current thinking about motor control. This will go some way toward substantiating my earlier comments about the possibility of incorporating the distinctive phenomenology of bodily awareness within a "third-person" perspective on agency.

Any planned motor movement directed toward an extrabodily object requires two basic types of information:

1. Information about the position of the target relative to the body
2. Information about the starting position of the relevant limb (the hand in the case of a reaching movement)

The first question to ask is how this position information is coded. The study of trajectory errors and velocity profiles of hand movements suggests that the first type of information is coded in extrinsic coordinates in a frame of references centered on the hand (Ghez et al. 2000). Intended reaching movements are coded, roughly speaking, in terms of their goal and end point, rather than the means by which that end point is to be achieved. This coding involves hand-centered vectors, rather than the complex muscle forces and joint torques required for the action to be successfully carried out. One source of evidence for this is that hand movements directed at extrabodily targets have constant kinematic profiles, remaining straight and showing bell-shaped velocity curves with predictable acceleration at the beginning of the movement and deceleration as the target is approached (Morasso 1981). These kinematic profiles do not seem to be correlated with joint movements. There is considerable debate about whether the frame of reference on which target position is coded is egocentric or allocentric (Jeannerod 1997), but there is relatively little dispute that the coordinates are extrinsic rather than intrinsic (but see Uno et al. 1989 for the suggestion that the kinematic profiles observed by Morasso are consistent with the minimization of overall joint torque).

Turning to the second type of information, information about the starting position of limbs, the thrust of this essay has been that awareness of the body derived from somatic proprioception and somatosensation is not coded on either an object-centered or a body-centered frame of reference. The coordinates on which the location of body parts is coded are intrinsic rather than extrinsic. This leads us to an obvious second question: how is this type of bodily awareness involved in the control of action? The experienced spatiality of the body, as I have analyzed it, is closely bound up with awareness of the body's possibilities for action. The body presents itself phenomenologically as segmented into body parts separated by joints because these are the natural units for movement. But what we need to know are the details of the contribution that somatic proprioception makes to the initiation and control of action.

If the spatial dimension of proprioception and somatosensation is as I have described it, somatic proprioception clearly cannot provide information about the position of the relevant limb that will be sufficient to fix the initial position of the movement vector. Somatic proprioception and somatosensation provide information about how limbs are distributed, but this information will not fix the starting position of the hand in a way that allows immediate computation of the movement vector required to reach the target. There is no immediate way of computing the trajectory between the location of a limb given in terms of A-location and B-location, and a target location given in terms of extrinsic coordinates. As Merleau-Ponty puts it in a passage cited earlier, "the outline of my body is a frontier which ordinary spatial relations do not cross" (1962, 98). To put things somewhat more prosaically, acting effectively on the world requires some sort of translation between two fundamentally different coordinate frames. The translation required for the calculation of the movement vector will involve integrating information derived from the various mechanisms of bodily awareness with visually derived information. This yields a testable prediction, namely, that subjects who are prevented from seeing their hands before making a reaching movement to a visible target should not be capable of making accurate movements. And this in fact is what experimenters have found (Ghez et al. 1995). The fact that information derived from bodily awareness is not sufficient to guide and control action is powerful evidence that there is no single spatial coordinate system that encompasses both bodily awareness and external perception.

Does the specific proposal that the coordinate system of bodily awareness should be understood in terms of A-location and B-location (as distinct from the general proposal that the spatiality of the body is fundamentally different from the spatiality of the perceived world) link up in any interesting ways with the empirical study of action?

Many researchers into motor control currently think that we need to distinguish the kinematics of motor control from the dynamics of motor control (Bizzi and Mussa-Ivaldi 2000). Movements are planned in purely kinematic terms, as a sequence of positions in peripersonal space that the hand will successively occupy during the performance of the movement. Clearly, however, the actual execution of the movement depends on these extrinsically specified feedforward motor commands being implemented by intrinsically specified muscle forces, joint angles, joint torque, and so forth. The transition from extrinsically specified coordinates to intrinsically specified coordinates comes when the nervous system computes the dynamical implementation of the kinematically specified goal. Various proposals have been made about how this computation is achieved.[18] One traditional assumption is that this is a process of reverse engineering, so that the calculation of the muscle forces and joint angles required to implement the movement is achieved by working backward from the trajectory of the end point. There are obvious problems of computational tractability here. The problem does not have a unique solution, and in any case there are likely to be considerable difficulties in factoring in biomechanical factors due to fatigue and other variables. Accordingly it has been suggested that the translation into intrinsic coordinates does not depend on the solution of complex inverse-dynamic and inverse-computations but instead involves translating the targeted end point into a series of equilibrium positions (Feldman 1986). The basic thought here is that muscles and reflexes work as springs in ways that allow effector limbs to be treated as mass-spring systems that have adjustable equilibria. Motor planning, on this model, involves determining the equilibrium positions for the relevant effector limbs.

Whether the inverse-dynamic approach or the equilibrium approach is correct, it is precisely at this point that proprioceptively derived information about the distribution of body parts becomes crucial. The frame of reference of the intrinsic coordinates in which joint angles and equilibrium positions are coded seems much closer to the frame of reference of proprioceptive bodily awareness as I have characterized it than it is to the

18. For introductory surveys, see Brown and Rosenbaum 2002 and Wolpert and Ghahramani 2002.

Cartesian frames of reference on which movement end points are coded. This provides a good explanation of why proprioceptive and somatosensory feedback is able to play such an integral part in the smooth performance and correction of actions, as indeed in the development of internal models of limb dynamics. The feedforward commands directed at the hand are recursively structured in much the same way as proprioceptive feedback from the hand and intervening body segments. Motor commands to the hand need to specify appropriate angles for the shoulder, the elbow, and the wrist. Proprioceptive feedback about the B-location of the hand will equally specify the relevant joint angles. Comparison is straightforward. The crucial role of bodily awareness in the initiation and control of action comes at the point of transition between kinematic plan and dynamic instruction, as well as later on in the execution of the movement. What makes it possible for somatic proprioception to perform this role is that the awareness of the body it provides is coded on a frame of reference that maps straightforwardly onto the internal model of limb dynamics that specifies the body's potentialities for movement.

6   Conclusion

Let me draw the threads of the argument together. I began by considering two of the central themes in Merleau-Ponty's discussion of the body in *Phenomenology of Perception*. The first theme stresses the distinctiveness of how we experience our own bodies, and in particular the phenomenological differences between our awareness of the spatiality of our own bodies and our awareness of the spatiality of the extrabodily physical world. This theme is predominantly phenomenological. The second theme has to do with the relation between the phenomenological investigation of bodily awareness and the scientific study of the body. This second theme emerges particularly in Merleau-Ponty's development of the distinction between the objective body and the phenomenal body—between the body as a physical mass of bone, muscles, and nerves and the body as it is lived and experienced. As we saw, Merleau-Ponty develops this distinction in a way that places our first-person experience of our bodies and of our actions outside the domain of third-person physiology and scientific psychology.

The principal aim of this essay has been to try to accommodate the insights behind the first theme in *Phenomenology of Perception* in a way that keeps the body and bodily awareness "within the world," and hence without following Merleau-Ponty in the conclusions he draws from the distinction between the phenomenal body and the objective body. It is true that our experience of our own bodies and of our own agency has a number of very distinctive features that sets it apart from our experience of nonbodily objects. But these differences can, I suggested, be illuminated by thinking about the physiological and psychological mechanisms and information sources that underlie them. As we saw in the context of Merleau-Ponty's discussion of Schneider, careful distinctions between different types of body-relative information and different ways of representing the body show promise for dealing with the puzzles and problems that led Merleau-Ponty to the distinction between phenomenal body and objective body. More importantly, I proposed a way of thinking about the spatiality of bodily awareness that goes a considerable way to explaining the fundamental differences that Merleau-Ponty identified between our experience of our bodies and our experience of nonbodily objects. The key to these differences is that bodily locations are given on a non-Cartesian frame of reference. As brought out in the final section, this way of thinking about the phenomenology of bodily awareness has interesting and fruitful connections with current thinking about motor control.

References

Anscombe, E. 1957. *Intention*. Ithaca, NY: Cornell University Press.

Anscombe, E. 1962. On sensations of position. *Analysis* 22:55–58.

Armstrong, D. M. 1962. *Bodily Sensations*. London: Routledge & Kegan Paul.

Bermúdez, J. L. 1998. *The Paradox of Self-Consciousness*. Cambridge, MA: MIT Press.

Bermúdez, J. L. 2004. The phenomenology of bodily awareness. *Theoria et Historia Scientiarum* 7:43–52.

Bermúdez, J., A. J. Marcel, and N. Eilan, eds. 1995. *The Body and the Self*. Cambridge, MA: MIT Press.

Bizzi, E. 1999. Motor control. In *The MIT Encyclopedia of the Cognitive Sciences*, ed. R. A. Wilson and F. C. Keil. Cambridge, MA: MIT Press.

Bizzi, E. and F. A. Mussa-Ivaldi. 2000. Toward a neurobiology of coordinate transformations. In *The New Cognitive Neurosciences*, ed. M. S. Gazzaniga. Cambridge, MA: MIT Press.

Brand, M., and D. Walton, eds. 1976. *Action Theory*. Dordrecht, NL: Reidel.

Brown, L. E. and D. A. Rosenbaum. 2002. Motor control: Models. In *Macmillan Encyclopedia of Cognitive Science*, ed. L. Nadel. London: Macmillan.

Cassam, Q. 1997. *Self and World*. Oxford: Oxford University Press.

Chisholm, R. 1976. The agent as cause. In *Action Theory*, eds. M. Brand and D. Walton. Dordrecht: Reidel.

Cole, J. and J. Paillard. 1995. Living without touch and information about body position and movement. In *The Body and the Self*, ed. J. Bermúdez, A. J. Marcel, and N. Eilan. Cambridge, MA: MIT Press.

Davidson, D. 1980. *Essays on Actions and Events*. Oxford: Oxford University Press.

Dillon, M. C. 1988. *Merleau-Ponty's Ontology*. Bloomington: Indiana University Press.

Feldman, A. G. 1986. Once more on the equilibrium-point hypothesis (lambda model) for motor control. *Journal of Motor Behavior* 18:17–54.

Gazzaniga, M. S., ed. 2000. *The New Cognitive Neurosciences*. Cambridge, MA: MIT Press.

Ghez, C., J. Gordon, and M. F. Ghilardi. 1995. Impairments of reaching movements in patients without proprioception II: Effects of visual information on accuracy. *Journal of Neurophysiology* 73:361–372.

Ghez, C., J. W. Krakauer, R. L. Sainburg, and M.-F. Ghilardi. 2000. Spatial representation and internal models of limb dynamics in motor learning. In *The New Cognitive Neurosciences*, ed. M. S. Gazzaniga. Cambridge, MA: MIT Press.

Hsiao, S. S., T. Yoshioka, and K. O. Johnson. 2002. Somesthesis, neural basis of. In *Macmillan Encyclopedia of Cognitive Science*, ed. L. Nadel. London: Macmillan.

Jeannerod, M. 1997. *The Cognitive Neuroscience of Action*. Oxford: Blackwell.

Kenny, A. 1963. *Action, Emotion and Will*. London: Routledge & Kegan Paul.

Melzack, R. 1992. Phantom limbs. *Scientific American* 266:120–126.

Merleau-Ponty, M. 1962. *The Phenomenology of Perception*. London: Routledge & Kegan Paul.

Morasso, P. 1981. Spatial control of arm movements. *Experimental Brain Research* 42:223–227.

Nadel, L., ed. 2002. *Macmillan Encyclopedia of Cognitive Science*. London: Macmillan.

O'Connor, T. 2000. *Persons and Causes*. Oxford: Oxford University Press.

O'Shaughnessy, B. 1980. *The Will: A Dual Aspect Theory*. Cambridge: Cambridge University Press.

O'Shaughnessy, B. 1995. Proprioception and the body image. In *The Body and the Self*, ed. J. Bermúdez, A. J. Marcel, and N. Eilan. Cambridge, MA: MIT Press.

Paillard, J., F. Michel, and G. Stelmach. 1983. Localization without content: A tactile analogue of blindsight. *Archives of Neurology* 40:548–551.

Priest, G. 1998. *Merleau-Ponty*. London: Routledge.

Roberts, D. 2002. *Signals and Perception: The Fundamentals of Human Sensation*. Basingstoke: Palgrave Macmillan.

Semenza, C., and H. Goodglass. 1985. Localization of body parts in brain injured subjects. *Neuropsychologia* 23:161–175.

Shallice, T. 1988. *From Neuropsychology to Mental Structure*. Cambridge: Cambridge University Press.

Taylor, C. 1964. *The Explanation of Behaviour*. London: Routledge & Kegan Paul.

Uno, T., M. Kawato, and R. Suzuki. 1989. Formation and control of optimal trajectory in human multi-joint arm movement: Minimum joint-torque model. *Biological Cybernetics* 61:89–101.

Weiskrantz, L. 1986. *Blindsight: A Case Study and Implications*. Oxford: Oxford University Press.

Wolpert, D. and Z. Ghahramani. 2002. Motor learning models. In *Macmillan Encyclopedia of Cognitive Science*, ed. L. Nadel. London: Macmillan.

6   Bodily Awareness and Self-Consciousness

We are embodied, and we are aware of our bodies "from the inside" through different forms of bodily awareness. But what is the relation between these two facts? Are these forms of bodily awareness types of self-consciousness, on a par, say, with introspection? In this chapter, I argue that bodily awareness is a basic form of self-consciousness, through which perceiving agents are directly conscious of the bodily self.

The first two sections clarify the nature of bodily awareness. We get information about our bodies in many different ways. Some are conscious; others nonconscious. Some are conceptual; others nonconceptual. Some are first-personal; others third-personal. Section 1 taxonomizes these different types of body-relative information. Some philosophers have claimed that we have a "sense of ownership" of our own bodies. In section 2 I evaluate, and ultimately reject, a strong reading of this claim, on which the sense of ownership is a distinct and phenomenologically salient dimension of bodily awareness.

In sections 3 to 5 I explore how bodily awareness functions as a form of self-consciousness. Section 3 discusses the significance of certain forms of bodily awareness sharing an important epistemological property with canonical forms of self-consciousness such as introspection. This is the property of being immune to error through misidentification relative to the first-person pronoun. I explain why having the immunity property qualifies those types of bodily awareness as forms of self-consciousness (subject to two further requirements that I spell out). In section 4 I consider, and remain unconvinced by, an argument to the effect that bodily awareness cannot have first-person content (and hence cannot count as a form of self-consciousness). Finally, section 5 sketches out an account of the spatial

content of bodily awareness and explores the particular type of awareness
of the bodily self that it provides.

1   Types of Bodily Awareness

Normal subjects have many different ways of finding out how things are
with their bodies. Unfortunately, there is little consistency in the philosophical, psychological, or physiological literatures on how to label and
conceptualize them. This section offers a general taxonomy and explains
how it relates to discussions of proprioception within psychology and
physiology.

The body is a physical object and we can be aware of it in much the
same ways that we can be aware of any other physical object. The body can
be the object of vision, smell, or touch, for example. I will call these *third-
person forms of bodily awareness*. These forms of bodily awareness involve
the normal exercise of our ordinary, outward-directed sensory modalities.
At the same time, we have special ways of finding out how things are with
our bodies—ways that do not extend to any other physical object. Each of
us is aware of their body "from the inside," as it is standardly put. There
are several different forms of awareness here. I will term them collectively
first-person forms of bodily awareness.

As I am using the terms, "awareness" is synonymous with "consciousness." Both first- and third-person bodily awareness are conscious phenomena, although they may of course be recessive. We have many ways
of finding out about our bodies that are not conscious. Successfully executing most actions, for example, depends on constantly updated and very
fine-grained information about the position of the relevant limbs and
often the orientation of the body as a whole. This updating, and the information on which it is based, typically takes place below the threshold of
consciousness.

This type of information falls on the first-person rather than the third-
person side of the distinction. The systems that generate this type of
information operate only within the confines of one's own body. So, the
general category of body-relative information needs to be organized as in
figure 6.1.

In the first decade of the twentieth century, the physiologist Charles
Scott Sherrington introduced the concept of proprioception (Sherrington

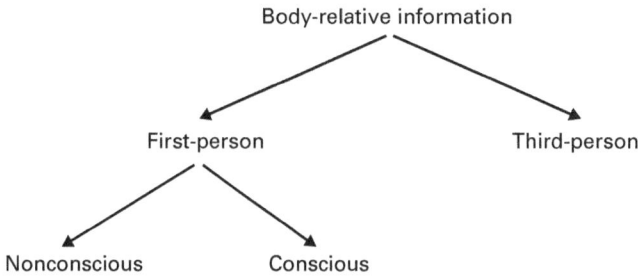

Figure 6.1
Body-relative information: the basic distinctions.

1907). Sherrington distinguished proprioception both from *exteroception* (the five, outwardly directed sensory modalities) and from *interoception* (our awareness of the internal states of our bodily organs, as in the sensations of hunger, thirst, and subcutaneous pain). For Sherrington, the function of proprioception is to provide information about limb position and movement and, through the vestibular system, about balance and related whole-body properties.

Proprioception, in Sherrington's sense, has both conscious and nonconscious elements. The vestibular system, which monitors balance and spatial orientation, is typically nonconscious (although disturbances of the vestibular system, such as motion sickness, certainly make their presence felt within consciousness). In contrast, we typically do have conscious awareness of how our limbs are distributed and whether they are moving. This awareness is coarser grained than the nonconscious information exploited in the online control of action.

Sherrington's reasons for separating out interoception and proprioception are primarily physiological. Interoception and proprioception are subserved by different neural systems. From my perspective, however, interoception counts as a form of first-person bodily awareness. Bodily sensations certainly provide one of the ways in which we are aware of our bodies from the inside. So interoception needs to be added to the taxonomy of body-relative information—under the first-person, conscious branch.

The nonconscious branch needs to include information about body morphology—information about the overall shape and size of the body. This sort of information is indispensable for planning and executing action. It is constantly changing during childhood and adolescence and remains plastic during adulthood. It can be modified by tool use (Cardinali et al. 2009), and also changes in response to drastic changes in the body (such as amputation) as well as to neuropsychological disorders such as hemispatial neglect (when patients ignore one side of their body).

Let me draw attention to a form of first-person conscious bodily awareness that has not received as much attention from philosophers as the somatosensory varieties. The psychologist J. J. Gibson gave the name *visual proprioception* to forms of self-specifying information that can be derived from the visual field of view. Vision presents the world in a fundamentally egocentric and perspectival way. The embodied self appears in visual perception as the origin of the field of view. This is secured through several features of the phenomenology of vision, including self-specifying structural invariants (such as the property one's limbs have of only being able to subtend a narrow range of visual solid angles); visual kinesthesis (the way in which changing patterns in the optic array specify the perceiver's movement through the environment); and the perception of affordances (higher-order invariants in the visual field that specify the organism's possibilities for acting in the environment). For more details on how visual proprioception counts as a form of bodily awareness, see Gibson 1979, Bermúdez 1998, and chapters 1–4 in this volume.

There are various additional ways in which the body is represented at the conscious level. People have an awareness of their body with strong evaluative and affective dimensions, for example. I will term this the *affective body image*. Disorders such as bulimia and anorexia seem to be pathologies of the affective body image. The affective body image is a paradigmatically first-person phenomenon. But it has a third-person analogue in the general beliefs that many people have about both the structure and function of different body parts. Some of these beliefs, particularly those tied to emotions such as shame, have a strong cultural dimension. A related but distinct type of body-relative information is semantic—semantic knowledge of the names of body parts. This is also third person, rather than first person.

I have organized the taxonomy of body-relative information up to now in terms of two distinctions—the first-person/third-person distinction and the distinction between conscious and non-conscious information. There is a further distinction to take into account. This is the distinction between conceptual and nonconceptual information about the body. The distinction between conceptual and nonconceptual content is not easy to pin down precisely (see Bermúdez 2007 and Bermúdez and Cahen 2015 for reviews of the extensive literature), but for present purposes I use it simply to mark the difference between representations of the body that are integrated with the propositional attitude system (and hence with reflection, planning, and emotional responses), on the one hand, and representations that are more closely tied to the online control of action, on the other.

In light of all this, I propose the taxonomy of body-relative information depicted in figure 6.2. There is much more to be said about the different elements of this taxonomy. It would be useful to map out the different sources of each type of body-relative information. What is the source, for example,

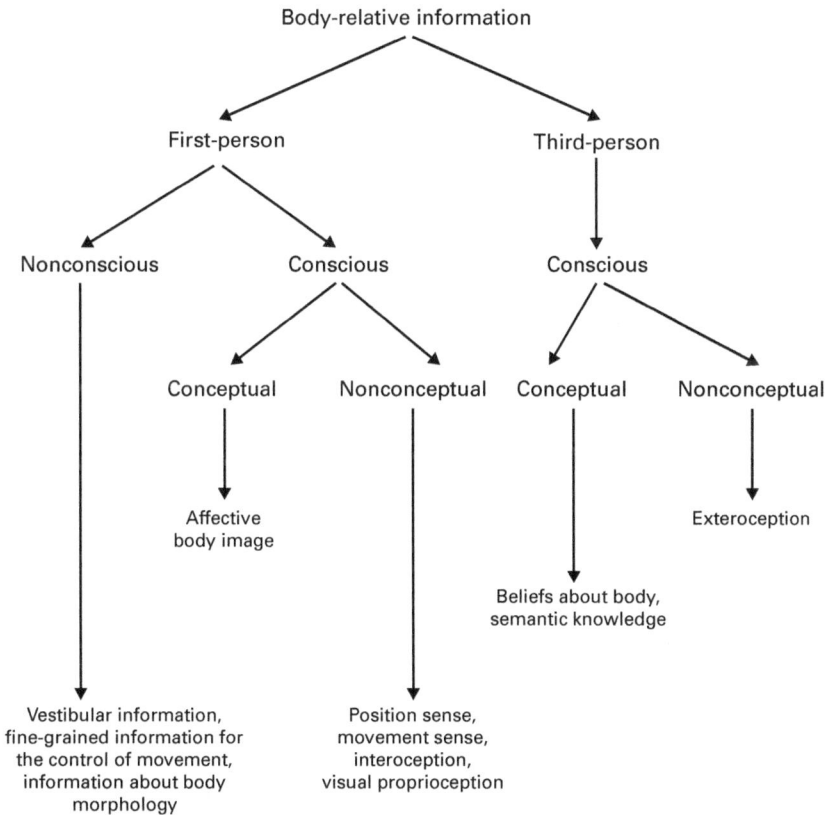

Figure 6.2
Body-relative information: a taxomomy.

of nonconscious information about body morphology? Where in the brain does it get processed? How is it integrated with other types of body-relative information in the control of action? But fortunately, answers to these questions (which are a long way from being settled) are not required to explore how bodily awareness counts as a form of self-consciousness.

2   A "Sense" of Ownership?

Many of the types of body-relative information identified in section 1 form part of our conscious experience. We are consciously aware of our bodily sensations (through interoception) and of the general disposition of our limbs. These forms of bodily awareness are all, one might say, phenomenologically salient. This section explores the relation between these phenomenologically salient forms of bodily awareness and what is often called the "sense of ownership" of one's own body.

There are two rather different conceptions of the sense of ownership current in the literature (although they are often not clearly distinguished). I will call them the *deflationary* and *inflationary* conceptions. They differ according to how they account for the phenomenological salience of the sense of ownership. Both accept that there is a positive phenomenology of ownership, but whereas the deflationary conception holds that it can ultimately be understood in terms of other aspects of bodily experience, the inflationary conception postulates the existence of an irreducible "feeling of mineness."

Here is a version of the deflationary conception proposed by Jérôme Dokic:

Bodily experience gives us a *sense of ownership*. Whatever property we can be aware of "from the inside" is instantiated in our own apparent body. Bodily experience seems to be necessarily short-sighted, so to speak, since it cannot extend beyond the boundaries of one's body. The very idea of feeling a pain in a limb which does not seem to be ours is difficult to frame, perhaps unintelligible. (Dokic 2003, 325; emphasis in the original)

As presented in this passage, the sense of ownership is really just a label for a higher-order property of somatosensation—the fact that the objects of proprioception and interoception are experienced within the confines of the body. This is a descriptive fact about the phenomenology of bodily awareness—a descriptive fact that a number of authors have partially analyzed in terms of the content of bodily sensations (e.g., Martin 1995;

Bermúdez 1998, and chapter 8 in this volume; as well as Dokic himself). If, as these authors maintain, bodily sensations are experienced as representing the state of the body at particular locations, then it is not surprising that they should have this higher-order property.

And one would expect, as Dokic points out, that this feature of somatosensation would lead to people finding bizarre the idea of feeling a pain in someone else's limb—and to other fairly standard features of how we *think* about the body and bodily sensations. On the deflationary conception of ownership, the sense of ownership consists, first, in certain facts about the phenomenology of bodily sensations and, second, in certain fairly obvious judgments about the body (which we can term judgments of ownership).

Certainly, it is a long way from these basic phenomenological facts and judgments of ownership to what I term the inflationary conception of the sense of ownership. Here is a statement of the inflationary conception from Shaun Gallagher:

> In non-observational self-awareness I do not require the mediation of a perception or judgment to recognize myself as myself. I do not need to reflectively ascertain that my body is mine, or that it is *my* body that is in pain or that is experiencing pleasure. *In normal experience, this knowledge is already built into the structure of experience.* (Gallagher 2005, 29; my emphasis)

As I read this passage, it states that bodily awareness incorporates a specific feeling of "myness." For Gallagher this feeling of "myness" is present both in bodily awareness and in introspection. Later on in his book he describes the sense of ownership as "a sense that it is I who am experiencing the movement or thought" (2005, 173) and emphasizes that this is a "first-order phenomenal aspect of experience" (174, n. 1).

Are there any reasons to accept this type of inflationary description of the phenomenology? One possibility would be to argue from pathological cases of "disownership." In alien hand syndrome, for example, patients deny that their hand is their own (Feinberg et al. 1998). This "disownership" is certainly phenomenologically salient. Perhaps what patients with alien hand syndrome are experiencing is the absence of the normal feeling of ownership? I suspect that something like this reasoning is behind the inflationary conception of ownership. It is not very compelling, however. There are all sorts of reasons why a patient might report that his hand does not feel to be his own. There is no particular reason for understanding a feeling of disownership as the absence of a feeling of ownership—at least, not without prior reasons for thinking that there is such a thing as the feeling of ownership.

Frédérique de Vignemont (2007) has offered positive arguments for the thesis that there is a positive phenomenology of ownership. She offers two arguments. One is derived from the normal case.

> Imagine the following situation. You close your eyes and someone takes your hand. Nothing in your experience tells you who is holding your hand. Yet, you feel this anonymous hand holding your own hand and nobody else's hand. There seems to be a phenomenological difference between your experience of someone else's hand and your experience, which could be explained by a sense of ownership. (de Vignemont 2007)

I am not sure this achieves quite what she wants it to, however. The basic starting point here must be that we do *not* experience someone else's hand. So it is not clear what the phenomenological difference is that the sense of ownership is being called on to explain. Do we need a feeling of myness to explain what is going on when I feel the pressure of someone else's hand on mine? If we do, then we need it to explain what is going on when I feel the pressure of the table on my hand. But I am not sure that we have anything here beyond the descriptive fact emphasized in the deflationary conception of ownership—namely, that sensations are typically experienced within the confines of the body.

A second argument comes from introspective reports of amputees wearing prostheses. Some amputees feel their artificial limb as their own. Others do not. We can make sense of this difference, according to de Vignemont, by assuming that the first group has a sense of ownership, while the second does not. This is not very compelling, however. Both deflationary and inflationary theorists hold that there is a positive phenomenology of ownership. The issue between them is how to understand that phenomenology. In particular, does it consist in a in a quale of ownership—a specific and irreducible feeling of "mineness"? Simply pointing out that amputees have a sense of ownership does not show that their phenomenology needs to be understood in the way proposed by the inflationary conception.

So, the arguments in support of the inflationary conception of the sense of ownership are not convincing. But are there any good arguments against it? I think that a line of argument canvassed by Elizabeth Anscombe in her paper "On Sensations of Position" (1962) can be adapted to show that the inflationary view is not sustainable.

Anscombe argues for the thesis that our knowledge of how our limbs are disposed and whether or not they are moving (position sense and movement sense) is "knowledge without observation," on a par with our knowledge of our own actions and intentions. The claim here is not simply that position sense and movement sense are forms of what I am terming first-person bodily awareness. That would hardly require argument. Nor is she denying that there are sensations of position and movement. That would quite simply be false. Her position, rather, is that our knowledge of limb position and movement is not based on proprioceptive and kinesthetic sensations. That is, it's not the case that we have proprioceptive and kinesthetic sensations and then, on that basis, arrive at conclusions about how our limbs are disposed and whether or not they are moving.

Anscombe is prepared to grant that we can speak of having the sensation of one's legs being crossed, but she thinks that this way of talking is ambiguous.

If we are considering an expression of the form "sensation of X," we need to ask whether the words "of X" are a description of the sensation content, or whether the sensation has some different content and X is what produces or always goes with it, etc. The sensation of going down in a lift is a sensation of sudden lightness and as it were of one's stomach's lurching upwards; "of going down in a lift" is not the internal description of the sensation. (Anscombe 1962, 56)

According to Anscombe, if proprioceptive and kinesthetic sensations ground knowledge of limb position and movement, then this can only be because their internal description stands in the right relation to the knowledge that they are being claimed to ground. And this, in turn, depends on the internal description being suitably independent of (or, as she puts it, separable from) the description of the fact known. We can know, through having the sensation of going down in a lift, that we are in fact going down in a lift because the sensation can be described in a way that makes no mention of lifts or downward motion—and, moreover, the occurrence of that sensation is a good (although not infallible) guide that one is going down in a lift.

The problem Anscombe identifies is that the vast majority of proprioceptive and kinesthetic sensations are not like the sensation of going down in a lift. They can only be internally described in very general terms, if at all—in terms of sensations of contact, muscle stretch, and so on. These internal descriptions completely underdetermine any conclusions that one might try to draw from them about how one's body is configured. They are simply not reliable guides in the required sense. Alternatively, bodily sensations can be, as she puts it, nonseparably described (as, for example, the sensation of having one's legs crossed). But under the nonseparable description they cannot ground our knowledge that our legs are crossed.

The issue here is not one of vocabulary, it should be emphasized. She is not claiming that we lack the descriptive tools to characterize a perfectly determinate sensation. We can capture the spirit of Anscombe's position without talking about descriptions at all. The claim, rather, is that there is really nothing interesting in common between all the different sensory experiences that we might have when our legs are crossed, say—other than that they are the sensations of having our legs crossed. There is no distinctive "my legs are crossed" qualitative feel that we might use as a sign that our legs are crossed. There is simply the sensation of one's legs being crossed, which might or might not be accompanied by any one of a whole range of "qualitative feels."

However it is formulated, I find this argument that proprioception and kinesthesia give us knowledge without observation very compelling. But be that as it may, the argument is completely devastating against the inflationary conception of the sense of ownership. According to the inflationary conception, there is a feeling of myness that explains some of the judgments that we make about the body—what I have termed judgments of ownership. Anscombe's argument shows us that this view is fatally flawed.

To the best of my knowledge nobody has claimed that the feeling of myness can be internally described in Anscombe's sense. As emphasized, this is not a vocabulary issue. It is not that we lack the conceptual or linguistic apparatus to describe the feeling of myness. What I am denying is that there is a perfectly determinate "quale" associated with the feeling of myness that we can identify and consider independently of the myness that it is communicating.

Given this, what work can the feeling of myness do? It is called on to do the job of grounding and underwriting what I have called judgments of ownership. But I think that Anscombe would be exactly right to object that a feeling of myness that can only be characterized or experienced in those very terms is not suitable for that job. It is not sufficiently independent of the fact that it is being claimed to justify.

The upshot of all this, I submit, is that the inflationary conception of the sense of ownership is neither supported by the considerations offered on its behalf nor capable of doing the work it is called on to do. We would be most unwise to go beyond the deflationary conception. There are facts about the phenomenology of bodily awareness (about position sense, movement sense, and interoception) and there are judgments of owner-ship, but there is no additional feeling of ownership. The remainder of this chapter will focus on exploring the relation between the phenomenology and the judgments, to elucidate how bodily awareness qualifies as a form of self-consciousness.[1]

3 Bodily Awareness as a Form of Self-Consciousness: Immunity to Error through Misidentification

Why should we think that (first-person) bodily awareness is a form of self-consciousness? In *The Paradox of Self-Consciousness* (Bermúdez 1998), I discussed what I termed the *simple argument*:

(1) The self is embodied.
(2) First-person bodily awareness provides perceptions of bodily properties.
(3) First-person bodily awareness is a form of self-perception.
(4) Therefore, first-person bodily awareness is a form of self-consciousness.

The crucial step here is the step from (3) to (4)—although there are some interesting issues concerning the precise relation between bodily awareness and the exteroceptive sense modalities (for further discussion see Shoemaker 1994 and Bermúdez 1998, sec. 6.3). The simple fact that bodily awareness involves perceiving something that happens to be the self is plainly not enough for it to count as an interesting form of self-consciousness. Self-perception falls short of self-consciousness, since one can perceive oneself without being aware that it is oneself that one is perceiving.

How do we get from self-perception to self-consciousness? One popu-lar strategy, pioneered by Gareth Evans (1982), is to stress that first-person bodily awareness shares an important epistemological property with

1. For further discussion of deflationary versus inflationary conceptions of owner-ship, see chapters 7 and 8 in this volume, particularly the former, which develops my objection to inflationary views in the context of responding to further argu-ments from de Vignemont.

canonical forms of self-consciousness, such as introspection and autobiographical memory. This is the property, originally highlighted by Wittgenstein and subsequently labeled and explored more systematically by Sydney Shoemaker, of being *immune to error through misidentification relative to the first-person pronoun* (Shoemaker 1968)—henceforth the IEM property.[2]

The IEM property is a property of judgments—of the judgment, for example, that my legs are crossed. It holds relative to the information on which those judgments are made. A particular judgment can have the IEM property when based on one type of information, and lack the property when based on a different type of information. The information sources that give rise to judgments with the IEM property all have the following feature: they provide information only about the self. These sources of information are such that, if we know from them that somebody has a particular property, we *ipso facto* know that we ourselves have that property. For the remainder of this chapter, I will assume that an information source has the IEM property when it gives rise to judgments that have the IEM property.

Introspection is an example of such an information source. If I know through introspection that someone is currently thinking about Southern Arizona, then I know that I am thinking about Southern Arizona. Introspection cannot provide information about anybody other than me. This does not mean that introspection and other comparable sources of information cannot be mistaken. They certainly can be mistaken. I might really be thinking about Eastern New Mexico, for example. But there is a certain type of error that they do not permit. Judgments made on the basis of them cannot be mistaken about who it is who has the property in question. It wouldn't make sense, for example, to wonder: someone is thinking about Southern Arizona, but is it me?

In chapter 7 of *Varieties of Reference*, Gareth Evans observed that certain types of first-person bodily awareness give rise to judgments with the IEM property. He concluded that position sense, interoception, and movement sense all count as primitive forms of self-consciousness. I have argued elsewhere that the same holds for visual proprioception (Bermúdez 2003, reprinted as chapter 4 in this volume). So, all four of the nonconceptual

2. There has been much discussion of the precise way to formulate the IEM property. See, e.g., Pryor 1999; Campbell 1999; Peacocke 1999; and the essays in Prosser and Recanati 2012.

first-person types of body-relative information have the IEM property.[3] Can we conclude from this that they are types of self-consciousness? Everything depends on the importance attached to the IEM property as an index of self-consciousness. It is certainly true that judgments with the IEM property are typically self-conscious. But that may simply be because they are typically expressed with the first-person pronoun—as opposed to reflecting special characteristics of the information sources from which they are derived.

It is also true that judgments with the IEM property play a foundational role in our thoughts about ourselves. Judgments with the IEM property reflect ways of finding out about ourselves that are exclusively about the self and that do not require identifying an object *as* the self. Self-conscious judgments that are susceptible to error through misidentification must ultimately be grounded in judgments that do have the IEM property. This is because judgments lacking the IEM property involve identifying an object as the self, and any such identification must be immune to error through misidentification on pain of regress.

But again, we are not entitled to draw conclusions from this about information sources with the IEM property. Some of these information sources are plainly forms of self-consciousness. It would be hard to deny that introspection is a form of self-consciousness, for example. But there are enough differences between introspection and bodily awareness to cast doubt on any quick extrapolation from the former to the latter.

A more plausible approach is via functional role. The distinctive functional role of self-conscious thoughts is relatively well-understood thanks to the work of Castañeda (1966, 1969/1994) and Perry (1979), among others. As these authors have brought out, a thought expressed with the sentence "I am *F*" has immediate implications for action not necessarily present in a thought expressible as "*a* is *F*," even when "I" and "*a*" are coreferential (pick out the same individual). Castañeda and Perry make a powerful case that these implications for action are (partly) constitutive of self-conscious thought. The absence of any gap between thought and action is an important part of what makes self-conscious thought self-conscious. It is, moreover, ultimately grounded in the IEM property, since there will always be a potential gap between thought and action whenever thoughts involve

3. Anyone skeptical about this is directed to chap. 2 of Cassam 1997, esp. secs. 6 and 7.

identification in a way that is not ultimately discharged in a thought with the IEM property.[4]

This gives a powerful reason for thinking that first-person bodily awareness is a form of self-consciousness, because it has similarly immediate implications for action. This is true of self-directed actions. There is no gap between feeling an itch in a certain place and knowing where to scratch. It also holds for actions whose target is not the body. There tends not to be a gap between knowing how one's limbs are distributed and knowing which reaching movement to make to a particular extrabodily location. It is true that visual calibration is typically required in order to fix the end point of the movement. But this itself reflects a form of bodily awareness, since the perspectival nature of vision provides relational information about the world on an egocentric coordinate frame. This is part of visual proprioception, as analyzed by J. J. Gibson and his colleagues and students.

There are two further respects in which visual proprioception has immediate implications for action. The first is the phenomenon of *looming* (of particular interest to Gibson, much of whose research into vision was inspired by his service as head of the Air Force Research Unit during the Second World War). Imagine that you are a pilot landing an airplane. You are looking ahead at the point on the runway where you anticipate landing. As you approach, the landing point remains stationary, but the magnification of the visual solid angle it subtends accelerates. At the same time, the field of view contains textured surfaces around the stationary aiming point. These surfaces radiate outward in what Gibson calls *patterns of optic flow*, expanding in a lawlike manner as the landing point approaches. These perceptual invariants give the pilot direct feedback and, in effect, control over the adjustments that he makes to the landing pattern. Looming and optic flow are key determinants in the control of almost every type of movement.

Affordances are another aspect of visual proprioception with immediate implications for action. The theory of affordances is a key part of Gibson's theory that the fundamentals of perceptual experience are dictated by the organism's need to act in the environment. Affordances are forms of information in the field of view that specify the organism's possibilities for action and reaction. They are properties that objects and surfaces have relative to

4. For further discussion, see Bermúdez 2017a.

the organisms that perceive them. According to Gibson, they are directly perceived rather than learned or inferred. Nonetheless, while having immediate implications for action seems necessary for something to count as a form of self-consciousness, it cannot be sufficient (even in conjunction with the IEM property). If it were sufficient then we would have the puzzling result that there are nonconscious forms of self-consciousness. This is because the workings of the vestibular system, for example, both have the IEM property and have immediate implications for action—but are typically nonconscious (except in cases of motion sickness, and so forth).

So, what else is required for self-consciousness? We could, of course, simply stipulate a consciousness requirement. But this would be unsatisfactory without some principled reason for imposing the requirement. Here is one suggestion, developing the earlier discussion of information sources with the IEM property. We have seen that information sources have the IEM property derivatively. They derive it from the IEM status of the judgments derived from them. The notion of a judgment being based on an information source has been left unexplained up to now. There are several forms the basing relation can take. One way of thinking about it is in terms of the thinker taking the deliverances of the information source as *evidence* for the judgment.

It seems clear that the basing relation does not always work like this. I might judge that I am in balance without that judgment being based on evidence. This could be a case where the deliverances of my vestibular system issue directly in thought (as opposed to my feeling in balance, through some sort of sensation of equilibrium). In this sort of circumstance we might say: I just know that I am not in balance. I claim that this is not based on evidence because there is no aspect of my conscious life to which I can point as the source of the judgment. I would suggest, then, that body-relative information sources only count as forms of self-consciousness when they generate conscious phenomenology that can be taken as evidence for first-person judgments with the IEM property. This immediately generates a consciousness requirement and produces the required result that all forms of bodily self-consciousness do indeed have to be conscious. It is a corollary that, for these purposes, we will have to separate out the conscious deliverances of the vestibular system from the nonconscious deliverances. Both can give rise to first-person judgments with the IEM property, but only the former qualify as instances of self-consciousness.

4 Objections?

Some authors have objected to thinking of different types of bodily awareness as forms of self-consciousness. Not all of these criticisms are directly
relevant to the line of reasoning that I have been canvassing. Anne Newstead, for example, has taken issue with Evans's insistence that a proper
understanding of bodily awareness is, as he puts it, "the most powerful
antidote to a Cartesian conception of the self" (Evans 1982, 220). She interprets this as trying to argue directly from the IEM status of bodily awareness to the truth of some form of materialism about the self (Newstead
2006). Unsurprisingly, she thinks that any such line of argument would
be question begging. The argument hinges on the IEM nature of bodily
self-ascriptions, but this requires assuming that bodily self-ascriptions
are immune to error through misidentification *relative to "I."* But this of
course is precisely what is at issue between the materialist and the Cartesian. The Cartesian will accept that bodily self-ascriptions are IEM but deny
that they are IEM relative to "I" (as opposed to being IEM relative to "my
body," say).

Newstead seems to me to be right in thinking that the prospects are dim
for a direct argument from bodily awareness to materialism about the self
(but see Cassam 1997, particularly chap. 2, for a subtle argument to the
effect that self-conscious thinkers have to be intuitively aware of themselves *qua* subjects as physical objects). Like almost everyone else (including, I think, Evans), I am simply taking it for granted that Cartesianism
about the self is false—and hence that bodily awareness is awareness of the
embodied self. The question I am interested in is whether this counts as a
self-conscious awareness of the embodied self.

Joel Smith has argued that bodily awareness cannot be self-conscious
awareness of the self in this sense. His argument is unusual in resting
neither on the metaphysics of the self nor on the epistemology of self-
consciousness. Instead he argues (rather imaginatively) from the nature
of imagination. Smith claims that it follows from two theses about imagination that the experiential content of bodily awareness is not first
personal—or, to put it another way, that bodily awareness does not present the body to me as my bodily self, and so cannot count as a form of
self-consciousness.

The first thesis on which Smith's argument rests is:

The Dependency Thesis

When I imagine a bodily sensation (or other instance of bodily awareness), I imagine experiencing that sensation.

The dependency thesis stands opposed, on the one hand, to the view that one cannot imagine a bodily sensation without having that sensation and, on the other, to the view that imagining a bodily sensation is a cognitive achievement rather than an experiential one. According to the dependency thesis, to imagine some form of bodily awareness is to imagine an experience. This is something that one can do without undergoing that experience, but nonetheless is sufficiently close to undergoing the experience that one can derive conclusions about experiential content from imaginative content—and vice versa.

The second thesis is:

The Imagination Thesis

When I imagine something about someone else, I am not imagining anything about myself.

The imagination thesis rests on a positive account of what it is to imagine someone else (S) having an experience. This imaginative project has two components.

(a) I (experientially) imagine from the inside.
(b) I (suppositionally) imagine that the subject of the experience is S.

Smith introduces the distinction between experiential and suppositional imagining with an example from Christopher Peacocke (1985). There is no difference in experiential imagination between imagining a suitcase and imagining a suitcase with a cat behind it. But there is a difference in suppositional imagination—in the second case but not the first we suppositionally imagine a cat behind the experientially imagined suitcase.

Smith ingeniously applies these two theses to bodily awareness. I can imagine someone else having a particular bodily sensation—feeling a pain in her tooth, for example. By the imagination thesis, I imagine the experience of toothache from the inside. The other person only enters the imaginative project at the level of suppositional imagination. As far as the experiential content of the imagining is concerned there is just the toothache. This means that the imagined experience has to be impersonal, because otherwise we could not imagine someone else having it. But, by the dependency thesis, the content of the imagining is structurally analogous to the content of the original experience (namely, the toothache). Since the imagined experience is impersonal, the original experience must be impersonal also.

The argument is summarized in the following passage:

> When I imagine being Napoleon having a pain, the very same piece of sensory imagination would serve equally well to imagine being Goldilocks having a pain. The difference between the two is a difference in what is suppositionally imagined, i.e. whose experience it is. This means that the occurrence of the experience in the imagination leaves open, fails to determine, the identity of the imagined experiencer. But this means that the imagined experience does not have first person content, for the first person concept serves precisely to determine the identity of the experiencer. First personal states have as their object the subject whose states they are. Once again, the conclusion is that neither imagined, nor actual, bodily awareness has first person content. My body is not presented to me as myself. (Smith 2006, 57)

The argument depends critically on how Smith interprets the consequences of applying the dependency thesis to imagining someone else's bodily awareness. The dependency thesis requires that, if the relevant bodily experience has a first-person content, then that first-person content will carry over to the content of imagining. He thinks that there are two ways in which this might occur.

(i)   "I imagine myself having a pain and then suppose that I am identical to Napoleon" (Smith 2006, 58).

(ii) "The occurrence of the first person in the imagined experience has, not me, but Napoleon as its object" (ibid.).

He is quite right to reject (i). We need to look more closely at the discussion of (ii), however.

Smith rejects (ii) on the grounds that it conflicts with the following principle.

(*)   "If I am in a state that has first person content, then that state has me as its object" (ibid.).

Principle (*) seems to be an analogue at the level of thought of the token-reflexive rule governing the first-person pronoun. And so it inherits the (considerable) plausibility of the rule. An initial reaction to (*), however, might be that it is incompatible with the concept of *quasi-memory* (*q*-memories) introduced by Sydney Shoemaker (1970). Shoemaker observes that it is at least conceptually possible (and, for all we know, perhaps nomologically possible) for a thinker's apparent memories to be causally derived from someone else's experiences.[5] We can imagine, in fact, a situation in which this is a widespread but intermittent practice, so that a thinker confronted with an apparent memory cannot immediately determine whether it is a genuine memory or a q-memory.

Shoemaker claims that in this sort of situation autobiographical memory would no longer be an information source with the IEM property. He is surely right in this (although wrong, I suspect, to extend this claim to autobiographical memory in the normal case).[6] But we should not follow Parfit in drawing the further conclusion that the possibility of q-memory shows that autobiographical memories do not have first-person contents (Parfit 1971).[7] Q-memories are first-person states. The q-remembering subject has an apparent memory of herself doing something. The problem that she faces is working out whether or not to take that apparent memory at face value—or, to put it in Smith's terms, whether or not she herself is the object of the first-person content.

So, principle (*) seems questionable in the case of quasi-memory. But it would certainly be unwise to extrapolate from quasi-memory to bodily awareness. Quite apart from any doubts about the ultimate coherence of q-memories, there are significant disanalogies between memory and bodily awareness as information sources. The content of memory remains poorly understood, but it might be thought to contain a significant doxastic element that is lacking in bodily awareness. Are there any more directly experiential apparent counterexamples to principle (*)? Vision seems to me to fit the bill. The first step in seeing why is to appreciate how deeply figurative

5. The discussion here is confined to what psychologists would typically call autobiographical episodic memories.

6. For further discussion, see Evans 1982, sec. 7.5, and Bermúdez 2017b.

7. Parfit writes: "When I seem to remember an experience, I do indeed seem to remember *having* it. But it cannot be a part of what I seem to remember about this experience that I, the person who now seems to remember it, am the person who had this experience. That is something I automatically assume. (My apparent memories sometimes come to me simply as the belief that *I* had a certain experience.) But it is something that I am justified in assuming only because I do not in fact have q-memories of other people's experiences" (Parfit 1971, 15). Evans rebuts this view convincingly (1982, 246–248).

it is to talk about the first person occurring in an experience. Neither the first-person pronoun nor the first-person concept appear in an experience. It would be more accurate to say that experiences have certain features that warrant certain types of first-person judgment.[8] Experiences are properly described as first person when they have those features. In the case of vision, these are the features that collectively make it correct to describe visual experiences as perspectival. We have already looked at some of them in the context of Gibson's notion of visual proprioception. The important point for the moment, though, is simply this. To say that the content of vision is perspectival is not to say that the content of visual experience specifies whose perspective it is. That is an external fact about the experience, rather than an internal fact about the content of the experience. By analogy, the meaning of the first-person pronoun specifies that it refers to the person responsible for a particular token utterance. It does not specify who that person actually is—which is a feature of the utterance's context, rather than of its meaning.

So, it is not just the possibility of quasi-memory that casts doubt on principle (*). It is also suspect in the case of vision. This surely weakens Smith's argument significantly. But it will not be conclusive to anyone who thinks that there are enough disanalogies between vision and the types of bodily awareness that Smith is considering for principle (*) to apply in the latter cases, even if not in the former. I end this section by arguing that the argument does not go through even if principle (*) is accepted.

The problem emerges when we ask: to which state does principle (*) apply? Smith's argument rests on applying principle (*) to the imagined bodily sensation—to the experience that Napoleon (or Goldilocks) is imagined to be undergoing. This, he thinks, is what forces the choice between (i) and (ii) above. But, by his own lights, we do not ourselves experience bodily sensations that we imagine. And so there is no sense in which we are in the state of pain, say, that we are imagining Napoleon being in. Hence there is nothing in the domain of bodily awareness to which principle (*) can apply.

8. The issues here, I take it, are orthogonal to discussions over whether the content of experience is conceptual or nonconceptual. A conceptualist about the content of experience can (and should!) deny that the first-person concept features in the conceptual content of experience.

So, what state are we in? The answer is obvious. We are in a state of imagining—the state of imagining that Napoleon is in pain. Is this a first-person state? I can see arguments both ways, but for present purposes it doesn't really matter.[9] The state of imagining is either first-person or not. If not, then there is plainly no problem and principle (*) falls completely out of the picture. But if it is first-person, on the other hand, there are no difficulties accommodating principle (*)—the state of imagining, construed first personally, certainly has me as its object.

I conclude, then, that Smith's argument fails. The thesis that bodily awareness can serve a form of self-consciousness is still standing. More needs to be said, though, about exactly how we are aware of ourselves in bodily awareness. We turn to this in the next section.

5 The Content of Bodily Awareness

The upshot of the discussion so far is that we should think about bodily awareness as a form of self-consciousness. The nonconceptual, first-person forms of body-relative information identified in section 1 have two key features in virtue of which they qualify as forms of self-consciousness. They have the IEM property in a way that allows the outputs of those information sources to serve as evidence for first-person judgments. And they have the immediate implications for action characteristic of self-consciousness. But we have so far said little about the sort of awareness of the bodily self that bodily awareness provides. That is the subject of this final section.

Let me begin by mentioning two very general ways in which bodily awareness counts as a form of self-consciousness. The first is that bodily awareness offers a direct, experiential way of grasping the structure and limits of the embodied self—and, as a direct consequence, of the boundary between self and nonself. The second is that several different types of bodily awareness are directly implicated in the control of action, thereby offering a way of grasping the body as the unique object that is directly responsive to the will. But how exactly do these emerge from the structure

9. We need to distinguish the state of imagining that Napoleon is in pain from the state of imagining oneself as Napoleon in pain. The latter is definitely first person, but (as we have seen from the discussion of the dependency thesis) Smith is focusing on the former, and here the issues are less clear.

of bodily awareness? And what other forms of consciousness of the bodily self does bodily awareness provide?

I begin tackling these questions with the observation that bodily awareness is a form of spatial awareness. It is spatial awareness because it provides information about the properties of the spatially extended body. This seemingly trivial observation holds the key to many of the distinctive properties of bodily awareness. As a spatially extended thing, the body is a physical object just like any other physical object. From the point of view of the embodied self, however, the experienced body is a very peculiar type of object. The distinctiveness of embodied experience has led some philosophers to drastic conclusions. Merleau-Ponty, for example, often seems to describe the experienced body (or, as he puts it, the phenomenal body) as standing outside the physical world (see, in particular, part 1 of Merleau-Ponty 1962 and Bermúdez 2005, reprinted as chapter 5 in this volume).

Considered from the perspective of metaphysics, this approach is unlikely to garner much support. But, from an epistemological point of view, it seems an accurate description of the relation in which we stand to our bodies "from the inside." The challenge, then, is to provide an account of the spatiality of bodily awareness that does justice both to the distinctive phenomenology of bodily awareness and to how it provides information about the spatially extended body. In previous work I have proposed an account that tries to do this (Bermúdez 1998, 2003). I sketch the basic framework here.

Since bodily awareness is a form of spatial awareness, we must be aware of our bodies relative to a particular frame of reference. I claim that much of what is distinctive about the phenomenology of bodily awareness is directly derived from the distinctiveness of that frame of reference. Our experience of bodily space is fundamentally different from our experience of nonbodily space. Spatial awareness always requires a frame of reference, and we are typically aware of objects in nonbodily space relative to egocentric frames of reference. When we perceive objects, we perceive them in terms of their distance and bearing from a point of origin (on what mathematicians call a system of polar coordinates).[10] There are many different egocentric frames of reference. These vary according to the point of origin.

10. For a helpful tutorial on frames of reference in a cognitive context, see Klatzky 1998.

An egocentric frame of reference might have its origin in the eye, for example, or in the hand. Different frames of reference will be useful for different tasks and much of the computational challenge of acting within the world is coordinating and integrating these different frames of reference.

This challenge is made all the greater because acting within the world requires coordinating information about the spatial layout of the world with information (derived from bodily awareness) about the spatial layout of the body. And, I claim, the frame of reference for bodily awareness is of a fundamentally different type. We do not experience our bodies on an egocentric frame of reference. There is no privileged point in the body that counts as *me*, serving as the point of origin relative to which the distance and bearing of, say, bodily sensations are fixed. We experience events within our bodies as spatial events, but the spatiality of bodily experience is fundamentally different from the spatiality of our experience of the world.

So how do we experience bodily space? This question has two dimensions. The first dimension has to do with how we individuate locations in bodily space. The question here is: What counts as a given location in bodily space? How do locations in bodily space relate to locations in "ordinary," physical space? Is there a way of thinking about locations in bodily space on which events taking place in two different locations in physical space correspond to a single location in bodily space? The second dimension has to do with how those locations are given in experience. And in particular, what is the frame of reference relative to which an event taking place at a given bodily location is experienced?

There are, I have suggested in previous work, two different ways of individuating locations in bodily space. They differ in the quantity of relational information that is taken into account. I term them A-location and B-location respectively.[11]

A-Location

The A-location of a bodily event is fixed relative to an abstract map of the body. It does not take into account how the body is actually disposed. So, for example, if I have a pain in my knee, then the A-location of that pain will be the same whether I am standing up or sitting with my legs crossed.

11. See also the presentation in chapter 5 of this volume. The remainder of this section has been rewritten for the current volume.

B-Location

Unlike its A-location, the B-location of a bodily event does take into account how the body is disposed. The pain in my knee will have a different B-location depending on the position of my knee relative to the rest of my leg (if I am standing with my leg off the ground, for example, as opposed to standing normally).

Neither the A-location nor the B-location of a given bodily event can be identified with a particular location in physical space. An itch in my elbow will have the same A-location however my body is disposed and wherever my body is located in physical space. And it retains the same B-location (relative to a specific disposition of my body) if I am suddenly transported two meters to the left.

One reason for distinguishing these various ways of individuating bodily location is well-supported neuropsychological evidence for a double dissociation between two ways of identifying bodily locations. The dissociation has been identified in deafferented patients (who have lost peripheral sensations in certain parts of the body). So, for example, Jacques Paillard's patient GL, who is almost completely deafferented from the neck down with residual sensitivity to some thermal stimuli, can identify the location of a thermal stimulus on a schematic body-diagram or describe it verbally (e.g., "It is in my arm"). But she is unable to reach to the stimulus. So, she is sensitive to the sensation's A-location without being sensitive to its B-location. Another patient, with deafferentation of the forearm due to a parietal lesion, showed the reverse pattern, able to reach to the location of a stimulus, but not to describe it or point to it on a body-diagram—showing sensitivity, in other words, to B-location but not to A-location.

Moving to the second dimension of how we experience bodily space, we need to think about how A-location and B-location are given in experience. For neither is a Cartesian frame of reference appropriate. The defining feature of a Cartesian frame of reference is that locations are specified relative to a point that serves as the origin, and which is where the x, y, and z axes intersect. The same holds for variants of Cartesian frames of reference, such as spherical and cylindrical coordinate systems, which deploy polar coordinates. But when we think about the space of the body, there is no privileged point that can serve as the origin for any such frame of reference. There is nothing that stands to the space of the body in the way that, for example, the eyes stand to visual space. For this reason questions that make perfect sense for vision and hearing make no sense at all when it comes to bodily experience. We can ask whether one sound is nearer than another, for example, but not whether this itch is nearer than that one.

The alternative model that I propose for thinking about the space of bodily experience begins with the body's articulation into moveable and (relatively) immovable body parts. Moveable limbs, such as the head, arms, and legs, are appended to an immoveable torso. Those moveable limbs are themselves articulated into further moveable body parts, such as the forearm, wrist, and fingers (themselves further articulated into separable segments). Joints are the articulation points. They are body parts that afford the possibility of moving further body parts. There are around 230 in the human body, in which the relatively immoveable torso is linked by joints to five moveable limbs (the head, two legs, and two arms), each of which is further segmented by means of further joints.

These joints provide the fixed points for specifying both A-location and B-location. So, a particular bodily A-location is given relative to the joints that bound the body part within which it is located. A particular point in the lower leg is specified relative to the knee and the ankle. It might be, for example, a point that lies on the surface of the skin at such-and-such a distance and direction from the wrist and such-and-such a distance and direction from the elbow. Specified in this way, a given bodily event will keep the same A-location irrespective of how the body as a whole moves, or of how the relevant body part moves relative to other body parts.

The B-location of a bodily event is fixed, in effect, by adding additional spatial information to the event's A-location. If a sensation, say, has an A-location within a moveable limb, then its B-location is fixed recursively relative to the joints that lie between it and the immoveable torso. The additional information for specifying B-location comes from the angle of the intervening joints, which might be rotational (as in the elbow) or translational (as in the knee). B-location is specified in a way that is immediately relevant to action, since muscles and tendons typically work to change joint-angles.[12]

So, there are fundamental differences between the frame of reference relative to which we experience our bodies and the frames of reference exploited in perceiving every other physical object. These differences go a

12. For further discussion of A-location, B-location, and bodily space, see chapter 8 in this volume.

long way toward explaining what is so distinctive about our experience of
our own bodies—both the general sense of distinctiveness that led Merleau-
Ponty to claim that the phenomenal body is not part of the objective world,
and certain specific features of the phenomenology of bodily awareness.

So, for example, it explains what was earlier described as the descriptive fact underlying the sense of ownership (in its deflationary construal).
It is part of the phenomenology of bodily awareness that sensations are
always experienced within the limits of the experienced body (which may
not always coincide with the real body, as we see in phantom limb and
other illusions). This is exactly what one would expect given the coding in
terms of A-location and B-location. There are no points in (nonpathological) body space that do not fall within the body. In contrast, it would be
mysterious if we thought about the spatial content of bodily awareness in
terms of distance and bearing from a point of origin. Such a way of representing the location of bodily events provides no basis for the distinction
between bodily space and extrabodily space. Moreover, it explains the phenomenological fact that we do not experience body parts in isolation, but
rather as attached to other body parts. Part of what it is to experience my
foot, say, as located at a particular place is to experience the disposition of
leg-segments in virtue of which it is at that place. This is exactly what one
would expect, if the B-location of the foot were part of the content of bodily
awareness. Again, it would be mysterious if the spatiality of bodily awareness were given in terms of coordinates relative to an origin.

So, by way of summary, let us return to the two modes of self-
consciousness identified at the beginning of this section. I suggested that
bodily awareness (a) provides a direct, experiential way of grasping the
structure and limits of the embodied self, and (b) presents the body as the
unique physical object that is directly responsive to the will. I hope to have
made clear how closely connected (a) and (b) are with the distinctive spatial
content of bodily awareness.

References

Anscombe, G. E. M. 1962. On sensations of position. *Analysis* 22:55–58.

Bermúdez, J. L. 1998. *The Paradox of Self-Consciousness*. Cambridge, MA: MIT Press.

Bermúdez, J. L. 2003. The elusiveness thesis, immunity to error through misidentification, and privileged access. In *Self-Knowledge and Privileged Access*, ed. B. Gertler,
213–231. Aldershot: Ashgate. Reprinted in this volume.

Bermúdez, J. L. 2005. The phenomenology of bodily awareness. In *Phenomenology and Philosophy of Mind*, ed. D. W. Smith, A. L. Thomasson. New York: Oxford University Press. Reprinted in this volume.

Bermúdez, J. L. 2007. What is at stake in the debate about nonconceptual content? *Philosophical Perspectives* 21:55–72.

Bermúdez, J. L. 2017a. *Understanding "I": Language and Thought*. Oxford: Oxford University Press.

Bermúdez, J. L. 2017b. Memory and self-consciousness. In *The Routledge Handbook of Philosophy of Memory*, ed. S. Bernecker and K. Michaelian. London: Routledge.

Bermúdez, J. L., and A. Cahen. 2015. Mental content, nonconceptual. In *Stanford Encyclopedia of Philosophy*. https://plato.stanford.edu.

Campbell, J. 1999. Immunity to error through misidentification and the meaning of a referring term. *Philosophical Topics* 29:89–104.

Cardinali, L., F. Frassinetti, C. Bozzoli, C. Urquizar, A. C. Roy, and A. Farne. 2009. Tool-use induces morphological updating of the body-schema. *Current Biology* 19:R478–R479.

Cassam, Q. 1997. *Self and World*. Oxford: Oxford University Press.

Castañeda, H.-N. 1966. "He": A study in the logic of self-consciousness. *Ratio* 8:130–157.

Castañeda, H.-N. 1969/1994. On the phenomeno-logic of the I. In *Self-Knowledge*, ed. Q. Cassam, 160–166. Oxford: Oxford University Press.

de Vignemont, F. 2007. Habeas corpus: The sense of ownership of one's own body. *Mind & Language* 22:427–449.

Dokic, J. 2003. The sense of ownership: An analogy between sensation and action. In *Agency and Self-Awareness*, ed. J. Roessler and N. Eilan, 321–344. Oxford: Oxford University Press.

Evans, G. 1982. *The Varieties of Reference*. Oxford: Oxford University Press.

Feinberg, T. E., D. M. Roane, and J. Cohen. 1998. Partial status epilepticus associated with asomatognosia and alien hand-like behaviors. *Archives of Neurology* 55:1574–1577.

Gallagher, S. 2005. *How the Body Shapes the Mind*. New York: Oxford University Press.

Gibson, J. J. 1979. *The Ecological Approach to Visual Perception*. Boston: Houghton Mifflin.

Klatzky, R. L. 1998. Allocentric and egocentric spatial representations: Definitions, distinctions, and interconnections. In *Spatial Cognition: An Interdisciplinary Approach* to the Representation and Processing of Spatial Knowledge, ed. C. Freksa, C. Habel, and K. F. Wender, 1–17. Berlin: Springer-Verlag.

Martin, M. 1995. Bodily awareness: A sense of ownership. In The Body and the Self, ed. J. L. Bermúdez, A. J. Marcel, and N. Eilan, 267–289. Cambridge, MA: MIT Press.

Merleau-Ponty, M. 1962. The Phenomenology of Perception. London: Routledge.

Newstead, A. 2006. Evan's anti-Cartesian argument: A critical evaluation. Ratio 19:214–228.

Parfit, D. 1971. Personal identity. Philosophical Review 80:3–27.

Peacocke, C. 1985. Imagination, possibility, and experience: A Berkeleian view defended. In Essays on Berkeley: A Tercentennial Celebration, ed. J. Foster and H. Robinson, 19–35. Oxford: Oxford University Press.

Peacocke, C. 1999. Being Known. Oxford: Oxford University Press.

Perry, J. 1979. The essential indexical. Philosophical Review 86:874–897.

Prosser, S., and F. Recanati, eds. 2012. Immunity to Error through Misidentification: New Essays. Cambridge: Cambridge University Press.

Pryor, J. 1999. Immunity to error through misidentification. Philosophical Topics 26:271–304.

Sherrington, C. S. 1907. On the proprioceptive system, especially in its reflex aspect. Brain 29:467–482.

Shoemaker, S. 1968. Self-reference and self-awareness. Journal of Philosophy 65 (19): 555–567.

Shoemaker, S. 1970. Persons and their pasts. American Philosophical Quarterly 7:269–285.

Shoemaker, S. 1994. Self-knowledge and inner sense. Philosophy and Phenomenological Research 54:249–314.

Smith, J. 2006. Bodily awareness, imagination, and the self. European Journal of Philosophy 14:49–68.

7 Bodily Ownership, Bodily Awareness, and Knowledge without Observation

Each of us experiences our own body in a distinctive way. Part of that distinctiveness is that we each experience our body and our limbs as our own. This is often characterized by saying that we each have a sense of ownership of our own bodies. But in what does that sense of ownership consist? Where does it come from? And how is it grounded? This complex of questions is often termed the *problem of bodily ownership.*

Some authors have taken what I have termed an *inflationary* approach to the problem. Inflationary theorists argue that we experience our bodies as our own in virtue of a distinctive feeling of "myness" or "mineness" that is incorporated into all bodily phenomenology, whether tactile, proprioceptive, homeostatic, or kinesthetic. The idea here is that there is a positive *quale* of bodily ownership. Frédérique de Vignemont has provided a thoughtful development of the inflationary view (de Vignemont 2013—see also her 2007). She takes issue with my defense in Bermúdez 2011 of a *deflationary* approach to bodily ownership. In that paper (reprinted as chapter 6 in this volume) I proposed an argument deriving from Elizabeth Anscombe's various discussions of what she terms knowledge without observation (Anscombe 1957, 1962). My basic argument there was that the putative feeling of mineness cannot be "separately described" (to use Anscombe's term) in a way that would allow it to ground those features of thought and experience that it is being called on to explain.

De Vignemont is not convinced and in her 2013 paper appeals to the rubber hand illusion to undercut my appeal to Anscombe. Section I of this essay restates and extends the case I made in 2011 against the putative

A substantially shorter ancestor of this paper was published in *Analysis* under the same title as Bermúdez 2015.

quale of ownership. Section II turns specifically to de Vignemont's objections, and in particular her claim that the rubber hand illusion reveals the existence of precisely the type of separately describable feeling of ownership that I denied was possible. In section III, I return to Anscombe's concept of separability, exploring some of the questions that it raises about the relation between bodily awareness and "ordinary" perceptual awareness.

I

It can be hard to disentangle what is at stake in discussions of the phenomenology of ownership. But here is a basic claim that I think would be accepted by almost all participants in the discussion:

(A) When we experience our bodies, we typically experience them as our own.

This way of experiencing our bodies as our own is immediate and seems to be built into the content of somatosensory experience. So, for example, when I experience my legs as crossed, my legs are given to me within experience as my own. I do not (in normal circumstances) experience crossed legs and then go on to identify those legs as my own. One index of this is that certain types of error are not possible when we experience our bodies in normal ways. In normal circumstances (with my information being proprioceptively derived, and so forth), I can't experience someone else's legs being crossed while misidentifying those legs as my own—and nor, alternatively, can I experience my legs being crossed while misidentifying those legs as someone else's. The impossibility of the second type of error is standardly described by saying that bodily experience is immune to error through misidentification relative to the first-person pronoun (Shoemaker 1968).[1]

Claim (A) is the starting point for discussion. The debate begins when we ask why claim (A) is true. This is where the inflationary and deflationary

---

1. For recent discussions of the complexities in Shoemaker's notion of immunity to error through misidentification, see the essays in Prosser and Recanati 2012. Shoemaker's notion was first applied to bodily awareness by Gareth Evans in his book *The Varieties of Reference* (Evans 1982, particularly §7.3). On the relation between bodily awareness and the immunity property, see Cassam 1995, Chen 2011, Smith 2006, de Vignemont 2013.

views come apart. Taking an inflationary perspective, de Vignemont maintains that claim (A) holds because our bodily experiences all share a common phenomenological feature. Here is her central claim:

(B) We experience our bodies as our own in virtue of a "felt 'myness' that goes over and above the mere experience of one's bodily properties" (2013, 643).

As she puts it in her article, when I touch the table my tactile sensations include not only sensations of resistance, texture, temperature, and location, but also a distinctive experience of the hand as my own—a "nonconceptual intuitive awareness of ownership" (2013, 650). According to (B), there is a distinctive quale of ownership that is incorporated in our experience of our own bodies, and it is through this quale that we experience our bodies as our own.

Claim (A) says, in effect, that ownership is phenomenologically salient. Claim (B) offers one account of this phenomenological salience, identifying it with a distinctive quale of ownership. To appreciate that these are two very different claims, consider an analogy from discussions of perceptual consciousness. An equivalent of Claim (A) might be, for example, the claim that when we experience blue things we typically experience them as blue. One (relatively popular) way of explaining that fact about experience might be to postulate the existence of a felt quale of blueness. But of course, there is a range of other possible explanations. Likewise, there are other possible models of explaining the phenomenological salience of ownership identified in Claim (A).

De Vignemont's explicit target in her paper is the deflationary view of ownership that has been articulated by various authors, including Michael Martin (1992) and me (Bermúdez 2011). According to the deflationary view,

(C) There is no distinctive qualitative experience of ownership in virtue of which we experience our bodies as our own.

Deflationary theorists accept (A)—that is, they accept that when we experience our bodies we experience them as our own. So, they accept that there is a phenomenology of ownership. But they deny that this phenomenology of ownership is epistemically based on a quale of ownership. As Martin puts it, "what marks out a felt limb as one's own is not some special quality that it has, but simply that one feels it in this way" (1992, 201).

Of course, one might reasonably ask for more detail. What exactly does it mean to say that one feels a limb to be one's own even though it does not have some special quality? I have gone into this question in more detail elsewhere (see particularly chapter 8 in this volume). But (in brief) the deflationary theorist plainly has to identify features of bodily awareness and bodily experience that can provide an experiential ground for the sense of ownership. Whereas the inflationary theorist, in effect, takes the sense of ownership to derive from an irreducible and unanalyzable phenomenological quality, the deflationary theorist, derives the sense of ownership from other, more fundamental facts about the phenomenology of bodily experience. Here is a way of making the distinction clear in a way that will be helpful for the subsequent discussion. For the inflationary theorist, the aspect of bodily experience in which the sense of ownership consists has to be elucidated through the concept of ownership. The deflationary theorist disagrees, holding that the sense of ownership can be grounded in aspects of bodily phenomenology that can be characterized without employing the concept of ownership.

How might the disagreement between (B) and (C) be resolved? Clearly some sort of argument is required, as trading intuitions about the putative (non-) existence of a sensation is unlikely to be successful. In my 2011 paper, I adapted a powerful line of thought from Anscombe in support of (C). In effect, I used Anscombe's discussion of why bodily awareness counts as knowledge without observation to argue that there could not be a quale of ownership underwriting the phenomenology of ownership. Anscombe is concerned to argue that how we learn about our bodily states through bodily sensations is very different from how we learn about the world through, say, visual perception. Her basic line of argument can be adapted, I claim, to argue against the possibility of any quale of ownership doing the job that the inflationary theorist thinks it can do. (This needs to be emphasized. The claim is that, even if there were such a thing as a quale of ownership, it would be an idle wheel, serving no explanatory purpose.)

Let's start with Anscombe's reasons for thinking that bodily awareness is knowledge without observation. Here is her presentation of the view that she rejects (and she explicitly says that we could just as well speak of knowledge without clues as of knowledge without observation):

He [David Braybrooke] thinks that feelings of resistance, weight and pressure serve as clues by which one judges that one's legs are crossed, when they are crossed and one knows it in the ordinary way. (Anscombe 1962, 55)

The view she is attacking sees judgments about limb position and how one's body is disposed as ultimately derived by a process of inference that starts with bodily sensations.

What is wrong with the idea that bodily sensations serve as an inferential basis (clues) for how one's limbs are disposed? The problem, according to Anscombe, is that bodily sensations are not, as she puts it, "separable":

When I say: "the sensation (e.g. of giving a reflex kick) is not separable" I mean that the internal description of the "sensation"—the description of the sensation-content—is the very same as the description of the fact known; when that is so, I should deny that we can speak of observing *that* fact by means of the alleged sensation. (Anscombe 1962, 56)

Anscombe's point, as I understand it, is that for very few, if any, proprioceptive and kinesthetic sensations is it possible to provide internal descriptions that can serve as a guide to how one's limbs are disposed. Bodily sensations can normally only be described either in very general internal terms (e.g., sensations of pressure, contact points, muscle stretch), or in very specific external terms (e.g., the sensation of having one's legs crossed). Described the first way, bodily sensations are too general and vague to be the epistemic basis for one's awareness of limb position. But described the second way, they simply recapitulate the very knowledge that they are supposed to be grounding and so are not sufficiently independent to provide an epistemic basis. Under neither horn of the dilemma can bodily sensations do the work required to justify judgments about how one's body is disposed.

The epistemological background here is that (epistemic) grounding must satisfy the twin constraints that I term *focus* and *independence*. The focus constraint is, in effect, that nothing can serve as a ground or warrant unless its content is suitably aligned with the content of that for which it serves as a ground or warrant. The notion of "suitable alignment" can, of course, be fleshed out in many different ways, but at a minimum a content *a* can be suitably aligned with a content *b* only if the former can serve as evidence for the latter. Anscombe's claim, then, is that when bodily sensations are described internally, they cannot satisfy the focus constraint. To the extent that they have a content at all, that content is too vague and nonspecific to serve as evidence for one's knowledge of how one's limbs are disposed.

The independence constraint goes in the opposite direction. In effect, what it requires is that a ground or warrant must be capable of providing independent support for that for which it is a ground or warrant. And a necessary condition on a content *a* providing independent support for a content *b* is that the two contents be distinguishable (or separately describable, in Anscombe's phrase). If a content *b* simply duplicates a content *a*, then this requirement of distinguishability and independence is not satisfied—any more than one justifies an assertion by simply repeating it. And yet (says Anscombe) we only get duplication when bodily sensations are described externally. If I say that I know that my legs are crossed because I feel that they are crossed, then the appeal to bodily sensation adds no new information.

In effect, Anscombe offers a dilemma for the view that she opposes. Bodily sensations must be described either internally or externally. When described internally, they fail the focus constraint. But when described externally, they fail the independence constraint. In my 2011 paper, I applied a version of Anscombe's dilemma to de Vignemont's postulation of a "non-conceptual intuitive awareness of ownership."

It is highly implausible, I claimed, that there is a determinate quale of ownership that can be identified, described, and considered independently of the mineness that it is supposed to be communicating. Certainly no one has provided such an internal description. And this is why inflationary theorists tend to talk about a quale of mineness, or a preflective awareness of oneself as the owner of one's limbs and body. So, in effect, inflationary theorists are committed to the feeling of mineness being externally describable. And yet a feeling of mineness that can only be described in those very terms is not sufficiently independent of the phenomenon that it is claimed to justify. So, the postulated "non-conceptual intuitive awareness of ownership" falls foul of Anscombe's dilemma.

II

De Vignemont (2013) raises two objections to my argument. The first is that I overstate the import of Anscombe's argument, even assuming it to be sound. The argument cannot show that there is no intuitive awareness of ownership. The most it can show is that such an intuitive awareness can-not serve as an epistemic basis for our judgments of ownership. This is a fair point. But one might reasonably wonder what the point is of postulat-ing an intuitive awareness of ownership if it demonstrably cannot do any explanatory work. And de Vignemont herself does propose the quale of ownership as "a useful, simple explanatory tool, which allows for a single unified explanation of ownership illusions, for phenomenological differ-ences between sensations in one's limbs and in tools, and for disownership pathologies" (2013, 650). *Tu quoque!*

More persuasively, de Vignemont argues directly that there really is a separable awareness of ownership. Her argument is based on an understand-ing of perceptual awareness (and hence knowledge through observation) that she finds in an intriguing paper by Edward Harcourt (2008). As Har-court puts it, "where there is perception, there must be belief-independent perceptual appearances" (Harcourt 2008, 309). The existence of belief-independent perceptual appearances is shown in turn by the existence of perceptual illusions, where things perceptually appear one way while one knows (and hence believes) that that is not how they really are.

As an observation about the nature of perception, this seems unassail-able. De Vignemont thinks that it helps us understand the relation between separability and ownership because if we can find belief-independent appearances of ownership, then those will count (she claims) as examples of the type of separable description of the quale of ownership that I have denied exists. She writes:

> For experiences of ownership to be separately describable there must be cases in which one reports feeling as if a body part belonged to one while correctly judging that this is not one's body part. (2013, 644)

And, she argues, there are indeed such cases. Her prime example is the rub-ber hand illusion, first described by Botvinick and Cohen (1998) and much replicated since.[2]

The rubber hand illusion illustrates the dominance of vision over touch. To generate it, subjects are seated in front of a table on which there is a rub-ber left hand. Their own left hand is hidden by a screen. The experimenter simultaneously and synchronously use paintbrushes to stroke the subject's

---

2. For further discussion of the Rubber Hand Illusion and related whole body illu-sions, see Essay 8 below, which also provides extensive references.

concealed hand and the rubber hand. Typically, after a couple of minutes subjects report feeling sensations of touch in the rubber hand (Botvinick and Cohen 1998). When questioned, a significant proportion report feeling as if the rubber hand belongs to them. At the same time, of course, subjects are perfectly well aware that the rubber hand is not a part of their own bodies. So, we have a belief-independent appearance of ownership and (according to de Vignemont) precisely the separability that Anscombe denies.

Of course, the plausibility of the argument here rests directly on the plausibility of de Vignemont's interpretation of Anscombe's separability criterion, and it seems to me that de Vignemont misses the real point of Anscombe's discussion. In the second of the two passages quoted earlier, Anscombe certainly equates nonseparability with the identity of the sensation content and the description of the fact that is known—as she puts it, what blocks separability is the fact that "the internal description of the 'sensation'—the description of the sensation-content—is the very same as the description of the fact known" (1962, 56). *Pari passu*, for separability to be achieved, there must be the right kind of gap between the description of the sensation and the description of the fact for which the sensation is claimed to be evidence. And certainly, when appearance and reality diverge (as they do in the rubber hand illusion), then there is a gap *of some kind* between how things seem to the subject and how things really are, just as there is in any perceptual or quasi-perceptual illusion. But is it a gap of the right kind to secure separability, in Anscombe's sense?

I think not. When Anscombe writes about separability, she is focusing on something completely different. When, in cases of illusion, there is a gap between appearance and judgment, the content of the appearance is different from the content of the judgment. The appearance is that, say, the rubber hand is mine, while the judgment is, of course, that the rubber hand is not mine. And so, the appearance and the judgment contradict each other. This means that the appearance cannot provide any sort of grounding or support for the judgment. But Anscombe is trying to elucidate what would have to be the case for an appearance to ground or support a judgment in such a way that it would be appropriate to describe the appearance as a way of coming to know a fact about one's body. Let's look at this in more detail.

Extrapolating from what Anscombe says about bodily sensations and the associated judgments, we can see how it can be applied to the phenomenology of ownership. The starting point is that, when we look at the phenomenology associated with judgments of ownership it takes the form of

Sensations that ——

Feelings that ——

In both cases the "——" is a placeholder for a propositional content about ownership (e.g., "this hand is mine"). The sensation content, as it were, is the same as the content of the judgment of ownership. This is why, Anscombe believes, the sensation content cannot provide an epistemic basis for the judgment. Her point is that what is doing the justifying must be sufficiently independent of what is being justified to provide genuine epistemic support.

It is true that in the rubber hand illusion, the sensation content is not the same as the content of the associated judgment, because subjects typically experience the rubber hand as theirs while knowing perfectly well that it is not. So, the sensation content is certainly not identical with the judgment content. Does this make sensation content and judgment content sufficiently independent to allay Anscombe's concerns?

Again, I don't think so. The sensation content and judgment content are distinct, but the former is not in any sense serving as an epistemic basis for the latter. The epistemic basis for the judgment content is completely different, as it would have to be, given that the effect of the judgment is in essence to override the sensation content. So really the rubber hand illusion is orthogonal to Anscombe's argument. While it is true that the rubber hand illusion can be interpreted with some plausibility as a belief-independent appearance of ownership, but this does not make the phenomenology separately describable in a way that would allow us to talk about a quale of ownership in the way that de Vignemont wants.

III

At this point, however, a new set of problems emerges. In particular, one might think that the cure is in danger of killing the patient, because it looks as if the basic distinction we began with between knowledge without observation and knowledge through observation is in danger of disappearing. Let me explain.

The distinction between knowledge without observation and knowledge
through observation is intended to highlight the differences between how
we come to find out about (for example) our own bodily states and our
own intentions, on the one hand, and how we find out about the world
through ordinary (outwardly directed) perception, on the other. Only in
the latter case, Anscombe and others have thought, is it appropriate to talk
about knowledge through observation. But now, given the epistemic interpretation emphasized in the previous two sections, it looks as if ordinary
perceptual knowledge may come out as knowledge without observation.
The problem is that the epistemic basis for perceptual knowledge is typically taking perceptual experience at face value.[3] To take perceptual appearances at face value is to judge that the world is as it appears in perception.
That is to say, it amounts to forming a judgment whose content is the same
as the content of the perceptual appearance on which it is supposed to be
based. But now it seems as though one can raise for ordinary perceptual
knowledge exactly the same questions as were raised in section 1 for bodily
awareness and the putative *quale of ownership*. Does not ordinary perceptual
knowledge fail what I termed the independence constraint, because the
content of perceptual awareness is not sufficiently independent of the content of perceptual knowledge to provide evidential support for it? And if so,
does not knowledge through observation collapse into knowledge without
observation?

In fact, the distinction between knowledge without observation and
knowledge through observation seems to be under threat also from the
opposite direction, with the former looking as if it might collapse into the
latter. The problem here is that the discussion of the rubber hand illusion
seems to have gone a long way toward assimilating the phenomenology
of ownership (and of bodily awareness more generally) to the phenomenology of ordinary perceptual knowledge. In both cases, there are belief-
independent perceptual appearances.

Putting these two problems together yields the following challenge.
We have two ostensibly very different forms of experience (taking "experience" in the broadest of senses). We have our experience of our own bodies

3. See chapter 3 in this volume for more on the idea of taking experiences at face value,
with particular reference to Peacocke's (1999) characterization of
representation-dependent judgments.

(including the sense of ownership), on the one hand, and perceptual experience of the external world, on the other. In each case, we have both belief-independent appearances and judgments. So, is there really the kind of epistemic difference between these two forms of experience that Anscombe envisaged? If so, in what does it consist? And finally, can that difference be spelled out in a way that will support my earlier arguments against the possibility of a quale of ownership?

John McDowell, in an interesting paper that intersects with many of the themes of this discussion, offers a radical answer. In essence, his view is that there are no (sensory) appearances of, for example, limb position. As he puts it, "the presence to one of the position of a limb, when one knows it in the relevant way, has no sensuously qualitative character" (McDowell 2011, 148). (McDowell does not explicitly consider knowledge of ownership, but I am sure that he would take the same points to apply. I cannot imagine that he would accept that there could be such a thing as a quale of ownership.)

McDowell has two connected reasons for denying that there are appearances of limb position and the disposition of our bodies. The first (which derives from a line of thought that he finds in Anscombe's 1964 paper "Substance") is the claim that bodily awareness does not involve the apprehension of secondary qualities, while it is constitutive of perceptual awareness that it involve such apprehension. This phenomenological claim has been disputed (e.g., by Michael Ayers—see Ayers 1991, vol. 2, 285) and McDowell backs it up with some general reflections on the nature of perceptual knowledge.

For McDowell, perceptual knowledge is essentially receptive. It is a way in which the knower is affected through the senses by what is known. Knowledge of limb position and ownership, in contrast, is self-knowledge of oneself as a bodily agent: "In receptive knowledge, what is known is other than the knower; or if that is not so it is known *as other*. This is exactly not so with this knowledge of limb position. This knowledge is *self*-knowledge; what is known is the self-conscious bodily being who is the knower" (McDowell 2011, 142).

There is much to dispute in these reflections, however. McDowell is thinking in very Aristotelian terms of individual senses and their proper sensibles (the secondary qualities, each of which can be apprehended only by one sense). On this view, each sense has its own sense organ and a corresponding proper object. The proper object of vision is the secondary quality of color. The proper object of hearing is the secondary quality of sound. And so on.[4] The phenomenology of perception is much more complex and integrated than that neo-Aristotelian picture suggests, however. The boundaries between proprioception and exteroception are too blurred to carry the kind of distinction that McDowell is trying to impose with his comments about receptivity.

It is true that bodily awareness is self-knowledge. But this self-knowledge is not isolated in the way that, for example, our knowledge of our own thoughts can be. Rather, our knowledge of how our bodies are disposed is closely bound up with our awareness of the external environment. The sense of touch, for example, informs us both about limb disposition and about the configuration of outer objects, while the vestibular system tells us how our bodies are disposed relative to gravity and to supporting surfaces. At the same time, as I have stressed in other places (e.g., Bermúdez 1998 and chapter 5 in this volume), bodily awareness has a fundamental role to play in structuring exteroceptive perception. We do not gain perceptual knowledge of the external environment through the disparate and unconnected contributions of different senses, but rather through what Michael Ayers has termed "an integrated sensory field" that ineliminably incorporates bodily specific information derived from the different forms of bodily awareness.[5] What integrates the various sensory modalities is that they collectively represent a single space containing three-dimensional objects. Our experience of this space is structured by our experience of our own bodies. This is exactly what one would expect, given that the body is an object among others and that bodily awareness is an important element in our understanding of how we can act on distal objects.

But now this discussion of how integrated proprioception and exteroception are seems to put us in even greater danger of losing the distinction between knowledge through observation and knowledge without observation. To see how the distinction can be preserved we need to go back to bodily experience and how it differs from (externally focused) perceptual experience.

4. The *locus classicus* for this view is Aristotle's *De Anima*, Bk. II, chap. 6.

5. See, e.g., Ayers 1991, particularly at chap. 21 of vol. 1. J. J. Gibson has effectively criticized the psychological equivalent of Aristotle's view of proper sensibles (i.e., Müller's doctrine of specific nerve energies) in, for example, Gibson 1966.

We have seen (and endorsed) Anscombe's reasons for thinking that bodily sensations cannot be "clues" on the basis of which we infer or otherwise derive judgments about the body. Any such proposal faces a dilemma, depending on whether it proposes to characterize the content of bodily sensations internally or externally. When the content of bodily sensations is characterized internally, it falls foul of the focus constraint, while when characterized externally it runs into the independence constraint.

That insight alone is not going to yield the distinction that we are looking for, since it is fairly clear that perceptual sensations cannot be clues either. The only way in which perceptual sensations could be clues in the sense that Braybrooke proposed, and Anscombe criticizes, would be if some form of sense datum theory were true, and that surely is not a viable position. But thinking further about why both types of sensation cannot serve as clues will point us in the right direction, because it turns out that they each fail to function as clues in importantly different ways.

One key characteristic of bodily experience is that the bodily location of sensations is part of their phenomenological content. We experience a tingle in the knee, for example, or a pain in the neck. There are different models of the spatial content of bodily awareness, but all agree on the basic point that sensations are experienced on a body-relative frame of reference.[6] Moreover, it is not just that bodily sensations are experienced at particular body parts. Our experience of the spatial location of a sensation is given in terms of the spatial location of the body part in which it is located. The tingle in my knee is experienced at a particular point in space (in front of the chair and below the desktop) because that is where I experience the knee to be. This means that knowledge of limb position is an integral part of the content of bodily sensations. This is why sensations cannot serve as clues, or provide any other inferential or quasi-inferential basis for knowledge of limb position. McDowell himself appreciates this point, writing:

It is not that one knows where a felt tingle, say, is, independently of knowing how one's body is disposed in space, so that an aggregation of such knowledge of the location of objects of sensation—or, better, of the sensations themselves—might enable one to get to know how one's body is disposed in space. That gets things backwards. One locates these sensations in space only by locating them in one's

6. See, e.g., O'Shaughnessy 1980; Martin 1995; Cassam 1995. For my own model, see chapters 5 and 8 in this volume.

own body. Spatially organized awareness of one's bodily self is a presupposition for the capacity to locate bodily sensations, not something enabled by that capacity. (McDowell 2011, 145)

In effect, McDowell is eloquently affirming the independence constraint.

A similar point can be made about the phenomenology of ownership. The starting point for this essay was the following observation:

(A)   When we experience our bodies, we typically experience them as our own.

Another way of formulating (A) would be to say that ownership is an integral part of the content of somatosensory awareness. And, just as with bodily sensations and limb position, the independence constraint entails that our bodily experiences cannot serve as an inferential or quasi-inferential basis for our sense of ownership.

So, knowledge of limb position is an integral part of the content of bodily sensations and ownership is an integral part of the content of somatosensory awareness. This in itself is not enough to distinguish the two forms of awareness from ordinary perceptual awareness because we can make the parallel observation that knowledge of the layout of objects in the external environment is an integral part of the content of perceptual awareness? After all, we typically learn about the layout of objects in the external environment through taking our perceptual experience of the world at face value. However, the independence constraint does not apply here in the same way, because there is a crucial difference, which I will now explain.

The content of the perceptual awareness of the world that (assuming it is veridical) yields knowledge when taken at face value is propositional content. When I come to know that φ through perception, what I perceive is the same as what I come to know—namely, that φ holds. Here "φ" is a placeholder for some characterization of a propositional content, with the details to be filled out according to your preferred theory of propositions. When I come to know through perception that the cat is on the mat, for example, this is because I see that the cat is on the mat. More generally, when we specify the propositional content of ordinary exteroceptive perceptual awareness, we do so using the very same concepts and language that we use to spell out the content of the knowledge that is acquired through perception—and, of course, on the assumption that the conceptual/linguistic machinery that we use is itself reflected and applied in the perceiver's experience of the world. If this were all there were to the content of perceptual awareness, then the independence constraint would apply. But it is not, and so it does not.

As many commentators on perception have noted, there are other ways to characterize the content of perception, at least in the case of visual perception. Dretske, for example, famously distinguished epistemic seeing (the "seeing that φ" discussed in the previous paragraph) from simple seeing (Dretske 1969). Other theorists use the terminology of conceptual content as opposed to nonconceptual content (Evans 1982; Crane 1992; Peacocke 1992; Bermúdez 1998—see Bermúdez and Cahen 2015 for further references). For the authors mentioned, and many others, the nonconceptual content of perception provides a vital epistemic underpinning for the epistemic/conceptual/propositional content of perception. So, for example, on Peacocke's account, first put forward in his 1992, the possession conditions for observation concepts are given in part in terms of the appropriateness of applying them when enjoying perceptual experiences with relevant nonconceptual contents.

This is not the place to go into the complex debates surrounding the notion of nonconceptual content, or to engage with critics of the very idea such as John McDowell (1994). My point is a simple one. The fact that the content of ordinary, exteroceptive perceptual awareness is not exhausted by its propositional content opens up the possibility of finding a further epistemic basis for the propositional content of perception. This gives precisely the "separability" that Anscombe emphasized and that was discussed in sections I and II above.

The nonconceptual content of (visual) perception meets both of the key constraints identified earlier. It meets the focus constraint because, on all ways of developing the notion, nonconceptual content is representational. It represents the world as being a certain way, and so it is exactly the right sort of thing to provide evidential support for perceptual judgments. At the same time, there is no danger of an identity of content between the non-conceptual content of perception and the content of perceptual judgments and perceptual knowledge. The nonconceptual content of perception can provide evidential support for perceptual beliefs and perceptual knowledge because the two types of content represent the environment in fundamentally different ways. This is how the independence constraint is satisfied.

In contrast, as I have emphasized, there is no such possibility of finding within the content of bodily awareness an independent epistemic basis either for judgments about how one's body is disposed, or for judgments of ownership.[7] This is why I have described these forms of awareness as nonseparable, in Anscombe's sense. In both of those cases we are confronted with what is in effect a phenomenological given. There is no way of characterizing the content of bodily sensations that can exclude the fact that we experience bodily sensations at particular locations in particular body parts. Likewise, there is no way of characterizing the content of our experience of our own bodies that can exclude the fact that we experience our bodies as our own.

I should emphasize that the key issue here is not the distinction between conceptual content and nonconceptual content. It is most definitely not the case that the nonconceptual content of perception satisfies the independence constraint simply in virtue of being nonconceptual. To say that a content is nonconceptual is (as standardly construed) to say that a subject can be in a state with that content even though she does not possess the concepts required to specify it.[8] So, for example, Christopher Peacocke's model of scenario content characterizes the nonconceptual content of visual perception in terms of ways of filling out space around the perceiver. This model can accurately describe the (nonconceptual) content of how a subject sees the world even when that subject lacks some or all of the concepts required to set up or employ the model. But the fact that the subject lacks these concepts is not what secures the satisfaction of the independence constraint. Rather, the independence constraint is satisfied because there is sufficient distance between a description of the world given in terms of scenario content, and the (conceptual) description of the world for which the scenario content provides evidence and grounding.

For this reason, the question of whether or not bodily awareness is nonconceptual is orthogonal to my overall argument. As it happens, I think that it is.[9] But that cannot close the gap between bodily awareness and ordinary

7. This is not to say, though, that bodily awareness might not be able to provide an epistemic basis for other types of judgment. To my mind that remains an open question.

8. For further discussion see Bermúdez and Cahen 2015.

9. See chapter 1 in this volume, for example.

perceptual awareness. My point is that the content of bodily awareness cannot be accurately characterized at any level, or with any conceptual machinery, in ways that do not reflect the very facts about limb position and ownership that the content of bodily awareness might be called up to justify. That is what it means to say that knowledge of limb position and ownership of one's limbs is a phenomenological given. And it is for that reason that the (nonconceptual) content of bodily awareness does not stand to the (conceptual) content of judgments about limb position and ownership in the same way as the (nonconceptual) content of visual perception stands to the (conceptual) content of perceptual knowledge.

And so, to summarize the discussion in this section, there is a meaningful and important distinction between bodily awareness and knowledge of limb position, on the one hand, and ordinary, exteroceptive perceptual awareness, on the other. The terminology of "knowledge through observation" and "knowledge without observation" may not be entirely happy, but it certainly marks a real distinction. Moreover, circling back to the principal argument of this essay, understanding the distinction properly shows why there is no utility to postulating a quale of ownership in the way that de Vignemont proposes. Everybody agrees that we experience our bodies as our own. Such a "sense of ownership" is part of the phenomenology of experience. But it does not follow from this that, as de Vignemont proposes, we have such a sense of ownership in virtue of a "felt 'myness' that goes over and above the mere experience of one's bodily properties" (2013, 643). In fact, for the reasons I have brought out, such a quale of ownership would be an idle wheel with no explanatory power.

References

Anscombe, G. E. M. 1957. *Intention.* Oxford: Blackwell.

Anscombe, G. E. M. 1962. On sensations of position. *Analysis* 22:55–58.

Anscombe, G. E. M. 1964. *Substance: Collected Philosophical Papers.* Vol. 2. Oxford: Blackwell.

Ayers, M. 1991. *Locke: Epistemology and Ontology.* 2 vols. London: Routledge.

Bermúdez, J. L. 1998. *The Paradox of Self-Consciousness.* Cambridge, MA: MIT Press.

Bermúdez, J. L. 2011. Bodily awareness and self-consciousness. In *Oxford Handbook of the Self*, ed. S. Gallagher, 157–179. Oxford: Oxford University Press.

Bermúdez, J. L. 2015. Bodily ownership, bodily awareness and knowledge without observation. *Analysis* 75:37–45.

Bermúdez, J. L., and A. Cahen. 2015. Mental content, nonconceptual. In *Stanford Encyclopedia of Philosophy*. https://plato.stanford.edu.

Botvinick, M., and J. Cohen. 1998. Rubber hands "feel" touch that eyes see. *Nature* 391:756.

Cassam, Q. 1995. Introspection and bodily self-ascription. In *The Body and the Self*, ed. J. L. Bermúdez, A. J. Marcel, and N. M. Eilan, 311–336. Cambridge, MA: MIT Press.

Chen, C. K. 2011. Bodily awareness and immunity to error through misidentification. *European Journal of Philosophy* 19:21–38.

Crane, T. 1992. The nonconceptual content of experience. In *The Contents of Experience*, ed. T. Crane. Cambridge: Cambridge University Press.

de Vignemont, F. 2007. Habeas corpus: The sense of ownership of one's own body. *Mind & Language* 22:427–449.

de Vignemont, F. 2013. The mark of bodily ownership. *Analysis* 73:643–651.

Dretske, F. 1969. *Seeing and Knowing*. London: Routledge.

Evans, G. 1982. *The Varieties of Reference*. Oxford: Oxford University Press.

Gibson, J. J. 1966. *The Senses Considered as Perceptual Systems*. Boston: Houghton Mifflin.

Harcourt, E. 2008. Wittgenstein and bodily self-knowledge. *Philosophy and Phenomenological Research* 77 (2): 299–333.

Martin, M. 1992. Perception, concepts, and memory. *Philosophical Review* 101:745–763.

Martin, M. 1995. Bodily awareness: A sense of ownership. In *The Body and the Self*, ed. J. L. Bermúdez, A. J. Marcel, and N. M. Eilan. Cambridge, MA: MIT Press.

McDowell, J. 1994. *Mind and World*. Cambridge, MA: Harvard University Press.

McDowell, J. 2011. Anscombe on bodily self-knowledge. In *Essays on Anscombe's Intention*, ed. A. Ford, J. Hornsby, and F. Stoutland. Cambridge, MA: MIT Press.

O'Shaughnessy, B. 1980. *The Will: A Dual Aspect Theory*. Cambridge: Cambridge University Press.

Peacocke, C. 1992. *A Study of Concepts*. Cambridge, MA: MIT Press.

Peacocke, C. 1999. *Being Known*. Oxford: Oxford University Press.

Prosser, S., and F. Recanati, eds. 2012. *Immunity to Error through Misidentification: New Essays*. Cambridge: Cambridge University Press.

Shoemaker, S. 1968. Self-reference and self-awareness. *Journal of Philosophy* 65 (19): 555–567.

Smith, J. 2006. Bodily awareness, imagination, and the self. *European Journal of Philosophy* 14:49–68.

8 Ownership and the Space of the Body

In the last twenty years a robust experimental paradigm has emerged for studying the structure of bodily experience, focusing primarily on what it is to experience one's body as one's own. As in many areas of psychology and cognitive science, induced illusions have proved highly illuminating. The initial impetus came from the rubber hand illusion (RHI) first demonstrated by Botvinick and Cohen (1998), subsequently extended by various researchers to generate illusions of ownership at the level of the body as a whole (for reviews, see Tsakiris 2010; Serino et al. 2013; Kilteni et al. 2015). The resulting experimental paradigms and results have allowed cognitive scientists to operationalize aspects of bodily experience previously explored either purely theoretically or as distorted in neurological disorders such as unilateral spatial neglect. Experiments have focused primarily on the experience of ownership (what it is to experience one's body as one's own) and the experience of agency (what it is to experience acting with and through one's body).

However, these illusion paradigms have not directly studied one important aspect of bodily experience, namely, how the space of the body is experienced. The experienced spatiality of the body is part of what marks out our experience of our bodies as unique physical objects (Bermúdez 1998, 2005, 2011). There is, of course, no objective difference between the space of the body and the space of the extrabodily environment. But the representation of spatial location in bodily experience is very different from the representation of spatial location in vision and other forms of exteroceptive perception. Understanding these differences is integral to understanding how bodily experience contributes to self-consciousness.

This essay identifies some problems with how ownership is discussed in the context of bodily illusions, and then shows how those problems can be addressed through a model of the experienced space of the body. Section 1 briefly reviews the bodily illusions literature and its significance for cognitive science and philosophy. Section 2 expresses reservations with the concept of ownership in terms of which the RHI and other illusions are standardly framed. I offer three hypotheses for the source of our putative sense of ownership. The main body of the essay develops the third hypothesis, which is that judgments of ownership are grounded in the distinctive way that we experience the space of the body.

I

Botvinick and Cohen (1998) introduced an experimental paradigm for inducing illusions of ownership that has been widely replicated and developed. Since 1998, over 200 papers have been published on the RHI, in which subjects see a rubber hand being stroked while their own hand, which they cannot see, is being synchronously stroked. Subjects reliably report both feeling sensations of touch in the rubber hand and feeling that the rubber hand is their own hand. A number of studies have suggested that these subjective reports correlate reliably with behavioral measures, including

• galvanic skin conductance response (Armel and Ramachandran 2003),
• temperature in the stimulated hand (Mosely et al. 2008)
• drift in the perceived location of the hand relative to the rubber hand (Tsakiris and Haggard 2005)

The subjective experience of subjects undergoing the illusion has also been studied psychometrically with a 27-item questionnaire subsequently put through a principal component analysis (Longo et al. 2008).

Further development of the RHI paradigm has explored the possibility of dissociating reports of ownership in the rubber hand and reports of agency with respect to the hand (Kalkert and Ehrsson 2012); the significance of postural and anatomical congruence between the real hand and the rubber hand (Costantini and Haggard 2007); and the possibility of eliciting the illusion without visuotactile stimulation (Kalkert and Ehrsonn 2012). In terms of understanding the mechanisms underlying the RHI, the main issue has been whether the experience of ownership is a bottom-up, stimulus-driven process, or whether it involves higher-order representations of the body, such as a long-term body image and/or an occurrent postural map

(Tsakiris 2010; de Vignemont 2014). Investigations of the neural underpinnings of the experience of bodily ownership have highlighted the role of the temporal-parietal junction (Ionta et al. 2014).

Comparable illusions have been induced for the sense of ownership of the entire body using head-mounted displays to create a virtual reality in which subjects see the world from a different spatial perspective. The illusion has been generated from different perspectives, both third person and first person, as illustrated in figure 8.1. In the full-body illusion, subjects can be brought to identify with a full-body avatar that they see being stroked at a spatial location in front of them (Lengenhagger et al. 2007). In the body-swap illusion, subjects reports a sense of ownership for a mannequin that they see being stroked in the location where they would expect their own bodies to be (Petkova and Ehrrson 2008). An interesting phenomenon noticed in studies of the full-body illusion is that the illusion persists when transposed into a third-person perspective—subjects can perceive being in front of their own bodies and even shaking hands with themselves.

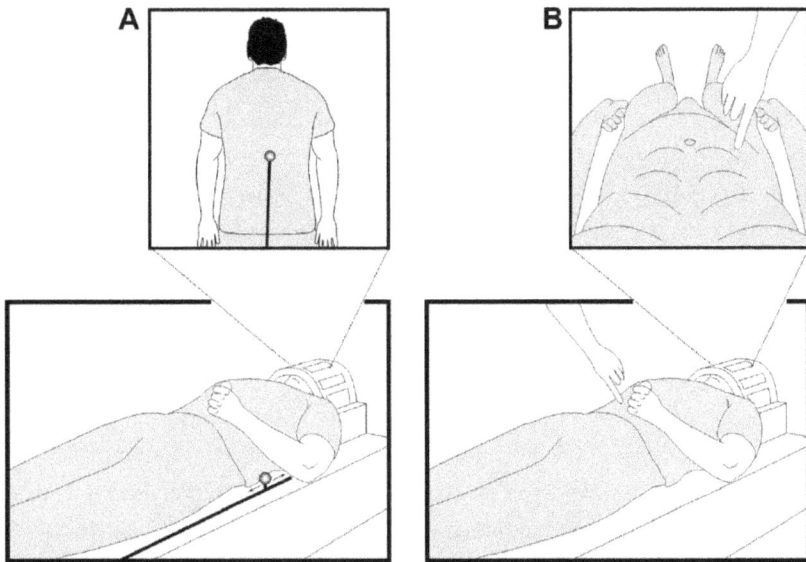

Figure 8.1
Illustration of the differences in perspective in the full-body illusion (A) and the body-swap illusion (B). From Serino et al. 2013.

One reason that the RHI and related experimental paradigms have generated such interest and excitement in the cognitive science community is that they offer a way of operationalizing and studying aspects of subjective experience that had stubbornly resisted experimental treatment in normal subjects. Previously, most of what was known about bodily experience came from neuropsychological studies of disorders such as *unilateral spatial neglect* (in which neurologically damaged patients neglect one side of their bodies, and indeed one side of peripersonal and external side—typically the side opposite the lesion), *somatoparaphrenia* (in which patients report disownership of body parts, typically on the contralesional side also) and *alien hand syndrome* (in which brain-damaged subjects report that someone else is moving their hands).[1] Although the study of neuropsychological disorders has been very illuminating, it has inherent disadvantages. Disorders such as somatoparaphrenia and alien hand syndrome are rare. It is hard to compare across cases since there is often significant additional brain damage that makes it difficult to disentangle the relative contributions of different disorders. And the reports of patients with severe brain damage can be challenging to understand and interpret.

From a more philosophical perspective, the structure of bodily experience has been studied by philosophers working within both analytical and phenomenological traditions—in fact, this has been one of the relatively few areas where there has been productive dialogue between the two traditions. Some of this work has been done more or less from the proverbial armchair (e.g., O'Shaughnessy 1980). But others have engaged more directly with the scientific study of the body. Merleau-Ponty, for example, was very well read in the neuropsychology of his day and rested important parts of his analysis of bodily experience in *The Phenomenology of Perception* (Merleau-Ponty 1968) on the detailed analysis of brain-damaged patients (most famously, the German war veteran Schneider). For more recent examples, see the essays in Bermúdez, Marcel, and Eilan 1995, as well as Gallagher 2005, Bermúdez 1998, 2011, and de Vignemont 2014. Many of these philosophers studying the body have converged on a small set of basic concepts and explanatory tools. These include different ways of thinking about the body image, as well as ideas of bodily ownership and

1. For reviews, see Corbetta and Shulman 2011 (spatial neglect), Vallar and Ronchi 2009 (somatoparaphrenia), and Scepkowski and Cronin-Golomb 2003 (alien hand syndrome).

bodily agency. These are precisely the notions that are operationalized and manipulated in the RHI and related bodily illusions.

II

The bodily illusions are standardly discussed as illusions of ownership—limb ownership in the case of the RHI and bodily ownership in the body-swap and full body illusions. It is clear that the RHI manipulates subjects' sense of their body parts belonging to them. If the rubber hand is experienced as being part of one's body, then it is natural to describe this as the experience of "owning" the rubber hand. But ownership is a rather tenuous and metaphorical concept in this context. We do not own hands, rubber or otherwise, in the way that we own personal property. And it is unlikely that any way of unpacking the metaphor that will work for limb ownership can be applied straightforwardly to so-called bodily ownership. Intuitively one might say that to feel ownership for a limb is to experience it as connected with the rest of one's body and as a part of one. But could that be the same sense in which we might feel ownership for our bodies as a whole? What would it mean to say that one experiences one's body as a part of oneself?[2]

Certainly, it seems impossible to extend to the body as a whole a *mereological* conception of ownership, as developed by Martin (1995). Martin defines the sense of ownership as a "phenomenological quality, that the body part appears to be a part of one's body" (1995, 269). This is perhaps one reason that some authors have proposed an account of ownership in terms of the locus of experience (with the emphasis more on ownership of bodily experiences, rather than on ownership of specific body parts). Gallagher, for example, writes of "the sense that I am the one who is undergoing an experience. For example, the sense that my body is moving regardless of whether the movement is voluntary or involuntary" (2000, 15).

Thinking about ownership in terms of the locus of experience is applicable both to individual body parts and to the body as a whole. However, there is a fundamental lack of clarity in the idea of a sense of ownership as it features in the literature. When, for example, it is said that subjects

2. For discussion at the neural level of the relation between ownership of the whole body and ownership of particular body parts, see Petkova et al. 2011 and Gentile et al. 2015.

in the RHI have a sense of ownership of the rubber hand, does this mean that there is a specific feeling of ownership—a qualitative "feel" that one has in all and only those body parts that one experiences as one's own? This is how some authors have described the phenomenology of ownership (see, e.g., Gallagher 2005 and de Vignemont 2007, 2013). But I have argued elsewhere that the feeling of ownership is a philosophical fiction (Bermú-dez 2011, 2015). If there is no such specific feeling of ownership then the putative sense of ownership becomes something that itself needs to be explained, rather than a basic notion that can do explanatory work. We know that there are judgments of ownership (and judgments of disowner-ship, for that matter, as in somatoparaphrenia). If there is a specific feeling of ownership, then those judgments can be viewed as simply reports of the feeling (or perhaps as expressions of the feeling, depending on one's view of first-person phenomenological reports). But if there is no such feeling of ownership then some account needs to be given of what those judgments are based on. This will, in effect, be a substantive account of what the sense of ownership consists in.[3]

So, when subjects report ownership (or disownership) of limbs, or of their entire bodies, what are those judgments based on? Here are three hypotheses:

(1) Judgments of ownership are based on the experienced location of sensation.
(2) Judgments of ownership are based on the experience of agency.
(3) Judgments of ownership are based on the experienced spatiality of the body.

This section explains why (1) and (2) are unconvincing. The remainder of the essay will focus on (3).[4]

3. For a broadly similar overall strategy, see Alsmith forthcoming, although he develops an account of judgments of ownership rather different from that proposed here. Alsmith's account of the RHI in terms of spontaneous imagining is somewhat plausible, but it is unclear how it would extend to nonillusory judgments of ownership.

4. The difference between (1) and (3) will become clear in section IV, but in brief the distinction is this. To base a judgment of ownership on the experienced location of sensation is to say that you take to be your own the body parts in which you feel sensations. In contrast, to base a judgment of ownership on the experienced spatial-ity of the body is to base it on the distinctive way in which bodily locations are experienced relative to nonbodily locations.

The idea behind (1) is that we report ownership of those limbs and body parts where we experience sensations. This idea goes back (at least) to the seventeenth century. In his *Essay Concerning Human Understanding*, John Locke argues that our "thinking, conscious self" extends to all parts of the body "that we feel when they are touch'd, and are affected by, and conscious of good or harm that happens to them" (Locke 1689/1975, Bk. II, chap. 27, §11). On this view, the body is experienced as the locus of sensation, so that judgments of ownership follow the localization of sensations.[5] One aspect of Locke's account that needs to be brought out is his stress on the dimension of concern. For Locke, to experience individual body parts and one's body as a whole as parts of one's "thinking, conscious self" is *ipso facto* to feel an immediate concern for what happens to them. This affective aspect of ownership has been highlighted by de Vignemont (forthcoming).

However, experiencing sensations in a particular body part appears to be neither necessary nor sufficient for judgments of ownership. Somatoparaphrenia seems to show that it is not sufficient. Somatoparaphrenic patients deny ownership of a limb or even of an entire side of their body. Yet there are reports from somatoparaphrenic patients of feeling sensations in limbs that they deny are theirs (Aglioti, Smania, Manfredi, and Berlucchi 1996; Bottini, Bisiach, Sterzi, and Vallar 2002).[6] And there are examples from the bodily illusion literature showing that experiencing sensations in a particular body part is not required for judgments of ownership. The experiments described by Ferri et al. (2013) show that the illusion can be induced by subjects seeing a rubber hand being approached, even when there is no touch (either of the rubber hand or of their own hand).

The idea that there is a connection between ownership and agency is highly intuitive, so that we experience our body and body parts as our own to the extent that we act with them, or are capable of acting with them. Within the philosophical literature, this way of thinking about judgments of ownership has typically not been distinguished from the first

5. For more recent discussions, see Cassam 1995, 1997, and Hamilton 2013.

6. It may be that what somatoparaphrenic patients are denying is concern or care for the relevant body parts, rather than that those body parts are their own, which might suggest that bodily location and concern are not as inextricably connected as Locke (and others) have thought. It is rarely straightforward to interpret the reports of patients with somatoparaphrenia and comparable disorders.

hypothesis. There are some good reasons for this, as will emerge in the next three paragraphs—and also some more questionable ones, connected to the postulation of a sense of agency but also capable of being dissociated from the sense of ownership (see Gallagher 2005 for an influential formulation). To my mind, the putative sense of agency suffers from exactly the same explanatory problems as the putative sense of ownership. In any event, setting up a dialectic on which there are distinct and separable sense of ownership and agency obscures the potential role of awareness of agency in underwriting judgments of ownership.[7]

Whereas hypothesis (1) frames the body as the locus of sensation, hypothesis (2) frames the body as the locus of action. Nonetheless, the rubber hand illusion itself shows that judgments of ownership cannot be based solely on the *experience* of acting with specific body parts, since there is no active movement in the RHI. The experience of agency cannot be a necessary condition. It may be a sufficient condition, however. Kalkert and Ehrsonn (2012) showed that the RHI can be induced with active movement in the absence of sensory stimulation.

Still, hypothesis (2) seems too narrowly formulated. For one thing, focusing exclusively on the experience of agency is insufficiently distant from hypothesis (1), since a significant part of the experience of agency surely consists in kinesthetic and other bodily sensations. An alternative would be to take judgments of ownership to rest on the capacity for agency, rather than the experience of agency. The guiding idea here is that the body is the physical object uniquely responsive to the will, and so we take ownership to extend to body parts that we can act with directly.

One difficulty with this proposal is that there are body parts that we judge to be our own but that we act with only in a very attenuated sense (if at all), such as the spleen or the kidney. Another, perhaps more significant, challenge is operationalizing the capacity for agency, as opposed to the exercise of agency in action. What would be an adequate test of whether one experiences a body part as something that one can act with, in circumstances in which one does not actually move it? The problem is that it is not clear what would distinguish the judgment that I can act with *this* limb from the corresponding judgment of ownership (this is *my* limb)—and yet

7. But see Tsakiris, Prabhu, and Haggard 2006 for empirical explorations in the context of the RHI.

we need the former judgment to be the sort of thing that can ground the latter judgment.

A more promising approach, I think, would be to look for a phenomenon that might plausibly explain why both the experienced location of sensation and the experience of agency seem so important to judgments of ownership. This is where hypothesis (3) comes into the picture. Both forms of experience reflect the fact that we experience our bodies as distinctive physical objects. They also reflect (and possibly even contribute to) a very important source for that experienced distinctiveness, namely, the differences between how space is represented within the bounds of the body and how extrabodily space is represented—or, to put it another way, between how bodily locations are encoded and how nonbodily locations are encoded. So, the hypothesis that I will explore in this essay is that judgments of ownership track the distinctive spatiality of bodily experience.

III

This section focuses on two very general features of how bodily events are experienced. (I am understanding bodily events in a broad sense, to include sensations such as itches, pains, and so forth, as well as tactile experiences and proprioceptive/kinesthetic experiences of how one's limbs are disposed and/or moving.) The first feature I call *Boundedness*.

Boundedness

Bodily events are experienced within the experienced body (a circumscribed body-shaped volume whose boundaries define the limits of the self).[8]

8. Cf. Martin 1995. According to Martin, it is a distinctive feature of the phenomenology of the body that "in having bodily sensations, it appears to one as if whatever one is aware of through having such sensations is a part of one's body" (1995, 269). This is a clear statement of what I am calling Boundedness (and he uses that very term at p. 271). Martin describes this phenomenological feature as a sense of ownership. For reasons indicated above I do not find this terminology very helpful. Moreover, he does not provide an explicit account of what grounds this phenomenological feature, which he seems to treat more as an explanandum than as an explanans (entirely appropriately, given his broader philosophical aims in that paper). Accordingly I did not include his position as one of the three hypotheses about the grounds of judgments of ownership considered above.

The body-shaped circumscribed volume that defines the limits of the self is the experienced body. It can be, but need not be, identical to the physical body. There are many documented cases where the two diverge, and the divergence takes place in both directions. The boundaries of the bodily self in the experienced body can extend beyond the limits of the physical body. The experience of sensations in phantom limbs is a well-known example, indicating how the experienced bodily self expands to accommodate displaced sensation. Pathologies such as unilateral spatial neglect and somatoparaphrenia illustrate how the experienced body can be more restricted than the bounds of the physical body.

I should clarify how Boundedness is to be understood. It is not intended as a necessary truth about human somatic experience. There seem to be counterexamples in the literature. I am grateful to a referee for directing me to an interesting case presented by Cronholm (1951). Cronholm reports a phantom limb patient at the Carolinska Institut in Stockholm who appeared to be fully aware of the spatial boundaries of his *phantom* and yet who reported feeling a sensation in a region of space outside those boundaries. This case is highly unusual, but I would be surprised if it were unique. From my perspective, however, Boundedness is proposed as a general characterization of the phenomenology of bodily awareness. That it might be contravened in highly unusual circumstances is interesting, but not particularly damaging to the proposal, particularly given that Boundedness does seem to be respected in the overwhelming majority of pathological cases.

In any event, Boundedness captures a reciprocal, temporally extended, and plastic process. At any given moment the boundaries of the experienced body are relatively fixed. But viewed over time the experienced body is malleable and adaptable, responding to organic bodily growth, trauma, and the changing demands of movement and action. The technique of using *extended physiological proprioception* (EPP) in the design of prosthetics for amputees is an excellent illustration of the role that agency can play in redefining the limits of the experienced self. The inspiration for EPP comes from the familiar example of blind people using white canes not just as motility aids but also as tools for discovering the environment. Recognizing this type of transferred sensation as a potential tool for improving the effectiveness of prosthetic limbs, D. C. Simpson proposed EPP in the 1970s.

The basic idea of EPP is to design prostheses so that feedback information from the artificial limb is experienced proprioceptively. Agency is crucial, since the mechanism for achieving this is coupling the movement of the prosthetic with the residual movements available through the nearest intact joint so that there is a direct relation between the movement and position of the prosthetic limb and the movement and position of the anatomical joint. We can think about the movement of a prosthetic limb in input–output terms. The movement of the intact joint is the input and the new position of the prosthetic is the output. By designing the prosthetic limb so that the input and output are closely bound to each other, the output position can be sensed through proprioceptive feedback from the input movement. It appears that using the EPP technique to design prosthetic limbs improves their effectiveness (Doubler and Childress 1984).

There are no studies that I am aware of on the subjective experience of amputees with EPP, but we can obtain guidance from qualitative studies of patients with "ordinary" prosthetics. A study of thirty-five amputees in the UK specifically explored the experience of embodiment in wearers/users of prosthetics, with many of the patients reporting their phantom limbs merging with the prosthesis (Murray 2004). Here are some sample comments from amputees:

… because I don't feel as anything is really missing. So my prosthesis is "natural." (Murray 2004, 969)

When I put on a prosthetic, the phantom becomes the prosthesis to the extent that the not-foot [phantom] is in almost the same position as the Flexfoot [a brand of prosthesis], maybe slightly more rotated. The fit is so good, that it makes walking with the prosthesis easier because of the correspondence between the prosthetic leg and the phantom. (970)

… Many amputees feel that their artificial limb is somehow part of them, a simple example of this is that I wouldn't like just anyone putting their hand on my artificial knee, even though it is not actually part of my body's flesh, it is still mine even though it's a piece of plastic and metal. (970)

Interviewer When you say it's part of you now, what exactly do you mean by that?
Participant Well, to me it's as if, though I've not got my lower arm, it's as though I've got it and it's [the prosthesis is] part of me now. It's as though I've got two hands, two arms. (970)

This "merging" of phantom limbs with prostheses contrasts significantly with referred sensations in tool use and with the incorporation of tools in the body schema more generally. Here the prosthetic seems to be incorporated into the limits of the self, in the way that tools typically are not.[9]

The second general feature of how bodily events are experienced I term *Connectedness*.

Connectedness

The spatial location of a bodily event is experienced relative to the disposition of the body as a whole.

Connectedness presupposes Boundedness, but not vice versa. It is conceptually possible that we could experience bodily events within a space that defines the limits of the self and yet experience those events in isolation from everything else going on in that space. But that is not the normal phenomenology of the body. Bodily events are typically experienced relative to the background of the body as whole. In experiencing a pain in my knee, for example, I experience the pain as being in my leg, which in turn is disposed in a certain way relative to my torso. My torso itself is experienced as being disposed in a certain way relative to gravity and supporting surfaces. In this sense, therefore, bodily events are experienced within a holistic framework that, although sometimes recessive, is normally an ineliminable part of the content of experience. To motivate that thought, think how strange it would be to feel a sensation in your foot without having an idea of the angle of your foot relative to your lower leg, or of whether your leg is bent or straight at the knee.

The phenomena of both Boundedness and Connectedness can be readily identified in the bodily illusion experiments. So, for example, Boundedness predicts that subjects experience the rubber hand as incorporated into their own bodies—as opposed, for example, to being spatially discontinuous with their bodies. This is exactly how the phenomenology of the RHI is described by the subjects reviewed by Longo et al. (2008). Moreover, as Longo et al. observe, the rubber hand is typically experienced as displacing the subject's real hand. It is very rare for subjects in RHI experiments to report experiencing the rubber hand as a third, supernumerary hand (although see Ehrsson 2009 for a version of the RHI in which healthy

9. For further discussion of tools and bodily awareness, see de Vignemont and Farne 2010.

subjects seem to report experiencing two right hands). Interestingly, in the so-called invisible hand illusion, where referred sensations are elicited by stroking empty space, subjects report feeling the referred sensations in a hand that they cannot see, rather than outside the body (Gutersdam, Gentile, and Ehrsson 2013).

As this indicates, bodily awareness can only be manipulated within certain, structural limits. One limiting factor is what is sometimes called the long-term body-image (O'Shaughnessy 1980, 1995)—an implicit understanding of the large-scale, structural properties of the body (such as the property of having no more than two hands!). A number of studies have shown that the RHI is constrained by factors of anatomical plausibility. The illusion is extinguished, for example, when the rubber hand is of a different laterality from the subject's own hand (Tsakiris and Haggard 2005). This is another Boundedness effect.

Manipulations of the RHI paradigm also reveal Connectedness effects. Most significantly, postural mismatches can extinguish the illusion. The difference between a postural mismatch and an anatomical mismatch is important. In both cases the manipulation extinguishes the illusion by, in effect, revealing it to be impossible for the subject to be the owner of the rubber hand. This comes about because the rubber hand is placed in a position that conflicts with subjects' knowledge of their own bodies and how they are disposed. As we have seen the knowledge engaged in Boundedness effects is general knowledge of the structure of the body. In cases of postural mismatch, in contrast, the rubber hand is (as it were) anatomically viable. But it just couldn't be part of the subject's body because the disposition of the rubber hand is inconsistent with the subject's knowledge of how his actual hand and arm are disposed. Tsakiris and Haggard (2005), for example, established that the illusion disappears if the rubber hand is oriented at a 90° angle to the subject's actual hand. The angle of the rubber hand rules out its being attached to the subject's wrist and arm. This is a Connectedness effect, because if the position of the hand were not coded relative to the position of the wrist and so on there would be no inconsistency.

There are clear connections between, on the one hand, Boundedness and Connectedness and, on the other, the experienced location of sensation (hypothesis 1) and the experience of agency (hypothesis 2). One reason the experienced location of sensations seems so important for ownership is that (per Boundedness) sensations are typically experienced within the limits of the bodily self. Likewise for the experience of agency, which is standardly enabled by the experience of a connected and bounded body.[10] Boundedness and Connectedness are more general aspects of the phenomenology of bodily awareness, however. Letting them carry the explanatory weight allows us to think of judgments of ownership as multifactorial. The experience of agency and the experienced location of sensations both play a role in grounding judgments of agency. In the next section, we will see that both Boundedness and Connectedness are themselves ultimately grounded in certain very basic features of the spatiality of bodily experience.

IV

How is the space of the body represented? The general topic of somatic spatial representation has seen rapidly increasing attention from psychologists and neuroscientists over the last three decades. Researchers have pursued a number of different, but overlapping, questions highly germane to the discussion in earlier sections of bodily illusions and the phenomenology of bodily awareness, but the two lines of research do not always map cleanly and directly on to each other. The principal focus of research into bodily illusions is on how we experience our bodies as our own. The principal focus of research into the neuroscience of spatial representation has been on how the brain encodes information about the body and about the location of objects in the immediate distal environment to allow reaching and other motor behaviors. Of course, it is hard to imagine that the way we experience our bodies is not at least partially determined by how the brain encodes spatial information, but the fact remains that these are two different questions. This section disentangles some of these issues.

One much discussed issue is how we represent peripersonal space. Peripersonal space is standardly defined as the area of space around the body that is within reach—as opposed to extrapersonal space, which is out of reach. Whereas information about extrapersonal space comes primarily through vision, with contributions from hearing and smell, awareness of

10. I am focusing here on what might be termed direct agency. There are also cases where subjects have an indirect experience of agency (as might be experienced by drone pilots and other remote-tool-users) that do not seem to involve an experience of a connected and bounded body.

peripersonal space is much more multimodal. An elegant illustration of the difference between peripersonal and extrapersonal space comes from experiments on patients with unilateral spatial neglect. Neglect patients typically make significant errors when asked to bisect lines—since they neglect (typically) the left side of space, they will place the midpoint of the line far to the right of the true midpoint. Since these bisection tasks involve drawing a line they take place within peripersonal space. However, Halligan and Driver (1991) showed that a neglect patient with right hemisphere damage after a stroke, despite having the standard deficit when asked to *draw* a bisecting line, showed no deficit when asked to use a laser pointer to bisect a line in extrapersonal space.

There is considerable consensus that the representation of peripersonal space engages multiple frames of reference, depending on the relevant modality (Spence and Holmes 2004; Battaglia-Meyer et al. 2003). Information from vision is standardly represented in retinotopic coordinates (coordinates centered on the retina), while auditory and olfactory information is coded in head-centered coordinates (Cohen and Anderson 2002). Moreover, neuron recordings in macaque monkeys have identified arm-centered receptive fields in the premotor cortex (Graziano, Yap, and Gross 1994). These receptive fields move when the arm moves, rather than when the eyes move. So, the representation of peripersonal space is multilevel and varies according to modality and context.

Moreover, Noel et al. (2015) have shown that in the full-body illusion peripersonal space shifts to being centered at the location of the virtual body. However, one cannot draw direct conclusions about how the spatiality of the body is experienced from representations of peripersonal space. It is true that if a receptive field moves with the location of the arm, then the nervous system must have some way of keeping track of where the arm is. But it is perfectly possible, given the design of the studies, that the location of the arm is tracked visually, relative to a retinotopic reference frame. This would tell us nothing about how the body is experienced "from the inside" through bodily sensations, proprioception, and kinesthesis. And even if the location of the arm were tracked "from the inside," the question is still wide open as to the frame of reference relative to which this tracking takes place.

The question of how somatosensory spatial information is integrated with visual information has been prominent in studies of reaching.

Successful reaching depends on calibrating the represented location of the target with the represented starting point of the hand, to allow both the initial aiming and online monitoring and correction of the movement. There is evidence from psychophysics that successful reaching depends on remapping the target location from a retinotopic coordinate system into body-centered and/or hand-centered frames of reference (Soechting and Flanders 1989a, 1989b). Such remapping would plausibly make the calibration easier. But, as with the representation of peripersonal space, it does not really help with the question we are interested in. Exactly the same question arises. To say that a target location is relative to a hand-centered frame of reference just means that target location is coded on a coordinate system whose origin is some designated point in the hand. But that doesn't tell us how the nervous system encodes the location of the center of the coordinate system—let alone how the location of the hand is experienced "from the inside" relative to the rest of the body.

What is needed to complement ongoing research into how peripersonal space and reaching movements are neutrally encoded is a model of how normal subjects experience the space of the body. Such a model obviously needs to be consistent with the existing experimental literature, but also needs to go further in two key respects. First, it needs to focus on the phenomenological aspect of spatial awareness of the body. That is, it needs to focus on how subjects are conscious of bodily space—on what it is to experience a bodily sensation at a particular bodily location, for example, or how the layout of the body is presented in somatosensory experience. Second, it needs to explain why our experience of our own bodies has the properties of Boundedness and Connectedness.

V

The first issue that arises in modeling the spatial content of bodily awareness is determining a frame of reference and corresponding coordinate system. This section introduces two possible approaches.

The first approach is in essence a direct continuation of the modeling strategies discussed in the previous section in the context of peripersonal space and reaching. We looked at a number of different reference frames—retinotopic, head-centered, or centered on specific body parts such as the hand. These are all standard Cartesian frames of reference with three axes.

What distinguishes them is the point each takes as its origin. A natural extension of this approach would be to conceptualize the space of the body in a Cartesian frame with three axes, corresponding to the frontal, saggital, and transverse planes. A plausible candidate for the origin of the coordinate system would be the body's center of mass.

So, on this modeling strategy, to experience a bodily event at a particular bodily location is to experience it at a certain point (x, y, z) in a space whose origin is the body's center of mass, where that point is given in terms of its distance from the origin on each of the three axes. A variant (probably more plausible) would be to use a spherical coordinate system, generalizing two-dimensional polar coordinates, rather than Cartesian coordinates, so that the sensation is given as located at a point (r, θ, φ) where r is the radial distance from body's center of mass; θ is the polar angle (measured from a fixed zenith in the vertical direction opposite the pull of gravity); and φ the azimuth angle (measured from a fixed direction on a plane orthogonal to the zenith, and so at right angles to the pull of gravity). Cartesian and spherical coordinate systems are interconvertible, of course.

One advantage of this approach is that it allows the space of the body to be mapped straightforwardly onto peripersonal space. A target location perceived in hand-centered coordinates in peripersonal space can equally be described in Cartesian or spherical coordinates relative to an origin in the body's center of mass. And so, for example, it is computationally easy to plot the displacement required to move the hand from its current location to the target location, as well as to monitor the movement and adjust while it is in progress.

On the other hand, though, the approach has difficulty doing justice to how we actually experience our bodies. For one thing, as I have pointed out in previous work, our experience of our own bodies does not typically present a particular point as a privileged origin so that we experience particular bodily locations as being nearer than or further away from that origin (Bermúdez 1998, 2005, 2011). In fact, it is not clear that the concepts *nearer than* or *farther away from* have any applicability to the space of bodily experience. These comparative concepts have an implicit self-reference built into them, unless some other object is explicitly given as a reference point. To say that one thing is nearer than another is typically to say that it is nearer to *me*. Within a visual perspective this makes perfectly good sense, since the structure of the visual field implicitly defines a point that can serve as me for the purposes of comparison. But bodily awareness is not like this. The body's center of mass is important, of course, for balance, and so more generally for movement, but not in a way that makes it a candidate for calibrating distance and direction. And there is no other point in the body that can count as me relative to the rest of the body in the same way that the origin of the visual field counts as me relative to objects in the distal environment. So comparisons of distance and direction really only make sense in special circumstances (talking to the doctor, for example, where a reference point is typically assumed).

A second problem with the standard approach comes with accommodating Boundedness and Connectedness. According to Boundedness, bodily events are experienced within the experienced body (a circumscribed body-shaped volume whose boundaries define the limits of the self). So, from the perspective of conscious bodily experience, there is a marked distinction between bodily space and peripersonal space. Within the total volume of space defined by the limits of peripersonal space, those points that fall within the perceived space of the body are experientially privileged. They are, as Locke would put it, part of the conscious self. Yet this distinction is not at all captured within the model under consideration. Within the context of a frame of reference centered on the body's center of mass, the space defined is completely homogeneous. There is no distinction between a point that falls within the perceived space of the body and one that does not—between a point that falls within my left forearm, for example, and a point that is three inches to the right in extra personal space. The standard approach would admittedly allow bodily boundaries to be defined, but this would be (as it were) a purely geometrical way of marking the difference between bodily space and peripersonal space. It would not in any sense capture how the space of the body is experientially privileged.

The standard approach fares no better with Connectedness. According to Connectedness, the spatial location of a bodily event is experienced relative to the disposition of the body as a whole. It follows that experienced locations within bodily space are not experienced in isolation. So, when we experience our foot flexed at a certain angle we experience that flexing of the ankle relative to the disposition of the foot, the knee, and the hip, for example. That is to say, bodily experience is both relational and holistic. In contrast, spatial locations on the standard approach are purely particularist. A bodily location is given as a triple of numbers, either (x, y, z) or (r, θ, φ).

The coding of the location carries no information about what is going on elsewhere in the body.

For these reasons I have proposed a different model for thinking about how the space of the body is represented in conscious bodily experience. A starting point for the model is a distinction between two ways of thinking about bodily location. We can think about a given bodily location in a way that abstracts from the disposition at a time of the body as a whole. So, for example, we might think about an itch being located at the front of the shin. This is a location that the itch has as long as it endures, irrespective of whether or not the shin moves. Alternatively, one might think of the itch in a way that takes into account what the rest of the body is doing. In previous work I have termed these A-location and B-location, respectively (Bermúdez 1998, 2005, 2011).

A-location (1)

The location of a bodily event in a specific body-part relative to an abstract map of the body, without taking into account the current position of the body.

B-location (1)

The location of a bodily event in a specific body-part relative to the current position of relevant body-parts.

So, for example, if I have a pain in the middle finger of my left hand and then contract my bicep to raise my left hand by six inches, then the A-location of my pain remains unchanged, while the B-location changes. The A-location remains unchanged because the pain is still in the middle finger of my left hand. The B-location is different, however, because my left hand is now at a different angle relative to my elbow. Both A-location and B-location are body relative. If I move six feet to the left and then stand as I am standing here, the pain in the middle finger of my left hand will still have the same A-location and B-location.

The idea, therefore, is that we experience a given bodily event at a specific A-location and B-location. A-location and B-location are not independent of each other—two different aspects of a single type of experience rather than two different ways of experiencing bodily events. The A-location dimension of bodily experience does justice to Boundedness, while the B-location dimension speaks more to Connectedness. If we typically experience a bodily event at a specific A-location then it follows automatically that we experience it within the experienced body, because A-locations can only fall within the perceived limits of the body. By the same token, if we typically experience a bodily event at a specific B-location, then we gain immediate insight into the relation between that bodily event and the overall disposition of the body.[11]

Of course, the explanatory value of this model depends on giving a substantive account of A-location and B-location. In particular, we need an account of how the body is represented in somatosensory experience that will explain how and why we experience bodily events at specific A-locations and A-locations. I offer such an account in the next and final section.

VI

Extending Bermúdez 1998 and subsequent papers (2005, 2011), the previous section offered a general account of how the space of the body is represented in experience. This section offers a more detailed account that develops insights from two approaches to modeling the body—in biomechanics and robotics, on the one hand, and in Marr and Nishihara's model of object recognition, on the other.

The model proposed in *The Paradox of Self-Consciousness* (Bermúdez 1998) starts from how the body is articulated as a relatively immoveable torso connected by joints to moveable body parts. These joints range in size and scope from the knee and the neck, at one extreme, to the joints in fingers and toes, at the other. Joints afford the possibility of moving the body parts that they connect. There are around 230 joints in the human body, differing in the types of movement that they allow and in the degrees of freedom that they offer. The hip, for example, operates on all three planes and allows six different types of movement (abduction, adduction, extension, flexion, horizontal abduction, and horizontal adduction). The knee, like many of the finger joints, allows only flexion and extension in a single plane.

Joints provide the fixed points relative to which particular A-locations and B-locations can be specified.

---

11. B-location does not immediately yield Connectedness in its entirety, however, because of the restriction to *relevant* body-parts. Thanks to Adrian Alsmith for pressing me here.

A-location (2)

A particular bodily A-location is experienced in a given body part and speci-fied relative to the joint immediately controlling the movement of that body part.

So, for example, an itch in the palm of my hand is experienced in the palm of my hand and its location is specified relative to the wrist, since the wrist immediately controls the movement of the palm of my hand (as opposed to the elbow and shoulder, whose control is mediate rather than immediate).

B-location (2)

A particular B-location is a given A-location oriented in a certain way rela-tive to the rest of the body. It is specified recursively relative to the joints that lie between it and the immoveable torso.

The B-location of the itch in the palm of my hand is its A-location, supple-mented by specifying the angles of the wrist relative to the forearm, the elbow relative to the upper arm, and the shoulder relative to the torso.[12]

To flesh this general model out further, we can draw on two different but complementary approaches to modeling the body. The first comes from biomechanics and robotics, where the body is typically modeled as a system of rigid links connected by mechanical joints. Kinesiologists and roboticists have developed sophisticated tools for representing both bodily position at a time and movement over time in terms of the angles of the relevant joints (see, e.g., a standard biomechanics textbook such as Hall 2014).

The second derives from Marr and Nishihara's model of object rec-ognition in terms of matching three-dimensional object representations derived from vision with a stored catalog of three-dimensional represen-tations (Marr and Nishihara 1978). Objects are represented schematically

12. In the case of bodily events taking place in the torso, A-location and B-location will coincide. Localization in the torso has not been as well studied as in bodily extremities, such as the fingers and hands. But see van Erp 2008 for a study indicat-ing that stimulus locations on the torso may be coded in polar coordinates centered on the body's center of gravity. Van Erp suggests that, to compensate for constant distortion of the skin surface as the torso flexes and moves, the angular component of the polar coordinate is more salient than the distance component. As he puts it, as long as we move our hand in the correct direction we will hit the stinging mos-quito sooner or later!

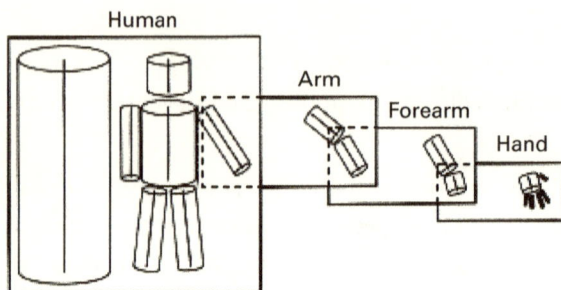

Figure 8.2
Marr and Nishihara's model of the human body as a hierarchy of generalized cones.
From Marr and Nishihara 1978.

as complexes of generalized cones (surfaces generated by moving a cross-section along an axis, maintaining its shape but possibly varying its size). The human body is represented as a hierarchy of generalized cones, as depicted in figure 8.2.

The suggestion I will develop is that *within bodily experience* the human body is represented in terms of generalized cones. This approach has two very significant advantages.

First, it allows us to fill in a gap in the general models of the body in robotics and biomechanics. Understandably, given what they are trying to achieve, kinesiologists and roboticists typically abstract away from the details of what goes on inside the limbs. From the perspective of studying human movement or programming artificial movement, it makes perfectly good sense to treat limbs as rigid links with no intrinsic properties. When studying the experienced space of the body, however, we obviously need tools for describing the location of bodily events that take place inside limbs. Modeling limbs as generalized cones allows us to do this in a way that is faithful to the anatomy of the body.

Second, if we think of limbs as generalized cones then we can use a cylindrical coordinate system, somewhat similar to the spherical coordinate system discussed earlier. Identifying a cylindrical coordinate system involves identifying an origin at the intersection of the longitudinal axis (along the cylinder's axis of symmetry) and a reference plane orthogonal to the longitudinal axis, with a specified reference direction. The location of a point x in the cylinder is given by the triple (ρ, φ, z) where (ρ, φ) are in effect the polar coordinates of x on the plane that passes through x and is parallel to the reference plane and z is the distance from the origin to x

along the longitudinal axis. As mentioned earlier, this is just one example of a number of interconvertible coordinate systems.

So, my proposal is that the space of the body is experienced relative to a model of body as a hierarchy of generalized cones linked by mechanical joints. Specifically, the hypotheses that I am making for A-location and B-location are as follows. First,

A-location (3)

The A-location of a bodily event in a given limb is fixed in a cylindrical coordinate system whose origin is at the midpoint (center of mass) of the joint immediately controlling the position of that limb.

The subject's awareness of the large-scale structure of her body (e.g., what O'Shaughnessy 1980 termed the *long-term body image*) in effect fixes the surface and volume of the cylinder, thus defining the potential bodily space within which bodily events can be experienced. In most normal cases, of course, there will be a close map between the physical boundaries of the body and the cylinder thus defined. But it is perfectly conceivable that a cylinder should be defined with its origin at the tip of an amputation. This seems to be what is happening when amputees feel sensations in prosthetic limbs, as discussed earlier in the context of extended physiological proprioception.

Second,

B-location (3)

The B-location of a bodily event in a given limb is fixed by supplementing its A-location with a chain of relative joint angles that collectively specify the location of the limb relative to the immoveable torso.

I am using the term "joint angle" as shorthand for whatever information is required to specify the disposition of a joint. It is likely, of course, to involve more than one coordinate, but no joint requires more than six (corresponding to the maximum number of degrees of freedom—three rotational and three translational). The degree of complexity will increase, however, when chains of joint angles are considered.

VII

To recap, experiments on bodily illusions raise important questions about what it is to experience one's body as one's own. Philosophers and cognitive scientists often refer to a sense of ownership that extends both to individual body parts and to the body as a whole. I do not find that this approach has much explanatory power, and thus proposed investigating the complex phenomenon of ownership by looking at the grounds for judgments of ownership. After discounting the idea that there is a specific feeling of ownership, three hypotheses emerged.

(1) Judgments of ownership are based on the experienced location of sensation.
(2) Judgments of ownership are based on the experience of agency.
(3) Judgments of ownership are based on the experienced spatiality of the body.

Hypotheses (1) and (2) give an important part of the overall picture, but I argued that neither is fully explanatory on its own. Hypothesis (3) identifies a phenomenon that is more fundamental, since both experiencing agency and experiencing sensations take place relative to experiencing the distinctive space of the body.

In developing hypothesis (3), I began with two large-scale features of the phenomenology of bodily awareness. According to Boundedness, bodily events are experienced within a circumscribed body-shaped volume whose boundaries define the limits of the self, while according to Connectedness, the spatial location of a bodily event is experienced relative to the disposition of the body as a whole. Developing an account of the spatiality of bodily experience that does justice to Boundedness and Connectedness took us to the idea that bodily events are experiences in terms of A-location and B-location, which I then glossed through combining biomechanical models of the body as rigid links connected by mechanical joints with the picture of the body loosely derived from Marr and Nishihara's model of object recognition. The space of the body is experienced, I suggest, relative to a model of the body as a hierarchy of generalized cones linked by mechanical joints.

Circling back, therefore, to the starting point of the essay, my main proposal is that the judgments of ownership that we make about our bodies and body parts are ultimately grounded in the fact that we experience the space of the body in this distinctive way that differs fundamentally from how we experience extrabodily events, even those in peripersonal space. With this proposal in view, let me end by identifying some important open questions for future work.

• How should the account of spatial content proposed in terms of A-location and B-location be developed into a full account of the content of bodily experiences?

• How should we spell out in detail the inferential or quasi-inferential relations in which bodily experiences stand to judgments of agency?

• How do those inferential or quasi-inferential relations compare to the relations between "ordinary" perceptual experiences and perceptual judgments?

• How should the account be extended to cases of *disownership*, as occur for example in somatopraphrenia and other disorders?

• Can a parallel explanatory strategy to that proposed here for the "sense of ownership" be extended to the putative "sense of agency"?

• If so, what role does the distinctive spatiality of bodily experience play in underwriting judgments of agency?

Acknowledgments

I am very grateful to Frédérique de Vignemont and Adrian Alsmith and to two anonymous referees for probing and helpful comments; to Patrick Haggard and Tony Cheng for their commentary at the December 2015 Copenhagen workshop; and to the other participants at the Copenhagen workshop.

References

Aglioti, S., N. Smania, M. Manfredi, and G. Berlucchi. 1996. Disownership of left hand and objects related to it in a patient with right brain damage. *NeuroReport* 8 (1): 293–296.

Alsmith, A. 2015. Mental activity and the sense of ownership. *Review of Philosophy and Psychology* 6 (4): 881–896.

Armel, K. C., and V. S. Ramachandran. 2003. Projecting sensations to external objects: Evidence from skin conductance response. *Proceedings of the Royal Society of London, Series B: Biological Sciences* 270 (1523): 1499–1506.

Battaglia-Mayer, A., R. Caminiti, F. Lacquaniti, and M. Zago. 2003. Multiple levels of representation of reaching in the parieto-frontal network. *Cerebral Cortex* 13 (10): 1009–1022.

Bermúdez, J. L. 1998. *The Paradox of Self-Consciousness*. Cambridge, MA: MIT Press.

Bermúdez, J. L. 2005. The phenomenology of bodily awareness. In *Phenomenology and Philosophy of Mind*, ed. D. W. Smith and A. L. Thomasson, 295–316. New York: Oxford University Press.

Bermúdez, J. L. 2011. Bodily awareness and self-consciousness. In *Oxford Handbook of the Self*, ed. S. Gallagher, 157–179. Oxford: Oxford University Press.

Bermúdez, J. L. 2015. Bodily ownership, bodily awareness and knowledge without observation. *Analysis* 75 (1): 37–45. doi:10.1093/analys/anu119.

Bermúdez, J. L., A. J. Marcel, and N. Eilan, eds. 1995. *The Body and the Self*. Cambridge, MA: MIT Press.

Bottini, G., E. Bisiach, R. Sterzi, and G. Vallar. 2002. Feeling touches in someone else's hand. *NeuroReport* 13 (2): 249–252.

Botvinick, M., and J. Cohen. 1998. Rubber hands "feel" touch that eyes see. *Nature* 391:756.

Cassam, Q. 1995. Introspection and bodily self-ascription. In *The Body and the Self*, ed. J. L. Bermúdez, A. J. Marcel, and N. M. Eilan, 311–336. Cambridge, MA: MIT Press.

Cassam, Q. 1997. *Self and World*. Oxford: Oxford University Press.

Cohen, Y. E., and R. A. Andersen. 2002. A common reference frame for movement plans in the posterior parietal cortex. *Nature Reviews Neuroscience* 3:553–562.

Corbetta, M., and G. Shulman. 2011. Spatial neglect and attention networks. *Annual Review of Neuroscience* 34:569–599.

Costantini, M., and P. Haggard. 2007. The rubber hand illusion: Sensitivity and reference frame for body ownership. *Consciousness and Cognition* 16 (2): 229–240.

Cronholm, B. 1951. Phantom limbs in amputees: A study of changes in the integration of centripetal impulses with special reference to referred sensations. *Acta Psychiatrica et Neurologica Scandinavica* 72 (Suppl.): 1–310.

de Vignemont, F. 2007. Habeas corpus: The sense of ownership of one's own body. *Mind & Language* 22:427–449.

de Vignemont, F. 2013. The mark of bodily ownership. *Analysis* 73:643–651.

de Vignemont, F. 2014. A multimodal conception of bodily awareness. *Mind* 123 (492): 989–1020.

de Vignemont, F. In press. *Mind the Body*. Oxford: Oxford University Press.

de Vignemont, F., and A. Farnè. 2010. Widening the body to rubber hands and tools: What's the difference? (Incorporer des objets et des membres factices: Quelle différence?) *Revue de Neuropsychologie* 2 (3): 203–211.

Doubler, J. A., and D. S. Childress. 1984. An analysis of extended physiological proprioception as a prosthesis-control technique. *Journal of Rehabilitation Research and Development* 21 (1): 5–18.

Ehrsson, H. H. 2009. How many arms make a pair? Perceptual illusion of having an additional limb. *Perception* 38 (2): 310–312. doi:10.1068/p6304.

Ferri, F., A. M. Chiarelli, A. Merla, V. Gallese, and M. Costantini. 2013. The body beyond the body: Expectation of a sensory event is enough to induce ownership over a fake hand. *Proceedings of the Royal Society of London, Series B: Biological Sciences* 280 (1765): 20131140.

Gallagher, S. 2000. Philosophical conceptions of the self: Implications for cognitive science. *Trends in Cognitive Sciences* 4 (1): 14–21.

Gallagher, S. 2005. *How the Body Shapes the Mind*. New York: Oxford University Press.

Gentile, G., M. Björnsdotter, V. I. Petkova, Z. Abdulkarim, and H. H. Ehrsson. 2015. Patterns of neural activity in the human ventral premotor cortex reflect a whole-body multisensory percept. *NeuroImage* 109:328–340.

Graziano, M. S. A., G. S. Yap, and C. G. Gross. 1994. Coding of visual space by premotor neurons. *Science* 266 (5187): 1054–1057.

Gutersdam, A., G. Gentile, and H. H. Ehrsson. 2013. The invisible hand illusion: Multisensory integration leads to the embodiment of a discrete volume of empty space. *Journal of Cognitive Neuroscience* 25 (7): 1078–1099.

Hall, S. 2014. *Basic Biomechanics*. 7th ed. New York: McGraw Hill.

Halligan, P. W., and J. C. Marshall. 1991. Left neglect for near but not far space in man. *Nature* 350 (6318): 498–500.

Hamilton, A. 2013. *The Self in Question: Memory, the Body, and Self-Consciousness*. Basingstoke: Palgrave Macmillan.

Holmes, N. P., and C. Spence. 2004. The body schema and the multisensory representation(s) of peripersonal space. *Cognitive Processing* 5 (2): 94–105.

Ionta, S., R. Martuzzi, R. Salomon, and O. Blanke. 2014. The brain network reflecting bodily self-consciousness: A functional connectivity study. *Social Cognitive and Affective Neuroscience* 9 (12): 1904–1913.

Kalckert, A., and H. H. Ehrsson. 2012. Moving a rubber hand that feels like your own: A dissociation of ownership and agency. *Frontiers in Human Neuroscience* 6: 40.

Kilteni, K., A. Maselli, K. P. Kording, and M. Slater. 2015. Over my fake body: Body ownership illusions for studying the multisensory basis of own-body perception. *Frontiers in Human Neuroscience* 9:141.

Lenggenhager, B., T. Tadi, T. Metzinger, and O. Blanke. 2007. Video ergo sum: Manipulating bodily self-consciousness. *Science* 317 (5841): 1096–1099.

Locke, J. (1698) 1975. *An Essay Concerning Human Understanding*. Ed. P. H. Nidditch. Oxford: Clarendon Press.

Longo, M., F. Schüür, M. P. M. Kammers, M. Tsakiris, and P. Haggard. 2008. What is embodiment? A psychometric approach. *Cognition* 107 (3): 978–998.

Marr, D., and H. K. Nishihara. 1978. Representation and recognition of the spatial organization of three-dimensional shapes. *Proceedings of the Royal Society of London* 200 (1140): 269–294.

Martin, M. 1995. Bodily awareness: A sense of ownership. In *The Body and the Self*, ed. J. L. Bermúdez, A. J. Marcel, and N. Eilan, 267–289. Cambridge, MA: MIT Press.

Merleau-Ponty, M. 1968. *The Phenomenology of Perception*. London: Routledge.

Moseley, G. L., N. Olthof, A. Venema, S. Don, M. Wijers, A. Gallace, and C. Spence. 2008. Psychologically induced cooling of a specific body part caused by the illusory ownership of an artificial counterpart. *Proceedings of the National Academy of Sciences of the United States of America* 105 (35): 13169–13173.

Murray, C. D. 2004. An interpretative phenomenological analysis of the embodiment of artificial limbs. *Disability & Rehabilitation* 26 (16): 963–973.

Noel, J.-P., C. Pfeiffer, O. Blanke, and A. Serino. 2015. Peripersonal space as the space of the bodily self. *Cognition* 144:49–57.

O'Shaughnessy, B. 1980. *The Will: A Dual Aspect Theory*. Cambridge: Cambridge University Press.

O'Shaughnessy, B. 1995. Proprioception and the body image. In *The Body and the Self*, ed. J. L. Bermúdez, A. J. Marcel, and N. Eilan, 175–203. Cambridge, MA: MIT Press.

Petkova, V. I., and H. H. Ehrsson. 2008. If I were you: Perceptual illusion of body swapping. *PLoS One* 3 (12): e3832.

Petkova, V. I., M. Björnsdotter, B. Gentile, T. Jonsson, T.-Q. Li, and H. H. Ehrsson. 2011. From part- to whole-body ownership in the multisensory brain. *Current Biology* 21 (13): 1118–1122. doi:10.1016/j.cub.2011.05.022.

Scepkowski, L. A., and A. Cronin-Golomb. 2003. The alien hand: Cases, categorizations, and anatomical correlates. *Behavioral and Cognitive Neuroscience Reviews* 2 (4): 261–277.

Serino, A., A. Alsmith, M. Costantini, A. Mandrigin, A. Tajadura-Jimenez, and C. Lopez. 2013. Bodily ownership and self-location: Components of bodily self-consciousness. *Consciousness and Cognition* 22 (4): 1239–1252.

Simpson, D. C. 1974. The choice of control system for the multimovement prosthesis: Extended physiological proprioception (EPP). In *The Control of Upper-Extremity Prostheses and Orthoses*, ed. P. Herberts, R. Kadefors, R. Magnusson, and I. Petyersen, 146–150. Springfield, IL: Charles C. Thomas.

Soechting, J. F., and M. Flanders. 1989a. Sensorimotor representations for pointing to targets in three-dimensional space. *Journal of Neurophysiology* 62 (2): 582–594.

Soechting, J. F., and M. Flanders. 1989b. Errors in pointing are due to approximations in sensorimotor transformations. *Journal of Neurophysiology* 62:595–608.

Tsakiris, M. 2010. My body in the brain: A neurocognitive model of body-ownership. *Neuropsychologia* 48 (3): 703–712.

Tsakiris, M., and P. Haggard. 2005. The rubber hand illusion revisited: Visuotactile integration and self-attribution. *Journal of Experimental Psychology* 31 (1): 80–91.

Tsakiris, M., G. Prabhu, and P. Haggard. 2006. Having a body versus moving your body: How agency structures body-ownership. *Consciousness and Cognition* 15 (2): 423–432.

Vallar, G., and R. Ronchi. 2009. Somatoparaphrenia: A bodily delusion. A review of the neuropsychological literature. *Experimental Brain Research* 192 (3): 533–551.

van Erp, J. B. F. 2008. Absolute localization of vibrotactile stimuli on the torso. *Perception & Psychophysics* 70 (6): 1016–1023.

9   Bodily Ownership, Psychological Ownership, and Psychopathology

Overview

Debates about bodily ownership and psychological ownership have typically proceeded independently of each other. This essay explores the relation between them, with particular reference to how each is illuminated by psychopathology. In sections 1 and 2, I propose a general framework for studying ownership that is applicable both to bodily ownership (*φ-ownership*) and psychological ownership (*ψ-ownership*). The framework proposes studying ownership by starting with explicit judgments of ownership and then exploring the bases for those judgments. Section 3 discusses John Campbell's account of ψ-ownership in light of that general framework, emphasizing in particular his fractionation (inspired by schizophrenic delusions) of ψ-ownership into two dissociable components. Section 4 briefly presents an account of φ-ownership that I have developed in more detail elsewhere. Section 5 explores the suggestion, originating with Alexandre Billon, that there needs to be an integrated account of φ-ownership and ψ-ownership because depersonalization disorders typically involve breakdowns of both φ-ownership and ψ-ownership. The argument from depersonalization is not compelling, but section 6 proposes a different way of reaching the same conclusion. Section 7 shows how reflecting on agency and practical reasoning offers a common thread between the models of φ-ownership and ψ-ownership discussed earlier in the essay.

1   Tools for Studying Ownership

Recent debates about ownership have been fueled by insights from a range of empirical sources. For discussions of bodily ownership the principal drivers have been the various illusions manipulating where subjects feel sensations and, consequently, their judgments about the extent of their body and what is (or is not) a part of them. In the rubber hand illusion, for example, subjects see a rubber hand being stroked while their own hand (which is out of sight) is synchronously stroked (Botvinick and Cohen 1998). It is a robust result that subjects report feeling sensations of touch in the rubber hand and feeling that the rubber hand is their own hand. In the full body illusion (Lenggenhager et al. 2007) subjects can be brought to identify with a full-body avatar that they see being stroked in front of them, while in the body-swap illusion subjects report a sense of ownership for a mannequin being stroked in the location where they expect their own bodies to be. These experimental paradigms have been hugely influential and are a rich source of insights and data. They offer tools for operationalizing aspects of subjective experience that can then be studied experimentally.

Earlier discussions of bodily ownership were driven much more by the psychopathology of bodily awareness (Bermúdez, Marcel, and Eilan 1995), and psychopathology remains a rich and complementary source for thinking about bodily ownership. Neuropsychologists have identified and studied a number of disorders in which bodily awareness in general, and ownership in particular, is distorted. Examples include *unilaterial spatial neglect* (where neurologically damaged patients neglect one side of their bodies, and indeed one side of peripersonal and external space, typically the opposite side to the lesion), *somatoparaphrenia* (where patients report disownership of body parts, typically on the contralesional side also), and *alien hand syndrome* (in which brain-damaged subjects report that someone else is moving their hands).

When we shift focus from bodily ownership to ownership of one's thoughts, emotions, and feelings, there is no equivalent to the rubber hand illusion and other illusions of bodily ownership. There are no experimental techniques for manipulating normal subjects' sense that the thoughts they are consciously thinking are their own. So here psychopathology is really the only source of data. Empirically minded philosophers have paid particular attention to delusions of thought insertion in *schizophrenia* (see, e.g., Graham and Stephens 1995; Campbell 1999a; Pacherie, Green, and Bayne 2006). *Cotard's syndrome* (a rare disease in which patients form the delusional belief that they do not exist, and/or are already dead) has also been studied in this context (Gerrans 2000; Billon 2016), as has the complex of symptoms known as *depersonalization*, in which patients feel varying degrees of detachment and disconnection from their own thoughts, emotions, and bodily states (Billon 2015).

Ownership illusions and psychopathology each have their advantages and disadvantages for the researcher. As already noted, while they do offer the great advantage of being experimentally tractable, ownership illusions exist only for bodily ownership. Moreover, they suffer from the disadvantage that subjects are typically aware of the illusion even while undergoing it. This is also a characteristic of many visual illusions, but it is potentially more concerning in this context. One reason for being interested in ownership is the light it can shed on high-level capacities such as self-consciousness. What we are exploring is the role that ownership plays in underwriting awareness of oneself as spatial entity and as a locus of mental and physical agency. This is a matter, broadly speaking, of the functional role of ownership. So an important part of what one is trying to do by looking at disorders of ownership is to make backward inferences from the functional role of disordered ownership to the functional role of normal ownership. But it is not obvious how to evaluate the functional role of an illusion that is known to be an illusion—not too many people really believe that the rubber hand is their own, for example, and so the illusion of ownership has a limited functional role. Delusions are not like illusions in this respect. Neuropsychological patients suffering from delusions conspicuously grapple with the challenge of integrating their delusional experience into an overarching cognitive and affective perspective on the world—and, according to one line of thought, how they do this is in many respects continuous with how they integrate nondelusional experience (Davies et al. 2001; Bermúdez 2001).

At the same time, though, trying to work backward from psychopathology to normal functioning brings its own problems. Many of the disorders that seem most illuminating from a theoretical point of view are actually very rare. Cotard's syndrome is a case in point. There are obvious methodological difficulties in classifying disorders and finding commonalities across patients who often have significant collateral impairments, in addition to the challenges of obtaining clear dissociation data and then making inferences to mental structure (as discussed, e.g., in Shallice 1988). And, in the last analysis, much of what is known about psychopathological disorders comes from the reports of severely impaired patients that are often very hard to understand.

For all these reasons, then, the most promising approach to the complex phenomenon of ownership is likely to be multifactorial and integrative. This essay is intended as a step in that direction.

2   A Framework for Thinking about Ownership

The terminology of ownership is widely used but nonetheless rather unclear. This section sets out a basic framework for characterizing the phenomenon of ownership and a general approach to explaining it.

As observed above, discussions of ownership in the empirical and philosophical literatures have pursued two parallel and often unrelated tracks. The first track has focused on bodily ownership, aiming to explicate what it is to take one's body as one's own, including ownership both of the body as a whole and of individual body parts. The second track has focused on the ownership of conscious thoughts, emotions, and feelings. In the following I will refer to these as φ-ownership and ψ-ownership, respectively:

φ-ownership

The phenomenon of taking one's body parts to be parts of oneself, and (correlatively) of taking one's body to be one's own.

ψ-ownership

The phenomenon of taking one's conscious thoughts, feelings, emotions, and other mental states to be one's own.

The description of ownership in terms of "taking" is deliberately neutral, so as not to prejudge one of the key questions in this area. Many discussions of both kinds of ownership begin with a supposed phenomenological datum, which is that we have (or so it is claimed) a "sense of ownership" for our bodies and for our mental states. Martin, for example, defines the sense of ownership as a "phenomenological quality, that the body part appears to be a part of one's body" (1995, 269). But what exactly is this supposed to mean? For some authors, the sense of ownership is a specific feeling of "mineness" that is supposed to be part of the content of introspection and bodily awareness. This feeling of mineness is proposed as an explanation of both φ-ownership and ψ-ownership (see, e.g., Gallagher 2005, 2017).

Elsewhere I have expressed doubts about both the coherence and the explanatory value of postulating a phenomenology of "mineness"

(Bermúdez 2011, 2015, 2017b – reprinted as Chapters 6, 7, and 8 in this volume). Be that as it may, it seems unwise to me to characterize the phenomenon of ownership in terms of a phenomenological sense of ownership. The basic notion is too unclear and there are too many conflicting intuitions in this area for that to be a secure starting point. If there is indeed something correctly describable as a sense of ownership then that will emerge as part of the explanation of ownership, rather than as part of the explanandum.

My counterproposal is that we start instead from explicit judgments of ownership—judgments of the form "That is my hand" or "I am thinking this thought," together with judgments of disownership, such as "That is not my hand," or the more problematic judgments made by patients suffering from delusions of thought insertion. It is plain that we all make judgments of ownership on a regular basis, and often have occasion to make judgments of disownership (at least in the realm of φ-ownership). Moreover, data about φ-ownership and ψ-ownership from experimental studies and from psychopathology typically come in the form of explicit verbal reports.

If we take our starting point to be judgments of ownership, then the obvious question to ask is: What are those judgments based on? This question in turn has two dimensions. On the one hand, it can be taken as asking a descriptive-causal question about the source or origins of those judgments. On the other, it can be taken to ask a normative question about the reasons for which those judgments are made. A full account of ownership will incorporate both dimensions—the descriptive-causal, on the one hand, and the reason-giving, on the other. My proposal, then, is that we tackle the problem of explaining ownership through explaining descriptive-causal and reason-giving bases for judgments of ownership.

With this framework in mind, the next two sections will outline John Campbell's account of φ-ownership and my own account of ψ-ownership, before turning to the more general question of how φ-ownership and ψ-ownership are related.

3 Campbell on ψ-Ownership

In a series of papers, John Campbell has proposed an interesting fractionation in the notion of ψ-ownership (Campbell 1999a, 1999b, 2002). His suggestion, inspired by the project of making sense of delusions of thought insertion in schizophrenics as well by general reflection on the nature of introspection, is that what we tend to think of a unitary phenomenon of ownership really has two components. One strand of what it is to take a thought (or other occurrent mental state) as one's own is that one be able to think of it as one's own—that one be able to ascribe the thought to oneself. This is, I think it is fair to say, the dominant conception of ψ-ownership, its most distinguished proponent being Immanuel Kant who famously wrote in the second edition of the Transcendental Deduction of the Categories that "The 'I think' must be able to accompany all of my representations."[1]

But reflecting on delusions of thought insertion suggests to Campbell that this cannot be all there is to ownership. Schizophrenic patients suffering from thought insertion report themselves as thinking thoughts that are not their own. Taking the reports at face value, the patients seem to be able to ascribe these thoughts to themselves. They do not deny that it is they themselves who are thinking the inserted thoughts (the "I think" does indeed accompany the inserted thoughts, which is why they are a source of such distress). What schizophrenics deny is that those thoughts that they are thinking are their own thoughts. If the possibility of self-ascription were all there is to ownership then these denials would be completely incoherent, which seems (among other problems) to trivialize a serious and disturbing disorder. So, in Campbell's words:

> At the very least, these reports by patients show that there is some structure in our ordinary notion of the ownership of a thought which we might not otherwise have suspected. The thought inserted into the subject's mind is indeed in some sense his, just because it has been successfully inserted into his mind; it has some special relation to him. He has, for example, some especially direct knowledge of it. On the other hand, there is, the patient insists, a sense in which the thought is not his, a sense in which the thought is some else's, and not just in that someone else originated the thought and communicated it to the subject; there is a sense in which the thought, as it were, remains the property of someone else. (Campbell 1999b, 610)

This second strand in the notion of ownership is causal. Part of what it is to take a thought to be one's own is to take oneself to be its author, the person who produced it. This dimension of ownership is missing in delusions

---

1. See the *Critique of Pure Reason* at B13. I have discussed different ways of looking at Kant's unity of apperception in Bermúdez 1994.

of thought insertion. The defining feature of schizophrenic patients with thought insertion is being introspectively aware of thoughts of which they do not take themselves to be the author.[2]

Considering this proposal through the lens of the general approach to ownership sketched in the previous section, it seems plausible to interpret Campbell as distinguishing two different types of judgment of ownership:

(1) "I am thinking this thought."

(2) "I am the producer of this thought."

To make a type-(1) judgments is to ascribe a thought to oneself. To make a type-(2) judgment is to claim authorship for that thought. What one might think of as a normal judgment of ownership ("I am thinking this thought" or "This is my thought") typically subsumes both dimensions of ownership.

Given this distinction between these two dimensions of ownership, the next step is to investigate the basis for each of them. Campbell (1999a) sympathetically discusses Frith's (1992) proposed explanation of schizophrenia in terms of a breakdown in normal mechanisms of action monitoring. According to influential models of motor control going back to the early nineteenth century, when people perform ordinary (i.e., bodily) actions a copy of the motor instructions (the *efference copy*) feeds into a comparator mechanism. This comparator uses the motor instructions to attenuate sensory and proprioceptive feedback. This is why, for example, the world does not appear to jump to the right every time we move our heads to the left. It is also one of the ways of identifying genuinely self-caused movements. Frith's proposal is that some analogue of this process exists at the level of thought, so that some form of cognitive efference copy feeds into a comparator mechanism, which then allows us to identify genuinely self-caused thoughts. These genuinely self-caused thoughts are, of course, the ones of which we take ourselves to be the authors. Delusions of thought insertion occur when the efference-copy/comparator mechanism for thoughts breaks down.

Frith's account certainly fits the general model I have proposed. It is an account of the basis for judgments of ψ-ownership (at least of what I have termed type-(2) judgments of ψ-ownership). What I want to emphasize,

2. For a broadly similar distinction, see Graham and Stephens 1995.

though, is that it can at best provide only a partial account.[3] As pointed out in section 2, the notion of a basis has both a causal-descriptive dimension and a reason-giving dimension. Frith's account, located as it is squarely at the subpersonal level, speaks to the first dimension but not to the second. It tells us about the subpersonal machinery that makes possible judgments of ψ-ownership. But the notion of a reason applies paradigmatically at the level of the person, about which Frith's account is silent.

There is an interesting question as to how we should think about the basis for Campbell's first dimension of ψ-ownership—the self-ascription dimension. I am attracted to the view that Kant's "I think" is, as it were, self-intimating, so that part of what it is to be introspectively aware of a thought is to be capable of ascribing it to oneself, but I will not explore that idea further here. The principal conclusion I want to draw from this discussion of Campbell is that there remains an open question about the reasons for which we typically take ourselves to be the authors of the thoughts that we are thinking. In the final section of this essay I will suggest an answer to this question.

5   A Model for Thinking about φ-Ownership

I've recently proposed an account of φ-ownership (Bermúdez 2017) grounded in earlier work on distinctive features of how the space of the body is experienced (Bermúdez 1998, 2005). The account starts from what I take to be two basic features of the phenomenology of bodily awareness. Here is the first:

Boundedness

Bodily events are experienced within the experienced body (a circumscribed body-shaped volume whose boundaries define the limits of the self).[4]

The experienced body has a degree of plasticity over time. At any given moment its boundaries are relatively fixed. But viewed over time it is malleable and capable of adapting to organic bodily growth, to trauma (such

3. Frith (2012) himself now makes more modest claims for the comparator theory.

4. Cf. Martin: "In having bodily sensations, it appears to one as if whatever one is aware of through having such sensations is a part of one's body" (1995, 269). He describes this as a "sense of ownership," but for reasons indicated above I find this terminology infelicitous.

as amputation), and the changing demands of movement and action. The experienced body does not always map cleanly onto the physical body. In some cases, such as prosthetic limbs, the experienced body can extend beyond the bounds of the real body. In other disorders, such as unilateral spatial neglect, portions of the real body fall outside the experienced body.

The second large-scale feature of the phenomenology of bodily awareness I term Connectedness:

Connectedness

The spatial location of a bodily event is experienced relative to the disposition of the body as a whole.

Part of what it is to experience, say, the heel of one's hand on the table is to experience the angle of the wrist and the degree of flexion in the shoulder and the elbow. Whereas Boundedness highlights the role of bodily boundaries in somatic experience, Connectedness highlights the role of limb disposition. The two principles jointly illustrate how individual bodily experiences incorporate an ongoing awareness of the body's limits and moment-to-moment layout. And of course the relation is reciprocal, since individual bodily experiences are an important element in generating that ongoing awareness.

Boundedness and Connectedness each emphasize different aspects of the spatial dimension of bodily experiences. Boundedness emphasizes the relation to the experienced spatial bounds of the body, while Connectedness emphasizes the relation to the body's experienced layout. Since there are no analogues of either for exteroceptive perception in any sensory modality, there seems to be something distinctive about how the spatial location of bodily events is experienced.[5]

This distinctiveness does not emerge if we think about how the space of the body is experienced in bodily awareness in the same way as we think about how the space of the external world is experienced in vision and

---

5. It is true that visual perception is inherently relational, in that the field of view is centered on the viewer's eyes. But this is not really an analogue of Connectedness, because the body is not experienced from a single origin. When we say, for example, that one thing looks nearer than another, this incorporates an implicit self-reference reflecting the origin of the visual point of view. Bodily experience, in contrast, does not allow such spatial comparisons. There is no privileged body part that counts as "me" for the purposes of describing, say, a pain as farther away than an itch.

other exteroceptive modalities. When the experienced spatiality of the body is discussed, it is standardly conceptualized in terms of a Cartesian frame with three axes, corresponding to the frontal, saggital, and transverse planes, with the body's center of mass serving as the origin of the coordinate system. This way of thinking about the space of the body, however, cannot do justice either to Boundedness or to Connectedness. There is no sense in which spatial locations that fall within the limits of the body are privileged (as Boundedness requires), and since each point is completely independent of every other there is no way in which it can accommodate Connectedness.

My proposed alternative model distinguishes two aspects of experienced bodily location, which I term A-location and B-location. Both presuppose a general map of the body as a relatively immoveable torso connected by joints to moveable body parts. To experience a bodily event (a pain, say) at a particular A-location is to experience it relative to such a map of the body, without taking into account the body's actual position. For this reason experienced A-locations can only be experienced within the boundaries of the body.[6] So, A-location corresponds most closely to Boundedness. The B-location of a bodily event is its A-location calibrated relative to the position of the rest of the body. A-location specifies a bodily event within a particular body part, while B-location fixes the location of that body part in terms of the angles of the joints that lie between it and the immoveable torso. So, the B-location of the pain in the ball of my foot is its A-location within my foot, supplemented by specifying the angles of the foot relative to the lower leg, and the lower leg relative to the upper leg.

This way of thinking about the spatiality of bodily experience is the key, I suggest, to understanding φ-ownership. The grounding here is both reason-giving and causal-descriptive. From the perspective of subjects' own experience and their reasons for making judgments of ownership, the salient fact is that we experience the space of the body in a manner fundamentally different from how we experience extrabodily space. This can help explain both judgments of ownership with respect to individual body parts and judgments about the body as a whole. The body parts we take to be our own are the body parts that fall within the experienced body—the body

---

6. I am assuming that the general map corresponds to the experienced body, rather than the real body. In this sense it corresponds to what O'Shaughnessy (1995) termed the *long-term body-image*.

parts within which bodily events can be A-located. At the same time, the B-location dimension of bodily experience reflects the way in which a constant awareness of the disposition of the body as a whole is a background part of bodily experience, and hence a powerful basis for taking one's body to be one's own.

From a subpersonal perspective, it is natural to look for a descriptive-causal explanation of φ-ownership in the mechanisms that make possible the experience of A-location and B-location. There is a significant body of work from both neuroscientists and neuropsychologists on which to draw. So, for example, neuropsychological and neuroimaging studies suggest that the right temporal and parietal lobes play an important role in supporting an abstract model of the body.[7] As far as B-location is concerned, there is a rich experimental literature on how limb position is coded for motor coordination and motor control, as well as on different sources of information about joint position.

The principal point that I want to emphasize for present purposes is that this approach ties φ-ownership very closely to the subject's awareness of the body's potentiality for action. From the perspective of action-planning and motor control, the most important variables are joint angles because, to a first approximation, muscles move limbs by changing joint angles. If, as I suggest, bodily events are experienced as having a B-location as well as an A-location, then an awareness of how one's body is configured from an agential point of view is built into the very structure of bodily experience.

5   Depersonalization Disorders and Breakdowns of Ownership

As mentioned earlier, discussions of φ-ownership and ψ-ownership have typically proceeded independently of each other. On the face of it this is puzzling. One of the principal grounds for judgments of ownership is the conscious experience of the body through bodily sensation, proprioception, kinesthesia, and the sense of touch. These experiences put us in touch with our own bodies. They are plainly somatic. At the same time, though, they are also psychological events. As psychological events, they are the sort of thing for which the question of ψ-ownership arises. So, φ-ownership and ψ-ownership intersect in potentially interesting ways.

7. See Tsakiris 2011, sec. 6, for a review and further references.

In recent work, Alexandre Billon has suggested an even closer connection between φ-ownership and ψ-ownership (Billon 2017). According to Billon, psychopathological disorders such as Cotard's syndrome and depersonalization suggest that we need a single, unified account of the two types of ownership. In Cotard's syndrome patients have a range of nihilistic delusions. They can deny that they exist, for example, or that they are thinking. Cotard's syndrome is complex, not least because it is very rare and the few patients who have been documented present a wide and not always consistent range of symptoms (Young and Leafhead 1996). Billon has argued with some plausibility, however, that there are close connections between Cotard's syndrome and the more common condition of depersonalization (Billon 2016). Patients suffering from depersonalization report a range of highly anomalous experiences that appear closely related to the delusions experienced by Cotard patients. Billon's thesis, in effect, is that Cotard's syndrome is the delusional counterpart of depersonalization, with Cotard patients taking at face value the content of the anomalous experiences characteristic of depersonalization.

From the perspective of ownership, the relevance of Cotard's syndrome and depersonalization is that they both often involve simultaneous breakdowns in φ-ownership and ψ-ownership. Depersonalization involves experiences both of *desomatization* and of *dementalization*. Patients report themselves as being alienated from their bodies as a whole, from individual body-parts, and from their thoughts and feelings. Here are some representative reports:

Desomatization (whole body)

"I do not feel I have a body. When I look down I see my legs and body but it feels as if it was not there. When I move I see the movements as I move, but I am not there with the movements. I am walking up the stairs, I see my legs and hear footsteps and feel the muscles but it feels as if I have no body; I am not there." (Dugas and Moutier 1911, 28, trans. in Billon 2017)

Desomatization (individual body parts)

She did not feel anything, or rather, she did not feel anything as she used to, so she had to touch herself. ... "When I wash myself, she said, my hand is insensitive [...] yesterday when I kissed my daughter, it didn't do me anything, my lips did not feel anything [...] my eyelids [she explained that she used to touch them every morning] are insensitive. [...] It is like a big void in my back, she says, while touching her spine, I do not feel 'my back.'" ... Touching her left side she said: "it is like insensitive." (Leroy 1901, 520–521, trans. in Billon 2017)

Dementalization

"I feel pains in my chest, but they seem to belong to someone else, not to me." (Mayer-Gross 2011, 114)

According to Billon, the fact that depersonalization disorders and Cotard's syndrome are pathologies of both ψ-ownership and φ-ownership suggest that there should be a unified, single explanation of the two types of ownership. At root, he thinks, there is one basic type of ownership that is compromised in these psychopathological cases.

Billon draws attention to complex and fascinating phenomena that will certainly need to be incorporated into a complete account of ownership. I am skeptical about his overall argument, however. Surely the most that we can conclude from depersonalization and Cotard's syndrome is that there needs to be a unified, single explanation of the simultaneous *breakdown* of ψ-ownership and φ-ownership. It is fallacious to conclude from the fact that two cognitive phenomena break down together that they are really two different aspects of a single phenomenon. There could be a simple physiological explanation for the simultaneous breakdown, for example, that in no way implies a common capacity that is impaired in each breakdown. So, for example, the two cognitive phenomena might be realized by overlapping neural networks such that damage to the first network interrupts the second. In effect, this is a wiring issue at the subpersonal level, which need not have implications at the personal level.

The history of so-called Gerstmann syndrome is instructive. As reported by Shallice (1988), for many years neuropsychologists identified a cluster of deficits associated with left parietal damage as a single clinical entity— including *aculculia* (difficulty in performing arithmetical calculations), *agraphia* (impairment in written communication), *left-right disorientation*, and *finger agnosia*. Shallice argues that these deficits do not seem to form a functional entity, however. To the extent that they cluster, it is due simply to a common anatomical basis.[8] Each of the deficits frequently appears

---

8. For a different perspective, see Rusconi et al. 2010, which offers a positive account of Gerstmann syndrome. It is not clear to me, however, that Rusconi et al. are clearly distinguishing between a syndrome in the sense of a cluster of symptoms that typically accompany each other, and the richer sense of syndrome in which the cluster of symptoms implicates the breakdown of a single, personal-level cognitive capacity. In fact, the Rusconi et al. hypothesis is that the cortical substrate for Gerstmann syndrome is a white matter lesion that disrupts connections between intraparietal and angular cortex.

outside of the cluster, and it does not seem possible to make a backward inference to a single common capacity that is disturbed in all of them.

Billon's claim is essentially an inference to the best explanation—namely that the best explanation of the simultaneous breakdown of φ-ownership and ψ-ownership is an impairment of the "sense of mineness." However, it seems to me that disorders of ownership display a similar pattern to the symptoms in Gerstmann syndrome. Even if it is the case that φ-ownership and ψ-ownership break down simultaneously in depersonalization, there are plenty of cases where they breakdown independently of each other. In fact, we have already considered a number of examples. Unilateral spatial neglect and somatoparaphrenia seem both to present breakdowns in φ-ownership without any compromise in ψ-ownership. In the opposite direction, thought insertion in schizophrenia is an example of a breakdown in ψ-ownership that is not normally accompanied by compromised φ-ownership. So, the psychopathology of depersonalization does not provide compelling reasons to think that there must be a unified account of φ-ownership and ψ-ownership.

6   The Relation between φ-Ownership and ψ-Ownership

Setting the argument from depersonalization aside, however, there are two more general reasons for thinking that accounts of φ-ownership and ψ-ownership must be closely integrated. First, the basic phenomena seem interdependent. As I will bring out in the following, φ-ownership presupposes ψ-ownership and vice versa. Second, from a broadly phenomenological point of view, our awareness of our own bodies and our awareness of our ongoing thoughts, emotions, and feelings are not simply co-conscious. They are part of what Michael Ayers (1991) has termed an integrated sensory field—a single, embodied perspective on the world.

Let me begin with the interdependence thesis. I have already hinted at how φ-ownership might be dependent on ψ-ownership. Probably the most important source for our taking our bodies and body parts as our own is our conscious bodily experience through somatosensation, proprioception, kinesthesia, and the sense of touch. These interoceptive mechanisms put us in touch with our bodies in a way that we are not in touch with nonbodily physical objects. But conscious bodily experiences are, of course, experiences. And as such they are themselves occurrent mental events, which means that the question of ψ-ownership arises for them. I take the body that I experience to be my body precisely because I take the experiences that I have of it to be my own experiences. The same holds, perhaps to a still greater extent, in the case of φ-ownership of individual body parts.[9] Here too the experience of φ-ownership rests on sensations and other qualitative events that are ψ-owned. To appreciate the point, consider this question: What would it be like to experience one's body as one's own as a function of feeling sensations in it, but without experiencing those sensations as one's own?

Does this dependence of φ-ownership on ψ-ownership mean that in some sense ψ-ownership is more fundamental than φ-ownership? Unfortunately not, since there is also a dependence in the other direction. Judgments of ψ-ownership take the form "This is *my* thought" or "I am thinking this thought." In these judgments, "I" functions, of course, as a referring expression. The referent of "I" is an embodied subject and hence the subject of bodily states that are taken to be the subject's own. So, I claim, ψ-ownership presupposes φ-ownership, in the sense that (for normal embodied subjects) the experience of ownership for one's thoughts and mental states proceeds via the experience of oneself as an embodied subject.[10]

One might wonder, though, whether this argument involves a fallacy of equivocation. After all, the fact that the "I" referred to is an embodied subject does not mean that using the expression "I" involves referring to oneself as an embodied subject.

9. This dependence of φ-ownership on ψ-ownership certainly emerges clearly in the model of φ-ownership sketched out in sec. 4, but it seems likely to be implicated in any alternative account. To take just one example, the hypothetical (and to my mind illusory) "feeling of mineness" that some authors have postulated is an occurrent mental state that the subject would need to φ-own. The same point applies, of course, if one thinks (with Zahavi and Kriegel 2015 that the "feeling of mineness" (which they term "for-me-ness") is not an experience itself, but rather an aspect of a core type of experience.

10. To be clear, the claim is that ψ-ownership presupposes φ-ownership for embodied subjects. Peacocke (2014) has argued, in effect, that there is no logical reason why disembodied subjects should not be capable of ψ-ownership. This issue is orthogonal to that considered here, however. There is no reason to think that an account of φ-ownership for embodied subjects would carry over to disembodied subjects, or vice versa.

On some accounts of what it is to use the referring expression "I" with understanding, embodied subjects cannot refer to themselves using "I" without grasping that they are embodied subjects.[11] But there is a more specific reason, not tied to any particular account of self-reference, for thinking that one cannot take oneself to be the subject of occurrent thoughts, emotions, and feelings without taking oneself to be the subject of bodily states. This reason emerges when we consider the phenomenology and the content of perceptual experience.

Starting with the phenomenology of perception, in his magisterial book *Locke* Michael Ayers makes some very salient observations about the multimodal nature of sensory experience (as a corrective to Locke's theory of sensitive knowledge and his very narrow conception of sensation). He writes:

> There are not, therefore, several sets of apparent directions, auditory, tactual, visual, proprioceptive, vestibular, and perhaps olfactory, which we learn, or are innately inspired, to associate or identify with one another. There is one space of which we can be aware in different, but essentially integrated, ways. The five (or more) senses are not distinct inlets for quite disparate, internally unconnected data. (Ayers 1991, 186–187)

Our sensory perspective on the world (what Locke termed our "sensitive knowledge") comes through what Ayers terms an "integrated sensory field," with the integration coming at the level of content. This is much stronger than the relatively familiar idea that sensory experiences across different modalities are co-conscious, or that perceptual experience is inherently relational and the perceiver's own body is one of the relata. The different sensory modalities are unified by the fact that they collectively represent a single spatial world of three-dimensional objects from a single embodied perspective. For that reason, our experience of our own bodies is integrated into the sensory field in multiple ways.

Our experience of our own bodies structures the experienced space of the nonbodily world in ways that J. J. Gibson brought out in his theory of ecological perception. The bodily self is a constant, framing presence in the content of visual perception. One reason is that particular body parts feature in distinctive, self-specifying ways in vision. Think of the arms obtruding into the visual array from below, or the nose that is the leftmost thing that can be seen by right eye and the rightmost thing that can be seen by

11. See, e.g., Evans 1982 and Bermúdez 2017a.

the left eye. Moreover, the experience of movement through the world is fixed by the interplay between bodily invariants and the changing pattern of optic flow. And finally, the theory of affordances emphasizes how much the perception of objects can be structured by the perceiver's potential for acting on them. To take a simple example, we see objects within periper-sonal space as being within reach.[12]

Interestingly, the line of thought that we find in Ayers has been sig-nificantly extended by Michael Tye (2003). Tye begins with a comparable notion of a unified sensory field: at any given moment, he writes, "there is just one experience here, described in two different ways. This experi-ence represents the sounds, smells, tastes, surfaces, and so on in the world around me in relation to my body, its parts and their boundaries, together with various bodily disturbances. My current experience is closed under conjunction *across the board*" (Tye 2003, 76). He then takes the idea of a single unified experience still further, to include both emotions and feel-ings and occurrent thoughts.

Tye argues that the phenomenology of conscious thought is the phe-nomenology of linguistic, auditory images, while awareness of one's moods and emotions comes via awareness of changes in one's perceptions of one-self and of the world. We are aware of our thoughts through their articu-lation in inner speech, and aware of our emotions and moods indirectly through the valence of how we experience the world and how we experi-ence our own bodies. Awareness of occurrent thoughts and other mental states, then, are really just further varieties of somatoperceptual experience, which makes them also part of the integrated sensory field (perhaps better termed the integrated somato-sensory-affective-cognitive field!).

This general picture of the phenomenology of introspection explains why one cannot take occurrent thoughts, emotions, and feelings to be one's own without taking oneself to be an embodied subject—and hence further explains the dependence of ψ-ownership on φ-ownership.[13] We cannot (in

12. For further discussion, see Bermúdez 1998 and chapters 1–4 in this volume.

13. The claim here is about the normal case. It is an interesting question (raised by Billon) how ψ-ownership would work for someone in a sensory deprivation tank, as envisaged by Anscombe. My hunch (and prediction) is that a lack of ongoing sen-sory feedback would not change the dependence of ψ-ownership on φ-ownership. No doubt, things would be very different for someone who had existed for his entire life in a sensory deprivation tank (which, in effect, is the thought experiment pro-

the normal case) experience ourselves as the owner of our perceptual experiences, thoughts, emotions, and so on, without experiencing ourselves as embodied. And to experience oneself as embodied is to experience oneself as the owner of one's body. So, the dependence between φ-ownership and ψ-ownership goes in both directions. This interdependence gives a *prima facie* reason for expecting accounts of ψ-ownership and φ-ownership to be integrated with each other. But what form might this integration take? The final section of the essay will propose a deep commonality *at the level of content* across the models of ψ-ownership and φ-ownership described in sections 3 and 4. The two types of ownership are tied together by the fundamental role that agency and practical reasoning play in each.

7   φ-Ownership and ψ-Ownership: The Common Thread

It seems unrealistic to expect a completely unified account of φ-ownership and ψ-ownership. Yet, as we have seen, the two phenomena are deeply interconnected, and one would expect this interconnection to be reflected in the accounts we give of them. The accounts of φ-ownership and ψ-ownership given in sections 3–4 seem on the face of things to be very different. This section will bring out, however, how the common thread of agency ties them together.[14]

As observed at the end of section 4, the proposed model of φ-ownership ties the experiential basis for bodily ownership very closely to the subject's awareness of their potentialities for action. What grounds judgments of φ-ownership is the fact that we experience the space of our bodies in the distinctive way that I have tried to capture using the Boundedness and Connectedness principles and the explanatory framework of A-location and B-location. This distinctive way of experiencing our bodies is closely tied to the body's agential capacities. The Boundedness principle, and with it the idea of A-location, incorporates (and contributes to) the subject's ongoing

---

posed by Avicenna—the so-called flying or floating man argument). But since this scenario is so far from the normal case, and since it is unlikely that any prediction made about that case will ever be tested, I am not sure that it helps to speculate about it.

14. For a different approach to the role of agency in self-awareness, see O'Brien 2007.

awareness of the limits of the bodily self, and hence the limits of what is directly responsive to the will. The Connectedness principle (and the idea of B-location) builds agential capabilities even more deeply into the spatial content of bodily experience, because it specifies bodily locations in terms of variables that are under the subject's direct control (i.e., in terms of the joint angles that specify the orientation of limbs and effectors). On the proposed account, therefore, *the spatial content of bodily awareness incorporates an awareness of the body's agential anatomy*.

With this in mind, let us turn back to Campbell's account of ψ-ownership, which it will be recalled distinguishes two dissociable elements in judgments of ownership—the self-ascription element ("This is my thought") and the authorship element ("I am the producer of this thought"). One question left hanging by Campbell's discussion of the authorship is how we should understand the reasons for which judgments of authorship are made (as opposed to an account, in terms of subpersonal efference copy and comparator mechanisms, of the enabling conditions of such judgments). To answer this question, I propose, we need to look more closely at mental agency.

To begin with a very general thought about ψ-ownership, an important part of what it is to take an occurrent thought as one's own is to take it as something that one can deploy in conscious reasoning. Ownership needs to be understood in terms of the active process of thinking. The comparison with delusions of thought insertion is instructive. Here are two famous and much-discussed reports of thought insertion:

I look out the window and I think that the garden looks nice and the grass looks cool, but the thoughts of Eamonn Andrews come into my mind.
    There are no other thoughts there, only his. ... He treats my mind like a screen and flashes thoughts onto it like you flash a picture. (Mellor 1970, 17)

I have never read nor heard them; they come unasked; I do not dare to think I am the source but I am happy to know of them without thinking them. They come at any moment like a gift and I do not dare to impart them as if they were my own. (Jaspers 1963, p. 123)

In both cases, the alienness of the inserted thoughts goes hand in hand with the patient's inability to integrate them into any kind of normal thinking process. Delusional patients are passive recipients of the thoughts, not active thinkers.

Returning to Campbell's distinction between two elements in ψ-ownership, the first element, introspective accessibility, is obviously a necessary condition for conscious deliberation. Only thoughts that we are aware of and that we ascribe to ourselves can occur in conscious reflection. But one of the lessons to be drawn from delusions of thought insertion is that introspective accessibility is not a sufficient condition. Part of the cognitive dissonance experienced by schizophrenic patients with these symptoms is that they experience (and are able to ascribe to themselves) thoughts that they do not know how to integrate with the rest of their cognitive and affective lives. A natural explanation of this cognitive dissonance, and certainly one compatible with Campbell's account, is that only occurrent thoughts that can feature as premises in reasoning are taken to be self-originated.[15] The sense of deep alienation that schizophrenic patients have from the thoughts that they claim to be inserted is tied to the fact that those thoughts resist the type of integration with other thoughts that would be required for the subject to be able to use them in deliberation.

The role of agency in ψ-ownership emerges when we think further about this deep connection between authorship and reasoning. Suppose that a judgment of authorship with respect to a particular occurrent mental state is based in large measure on its being available for reasoning. Reasoning can be practical or it can be theoretical, and it should be emphasized that the full range of conscious mental states that are ψ-owned can feature in both types of reasoning—feelings and emotions, for example, can function as quasi-evaluative premises in theoretical reasoning, just as they can feature more directly as motivators in practical reasoning. The connection with agency emerges even when the reasoning is theoretical, because theoretical reasoning is itself a form of mental action.[16]

But the real common thread between ψ-ownership and φ-ownership comes through practical reasoning. The core cases of practical reasoning issue in bodily action. Practical deliberation is deliberation about what one

15. This is also, broadly speaking, compatible with the account of thought insertion proposed by Graham and Stephens (1995), who suggest that schizophrenic patients deny the authorship of thoughts when those thoughts are inexplicable in terms of rest of their beliefs and desires. Their idea is that delusions of thought insertion can sometimes be the best way for the patient to make sense of profoundly anomalous experiences.

16. See further the essays in O'Brien and Soteriou 2009.

can do as an embodied subject through directly moving body parts in basic actions that themselves effect change in the environment. So the body is a background presence in practical deliberation. And it is so in ways that depend on the very two features of the spatial content of bodily awareness that (I have argued) are integral to φ-ownership.

First, the scope of practical deliberation is delimited by the structural constraints on the body's potential for action that are implicated at the level of A-location. Action planning is informed by a representation of the body that delimits the realm of the possible. What we are capable of moving in basic actions is the experienced body, which also fixes the boundaries of φ-ownership. At the same time (and this is the second point), implementing the results of action planning requires the constantly updated and ongoing awareness of how the body is oriented and how individual body parts are distributed that comes with B-location spatial content. These are precisely the agency-related factors that I have argued are central to φ-ownership. They give the starting points for bodily movements and hence for solving the complicated motor control equations of limb trajectory and movement end point.

Agency, therefore, is the common thread that links φ-ownership and ψ-ownership. There are more general lessons here for how we think about self-awareness. In an often-quoted phrase, Descartes states in the Sixth Meditation that "I am not merely present in my body as a sailor is present in a ship, but I am very closely joined, and as it were intermingled with it, so that I and the body form a unit."[17] The role of agency in φ-ownership and ψ-ownership offers a fresh perspective on the "substantial union" of body and mind. To take one's body as one's own is to be aware of it as directly responsive to the will, as the medium for effecting change in the physical world. To take one's thoughts, emotions, and feelings as one's own is to take them as potential premises in reasoning and deliberation—potential objects of mental actions and potential causes of bodily actions.

Acknowledgments

I am grateful for comments from Alexandre Billon and an anonymous referee.

17. Descartes, *Meditations on First Philosophy* (AT VII, p. 81), translated by John Cottingham in Descartes 1985, vol. 2, p. 56.

References

Ayers, M. 1991. *Locke: Epistemology and Ontology*. London: Routledge.

Bermúdez, J. L. 1994. The unity of apperception in the *Critique of Pure Reason*. *European Journal of Philosophy* 2:213–240.

Bermúdez, J. L. 1998. *The Paradox of Self-Consciousness*. Cambridge, MA: MIT Press.

Bermúdez, J. L. 2001. Normativity and rationality in delusional psychiatric disorders. *Mind & Language* 16:457–493.

Bermúdez, J. L. 2005. The phenomenology of bodily awareness. In *Phenomenology and Philosophy of Mind*, ed. D. W. Smith and A. L. Thomasson. New York: Oxford University Press. Reprinted in this volume.

Bermúdez, J. L. 2011. Bodily awareness and self-consciousness. In *Oxford Handbook of the Self*, ed. S. Gallagher, 157–179. Oxford: Oxford University Press. Reprinted in this volume.

Bermúdez, J. L. 2015. Bodily ownership, bodily awareness, and knowledge without observation. *Analysis* 75:37–45. Reprinted in this volume.

Bermúdez, J. L. 2017a. *Understanding "I": Language and Thought*. Oxford: Oxford University Press.

Bermúdez, J. L. 2017b. Ownership and the space of the body. In *The Subject's Matter: Self-Consciousness and the Body*, ed. F. de Vignemont and A. Alsmith. Cambridge, MA: MIT Press. Reprinted in this volume.

Bermúdez, J. L., A. J. Marcel, and N. Eilan, eds. 1995. *The Body and the Self*. Cambridge, MA: MIT Press.

Billon, A. 2015. Why are we certain that we exist? *Philosophy and Phenomenological Research* 91:723–759.

Billon, A. 2016. Making sense of the Cotard syndrome: Insights from the study of depersonalisation. *Mind & Language* 31:356–391.

Billon, A. 2017. Three challenges to recent theories of bodily self-awareness. In *The Subject's Matter: Self-Consciousness and the Body*, ed. F. de Vignemont and A. Alsmith. Cambridge, MA: MIT Press.

Botvinick, M., and J. Cohen. 1998. Rubber hands "feel" touch that eyes see. *Nature* 391:756.

Campbell, J. 1999a. Schizophrenia, the space of reasons, and thinking as a motor process. *Monist* 82:609–625.

Campbell, J. 1999b. Immunity to error through misidentification and the meaning of a referring term. *Philosophical Topics* 29:89–104.

Campbell, J. 2002. The ownership of thoughts. *Philosophy, Psychiatry & Psychology* 9:35–39.

Davies, M., M. Coltheart, R. Langdon, and N. Breen. 2001. Monothematic delusions: Towards a two-factor account. *Philosophy, Psychiatry & Psychology* 8:133–158.

Descartes, R. 1985. *Philosophical Writings*. Translated by J. Cottingham, R. Stoothof, and D. Murdoch. 3 vols. Cambridge: Cambridge University Press.

Dugas, L., and F. Moutier. 1911. *La Dépersonnalization*. Paris: Alcan.

Evans, G. 1982. *The Varieties of Reference*. Oxford: Oxford University Press.

Frith, C. 1992. *The Cognitive Neuroscience of Schizophrenia*. New York: Psychology Press.

Frith, C. 2012. Explaining delusions of control: The comparator model 20 years on. *Consciousness and Cognition* 21:52–54.

Gallagher, S. 2005. *How the Body Shapes the Mind*. New York: Oxford University Press.

Gallagher, S. 2017. Senses of the sense of ownership. In *The Subject's Matter: Self-Consciousness and the Body*, ed. F. de Vignemont and A. Alsmith. Cambridge, MA: MIT Press.

Gerrans, P. 2000. Refining the explanation of Cotard's delusion. *Mind & Language* 15:111–122.

Graham, G., and G. L. Stephens. 1995. Mind and mine. In *Philosophical Psychopathology*, ed. G. Graham and G. L. Stephens. Cambridge, MA: MIT Press.

Jaspers, K. 1963. *General Psychopathology*. Manchester: Manchester University Press.

Lenggenhager, B., T. Tadi, T. Metzinger, and O. Blanke. 2007. Video ergo sum: Manipulating bodily self-consciousness. *Science* 317:1096–1099.

Leroy, E.-B. 1901. Sur l'illusion dite dépersonnalisation. *L'Année Psychologique* 8:519–522.

Martin, M. 1995. Bodily awareness: A sense of ownership. In *The Body and the Self*, ed. J. L. Bermúdez, A. J. Marcel, and N. Eilan. Cambridge, MA: MIT Press.

Mayer-Gross, W. 2011. On depersonalization. *British Journal of Medical Psychology* 15:103–126.

Mellor, C. S. 1970. First rank symptoms of schizophrenia. *British Journal of Psychiatry* 117:15–23.

O'Brien, L. 2007. *Self-Knowing Agents*. Oxford University Press.

O'Brien, L., and M. Soteriou. 2009. *Mental Actions*. Oxford University Press.

O'Shaughnessy, B. 1995. Proprioception and the body image. In *The Body and the Self*, ed. J. L. Bermudez, A. J. Marcel, and N. Eilan. Cambridge, MA: MIT Press.

Pacherie, E., M. Green, and T. J. Bayne. 2006. Phenomenology and delusions: Who put the "alien" in alien control? *Consciousness and Cognition* 15:566–577.

Peacocke, C. 2014. *The Mirror of the World: Subjects, Consciousness, and Self-Consciousness*. Oxford: Oxford University Press.

Rusconi, E., P. Pinel, S. Dehaene, and A. Kleinschmidt. 2010. The enigma of Gerstmann's syndrome revisited: A telling tale of the vicissitudes of neuropsychology. *Brain* 133:320–332.

Shallice, T. 1988. *From Neuropsychology to Mental Structure*. Cambridge: Cambridge University Press.

Tsakiris, M. 2011. The sense of body ownership. In *The Oxford Handbook of the Self*, ed. S. Gallagher. Oxford: Oxford University Press.

Tye, M. 2003. *Consciousness and Persons*. Cambridge, MA: MIT Press.

Young, A. W. and K. M. Leafhead. 1996. Betwixt life and death: Case studies of the Cotard delusion. In *Method in Madness: Case studies in Cognitive Neuropsychiatry*, eds. P. W. Halligan and J. C. Marshall. Hove, UK: Psychology Press.

Zahavi, D., and U. Kriegel. 2015. For-me-ness: What it is and what it is not. In *Philosophy of Mind and Phenomenology*, ed. D. Dahlstrom, A. Elpidorou, and W. Hopp, 36–53. Routledge.

10   The Bodily Self, Commonsense Psychology, and the Springs of Action

The previous essays in this volume have all focused on primitive forms of self-consciousness. A recurring theme has been the extent to which what might initially seem to be low-level forms of awareness (of the environment, or of one's own body) actually count as forms of self-awareness and self-consciousness. The picture that I have proposed is one on which full-fledged, linguistic self-consciousness is built on a rich foundation of primitive, nonconceptual self-consciousness.

One way of putting the main theme of this volume is as a quasi-historical contrast between two very general models of the relation between the thinking self and the bodily self. On what might be termed the Cartesian model, there is a clear and sharp line between the thinking self and the bodily self—between the domain of thought and action, on the one hand, and the domain of sensation and behavior, on the other. The Aristotelian model, in contrast, offers a much more gradated view, on which there is a nested hierarchy of activities and different kinds of cognition and behavior. Descartes's "real distinction" between body and mind in his *Meditations* is very different from Aristotle's discussion of overlaps between the nutritive soul, the sensitive soul, and the rational soul in *De Anima*. At least as far as self-awareness of concerned, the picture that has emerged so far clearly favors a broadly Aristotelian model.

This paper is new for this volume. It is a composite of two earlier papers. One (Bermúdez 2005a) was written for a festschrifft for Paul Churchland, while the other (Bermúdez 2003) was originally delivered as a lecture at the Royal Institute of Philosophy in London. Neither paper on its own seemed to me to be worth reviving, but the composite raises (I hope) issues and arguments directly continuous with earlier essays in this volume.

Still, despite developing an overall model of the mind in terms of multiple and overlapping functions and capacities, Aristotle himself carved out an important and central role for deliberation and practical reason in how he thought about the thinking self. Key to his theorizing in this area are the concepts of what we would now call commonsense psychology (i.e., the concepts of *belief, desire,* and the other *propositional attitudes*). There are two reciprocal ideas: one about how actions are brought about (the springs of action) and one about how actions are explained. The springs of action, for Aristotle, are the propositional attitudes, as integrated with perception via the practical syllogism. Correlatively, explaining action takes place via identifying propositional attitudes that stand in the type of relation to the action that would be captured by an appropriate practical syllogism.

The focus of this essay is the role of the propositional attitudes as the springs of action and, correlatively, the role of the propositional attitudes in psychological explanation. Or, in a nutshell—the role of the propositional attitudes in the thinking self. The position that I will suggest is continuous with the position developed in the context of self-consciousness. Just as linguistic self-consciousness is the tip of the iceberg visible above the surface, so too do the propositional attitudes play a relatively restricted role in producing action and, *pari passu,* in explaining it.

The first section elucidates the concept of commonsense psychology, in a way that allows us to formulate more precisely the question about the role of the propositional attitudes in producing and explaining behavior. Section 2 offers a range of illustrations of how the springs of action may be finer grained than propositional attitudes, while sections 3 and 4 explore ways in which social understanding and social coordination can be achieved without the machinery of the propositional attitudes.

1 Modeling Commonsense Psychology

In its most general sense, the term "commonsense psychology" picks out the complex of social abilities and skills possessed by all normal, encultured, non-autistic, and non-brain-damaged human beings. These are the skills and abilities that allow us to navigate the social world. Taken in this very general sense, commonsense psychology is an *explanandum* rather than an *explanans*. We would expect it to be the sort of thing of which a theoretical account is given, rather than something that can itself do theoretical and explanatory work.

The expression "commonsense psychology" is used more determinately to characterize what is in effect a particular conceptual framework deemed to govern our social understanding and social skills, where this conceptual framework can be thought of as an account of what underlies the general abilities and skills just identified. Here are two useful characterizations of this second way of thinking about commonsense psychology:

> It has become a standard assumption in philosophy and psychology that normal adult human beings have a rich conceptual repertoire which they deploy to explain, predict and describe the actions of one another and, perhaps, members of closely related species also. As is usual, we shall speak of this rich, conceptual repertoire as "folk psychology" and of its deployment as "folk psychological practice." The conceptual repertoire constituting folk psychology includes, predominantly, the concepts of belief and desire and their kin—intention, hope, fear, and the rest— the so-called propositional attitudes. (Davies and Stone 1995, 2)

> Human beings are social creatures. And they are reflective creatures. As such they continually engage in a host of cognitive practices that help them get along in their social world. In particular, they attempt to understand, explain and predict their own and others' psychological states and overt behaviour; and they do so by making use of an array of ordinary psychological notions concerning various internal mental states, both occurrent and dispositional. Let us then consider folk psychology to consist, *at a minimum*, of (a) a set of attributive, explanatory and predictive practices, and (b) a set of notions or concepts used in those practices. (Von Eckardt 1994, 300)

The general idea here is that our skills in social understanding and social coordination are underpinned by the conceptual framework of propositional attitude psychology. We can make sense of other people and coordinate our behavior with theirs in virtue of our ability to apply the concepts of belief, desire, and so forth.

This general characterization leaves unanswered questions about how the conceptual framework of propositional attitude psychology is applied in practice. This brings us to a third way of thinking about commonsense psychology. This is where we find the much-discussed distinction between theory theorists and simulation theorists. A number of influential philosophers and psychologists accept the view that social understanding and social coordination rest on an implicitly known, and essentially theory-like, body of generalizations connecting propositional attitude states with overt behavior and with each other.[1] Paul Churchland is of course one of these, as are David Lewis, Frank Jackson, and Jerry Fodor. On this view (the so-called *theory theory*), social understanding involves subsuming observed behavior and what is known of a person's mental states under these generalizations in order to understand why they are behaving in a certain way and how they will behave in the future.

The theory theory has been challenged within both philosophy and psychology by the simulationist approach to commonsense psychology.[2] Simulationists hold that we explain and predict other agents by projecting ourselves into their situation and then using our own mind as a model of theirs. Suppose that we have a reasonable sense of the beliefs and desires that it would be appropriate to attribute to someone else in a particular situation, so that we understand both how she views the situation and what she wants to achieve in it. And suppose that we want to find out how she will behave. Instead of using generalizations about how mental states typically feed into behavior to predict how that person will behave, the simulationist thinks that we use our own decision-making processes to run a simulation of what would happen if we ourselves had those beliefs and desires. We do this by running our decision-making processes *off-line*, so that instead of generating an action directly they generate a description of an action or an intention to act in a certain way. We then use this description to predict the behavior of the person in question.

We can, therefore, distinguish three ways of construing commonsense psychology, as in table 10.1. The basic issue for this essay is the relation between the first construal of commonsense psychology and the second. To mark the distinction between the first and second construals, I will not treat the expressions "commonsense psychology" and "folk psychology" as synonyms. Instead, I will reserve "folk psychology" for the second

1. For philosophers, see, e.g., Churchland 1989, Fodor 1987, and Lewis 1994. For psychologists, see, e.g., Gopnik and Meltzoff 1997 and Perner 1993.

2. Gordon 1986 and Heal 1986 are key statements of the simulationist position. The principal readings in the debate between theory theorists and simulation theorists are collected in Davies and Stone 1995. Further essays will be found in Carruthers and Smith 1996. This collection includes interesting material from developmental psychologists and students of primate cognition. Currie and Ravenscroft 2002 develops a theory of imagination in the context of a simulationist approach to social understanding.

Table 10.1

1	The complex of skills and abilities that underlie our capacities for social understanding and social coordination.
2	A particular conceptual framework for explaining social understanding and social coordination in which the propositional attitudes are central.
3	A particular account of how the conceptual framework in (2) is applied in the service of explanation and/or prediction.

construal. Our question, then, is: What exactly is the domain of folk psychology? To what extent does social understanding and social coordination depend on the conceptual framework of the propositional attitudes?

Here are two conceptions of the domain of folk psychology—or, more accurately, the two ends of a spectrum of conceptions of the domain of folk psychology. At one end lies the narrow construal, according to which folk psychology is engaged only on those occasions when we explicitly and consciously deploy propositional attitude concepts in the services of explanation and/or prediction. At the other end of the spectrum lies the broad construal, which makes all social understanding and social coordination depend on attributing mental states and deploying those attributed states to explain and predict behavior.

The dominant conception of the domain of folk psychology among contemporary philosophers of mind is broad rather than narrow. Philosophers of mind tend to operate with a clear-cut distinction between understanding behavior in intentional terms, as rationalized by propositional attitudes, on the one hand, and understanding it as nonintentional, on the other. The standard examples in philosophy of mind textbooks of behaviors that are not to be understood in intentional terms are behaviors that are either reflexive or are not properly attributable to the agent. So one might distinguish, for example, between an arm-raising that is intentional, comprehensible as issuing from a particular nexus of beliefs and desires, and one that is the result of a reflex response, or of someone else lifting my arm for me.

The classical statement of this way of thinking about action is at the beginning of Donald Davidson's paper "Actions, Reasons, and Causes":

Whenever someone does something for a reason, therefore, he can be characterized as (a) having some sort of pro attitude toward actions of a certain kind, and (b) believing (or knowing, perceiving, noticing, remembering) that his action is of that kind. Under (a) are to be included desires, wantings, urges, promptings, and a great variety of moral views, aesthetic principles, economic prejudices, social conventions, and public and private goals and values in so far as these can be interpreted as attitudes of an agent directed towards actions of a certain kind. (Davidson 1963, 685–686)

The way in which this view is developed typically leaves no room for "thinking behavior" that is not (causally) generated by beliefs and desires. To the extent, then, that the activities of social coordination are thinking activities, the broad construal of folk psychology follows immediately. And indeed Davidson immediately follows the quoted passage by saying, "Giving the reason why an agent did something is often a matter of naming the pro attitude *(a)* or the related belief *(b)* or both" (Davidson 1963, 686).

This discussion suggests two independent but related strategies, therefore, for putting pressure on the broad construal of folk psychology. The first strategy is to challenge the basic claim that only the propositional attitudes can serve as the springs of (intentional) action. The second strategy is to challenge the claim that social understanding and social coordination can be achieved only through the conceptual framework of the propositional attitudes. The following explores these two strategies in turn.

2 Neural Representation, Microfeatures, and the Propositional Attitudes

Critical explorations of the role of propositional attitudes in psychological explanation would do well to begin with the writings of Paul and Patricia Churchland. I want to begin, not with Paul Churchland's "official" arguments for eliminative materialism (which seem typically to be pitched at level of the third construal of commonsense psychology, since they aim to show that folk psychology is a poor and nonpredictive *theory*), but rather with an illuminating passage in "Eliminative Materialism and the Propositional Attitudes" (Churchland 1981). Churchland is (implicitly) criticizing the idea that we can think of what a person believes in terms of the sentences to which that person would assent, so that we can use those sentences to characterize the *content* of what he believes, where this is, of course, simply a special case of the general principle that propositional attitudes have contents that can be specified by means of "that" clauses, where the complement of a "that" clause is a declarative sentence. He writes:

A declarative sentence to which a speaker would give confident assent is merely a one-dimensional *projection*—through the compound lens of Wernicke's and Broca's areas onto the idiosyncratic surface of the speaker's language—of a four- or five-dimensional "solid" that is an element in his true kinematical state. ... Being projections of that inner reality, such sentences do carry significant information regarding it and are thus fit to function as elements in a communication system. On the other hand, being *sub*-dimensional projections, they reflect but a narrow part of the reality projected. They are therefore *un*fit to represent the deeper reality in all its kinematically, dynamically, and even normatively relevant respects. (Churchland 1981, 129)

Churchland's point here is not that propositional attitude psychology is an impoverished theory, nor that it cannot be reduced to neuroscience, nor that it is limited in its explanatory scope (which are his official arguments against propositional attitude psychology). Rather, he objects that commonsense psychology rests on an untenable model of representation.

Cognition is, Churchland thinks, a form of information processing, and the representations over which that processing takes place are distributed in something like the way that representations are distributed over a large number of units and weights in an artificial neural network:

The basic idea is that the brain represents the world by means of very high-dimensional *activation vectors*, that is, by a pattern of activation levels across a very large population of neurons. And the brain performs computations on those representations by effecting various complex *vector-to-vector transformations* from one neural population to another. This happens when an activation vector from one neural population is projected through a large matrix of synaptic connections to produce a new activation vector across a second population of nonlinear neurons. Mathematically, the process is a process of multiplying a vector by a matrix and pushing the result through a nonlinear filter. (Churchland and Churchland 1998, 41)

Churchland is betting, in effect, that a complete account of neural computation will be defined over complex patterns of activation across large populations of neurons. This means that neural representations will have a huge number of degrees of freedom. There will be as many dimensions of variation in a neural representation as there are neurons whose activation values can vary independently. In mathematical terms, we need to consider neural representations as n-place vectors, where n is the number of neurons.

Philosophical discussion of the ramifications of the distributed nature of neural representations has tended to focus on the issue of whether mental representations are structured (see, e.g., the papers collected in Macdonald and Macdonald 1995). But there is a much more direct line of argument from the distributed nature of neural representation to eliminativism. Here is the possibility Churchland envisages:

Suppose that research into the structure and activity of the brain, both fine-grained and global, finally does yield a new kinematics and correlative dynamics for what is now thought of as cognitive activity. The theory is uniform for all terrestrial brains, not just human brains, and it makes suitable conceptual contact with both evolutionary biology and non-equilibrium thermodynamics. It ascribes to us, at any given time, a set or configuration of complex states, which are specified within the theory as figurative "solids" within a four- or five-dimensional phase-space. The laws of the theory govern the interaction, motion and transformation of these "solid" states within that space, and also their relations to whatever sensory and motor transducers the system possesses. (Churchland 1981, 129)

Churchland's basic claim is that this conceptual framework of solids within multidimensional phase space is incommensurable with the familiar framework of the propositional attitudes.

To see his point, suppose that we identify a locus of representational content at a very low level in neural network models. That is to say, suppose that we identify particular units, or small groups of units, as carrying out particular representational functions and tasks. This would be to make something like the "natural assumption" that Churchland sketches out in the following passage:

If we are to assign specific semantic or representational *contents* to collective units of this kind, a natural first assumption is that any unit must in some way inherit its overall content from the individual and more basic representational significance of each of its many constituting elements, namely, the activation level of each of its many neurons. After all, it is these individual neurons that are the recipients of information from the environment: either directly, through their interaction with ambient light, heat and various mechanical and chemical impingements; or indirectly, through their many synaptic connections with neurons earlier in the processing hierarchy. (Churchland and Churchland 1998, 83)

We can think of these units or groups of units as the representational primitives of the network—the place where we need to start if we are to build up to an account of the representational character of the network as a whole.[3] It is natural to think that these representational primitives will be

---

3. In fact, for reasons brought out in Churchland and Sejnowski 1992, the representational primitives are far more likely to be distributed across groups of units than to individual units. See their discussion of local coding versus vector coding in chap. 4 of that volume.

representing what are often called microfeatures of the environment. That is to say, they code features that are much more fine-grained than those encoded within the vocabulary that we employ to specify the content of propositional attitudes. These microfeatures are, to use the familiar jargon, subsymbolic.

This opens up a path for pursuing the first of the two strategies identified earlier. One way of challenging the basic claim that only the propositional attitudes can serve as the springs of (intentional) action would be to show that there are cases where the representations serving as the "springs of action" represent features of the environment that cannot be assimilated to those features represented in propositional attitude psychology. The remainder of this section points toward some relevant experimental findings and research programs. I will focus on five areas.

Two Visual Systems

Psychologists and neuroscientists agree that there are (at least) two different ways of thinking about how our perceptions of the environment feed into action. There is considerable controversy about precisely how we are to understand both the function and the neuroanatomy of these two pathways, but a definite consensus that some sort of distinction needs to be made between "vision for action" and "vision for identification."[4] Neuropsychological dissociations are an important source of evidence. Researchers have reported a double dissociation between the capacity to act on objects and the capacity to name them. Patients with optic ataxia are able to identify objects but are severely impaired in tasks that involve reaching objects or working out their orientation, while patients with various types of agnosia have the reverse impairment: they can act on objects but are often completely unable to identify them.

Relatedly, neuroanatomical evidence points toward a distinction between two visual pathways leading from the visual cortex—the dorsal pathway projecting to the posterior parietal cortex and the ventral pathway leading to the inferotemporal cortex. The functional distinction between the dorsal and ventral pathways was originally construed in terms of the distinction between "where" and "what," with the dorsal stream primarily involved

4. See the essays in section I of Prinz and Hommel 2002 for surveys of current thinking in this area. The tutorial by Rossetti and Pisella is particularly helpful. See also Jacob and Jeannerod 2003.

in computing distance and location and the ventral stream specialized for the type of color and form processing that feeds into object identification (Ungerleider and Mishkin 1982). Subsequent investigation suggested that the dorsal pathway is also involved in computing the "how" of action (Milner and Goodale 1995).

The "two visual systems" hypothesis offers an interesting example of how behavior can be explained in terms of the representation of micro-features. One of the striking pieces of experimental data that has emerged from investigation of the differences between vision for action and vision for identification is that the two systems can come into conflict. We see this, for example, in work that has been done on visual illusions, where the illusions have a much greater effect on perceptual reports than on action performance. The Ebbinghaus size contrast illusion is a case in point.

As the diagram in figure 10.1 indicates, a circle surrounded by other circles will appear smaller if the surrounding circles are enlarged. When (normal) subjects are presented with two circles of the same size, one of which is surrounded by small circles and the other surrounded by large circles, they will reliably judge the one surrounded by small circles to be larger than the one surrounded by large circles. Yet the illusion does not carry over to action. When subjects are asked to reach out as if they were going to pick up the circles, their grip aperture is constant for the two circles (Aglioti, DeSouza, and Goodale 1995). Similar effects have been observed with Müller-Lyer and Ponzo illusions. The dissociations between behavior and report in these visual illusions suggest that we respond to properties such as graspability that are a function of the size of the object and yet

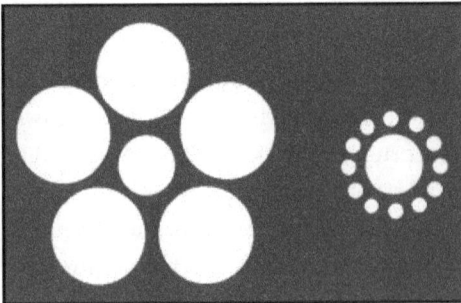

Figure 10.1
The Ebbinghaus size contrast illusion.

are clearly distinct from the object's perceived size. These are microfeatures that it is difficult to assimilate within the conceptual framework of commonsense psychology. It is a key tenet of commonsense psychology, for example, that we act on objects in virtue of how they appear to us, so that it is because an object looks a certain size to us that we make the appropriate hand movements for grasping it.[5] Yet the experimental evidence suggests that things cannot be as simple as this. If subjects acted on how objects appear to them (more strictly: on how they report objects appearing to them) then they would act differently in the two cases. Instead, it looks as if subjects are sensitive to properties of objects that are correlated with actual size but are independent of perceived size in a way that operates outside the realm of conscious awareness.

The Dimensional-Action System

The neuroscience of vision points to links between perception and action that are based on the representation of microfeatures and that shortcut anything that might plausibly be described as "central processing." Intriguing recent results in perceptual psychology provide further examples of such microfeature-based perception–action links.

Traditional information processing accounts make a sharp distinction between perceptual processing and post-perceptual processing and see all motor processing and response selection as falling clearly on the post-perceptual side of the divide. Whereas perceptual processing is widely held to involve the separate processing of microfeatures (with shape, form, color, and so on all being processed in neurally distinct areas), post-perceptual processing is thought to take place downstream of the "binding" of those microfeatures to form representations of objects. Yet some intriguing recent experimental evidence has led theorists to postulate highly specialized perception–action links that are explicitly tied to the perception of microfeatures (Cohen and Feintuch 2002). As with the dissociations discussed in the previous section, the experimental evidence seems to show that we can act on isolated features of objects in complete independence of other features of those objects. Researchers have known for a long time that there are regions of the mammalian visual system perceptually sensitive simply to color or to shape, but it has always been thought that we can only act on the world by somehow combining these separately processed features into

5. For further related discussion, see Clark 2001 and Briscoe and Schwenkler 2015.

representations of objects—into representations that operate at the symbolic level of commonsense psychology, rather than at the subsymbolic level of microfeatures.[6] This assumption appears to be called into question by research into the dimensional action system.

One representative set of experiments was carried out with the so-called flanker task interference paradigm. Subjects are instructed to make differential responses to types of object presented at the center of a display while ignoring peripheral distractors flanking the target object. In the experiments reported by Cohen and Shoup (1997) the targets and responses were as follows. The first response was to be made to the appearance either of a red vertical line or of a blue right diagonal line, while the second was to be made to the appearance either of a green vertical line or of a blue left diagonal line. So, if the target object had a vertical orientation the appropriate response could only be made on the basis of color, while if it was blue the appropriate response could only be made on the basis of orientation. The distractors were lines of varying colors and orientations.

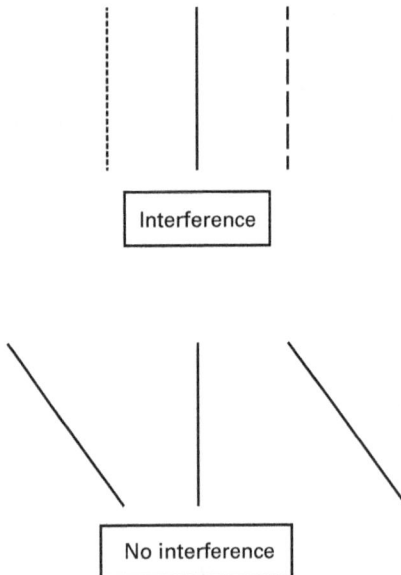

Figure 10.2
The flanker task interference paradigm. Short dashes = blue; solid lines = red; long dashes = yellow.

6. This assumption is what gives rise to the binding problem in the psychology and neuroscience of consciousness (Triesman 1996).

Strikingly, interference effects were observed only when the relevant responses for target and distractor were on the same dimension. So, for example, there would be an interference effect if a red vertical line were flanked by differently colored vertical lines, but not if it were flanked by red diagonal lines. Similarly, there would be interference if a blue left diagonal were flanked by other diagonal lines, but not if it were flanked by differently colored vertical lines. The conclusion drawn is that there are distinct processing channels linking the detection of individual microfeatures (a particular orientation, or a particular color) with particular responses. These processing channels operate without any "binding" of the relevant microfeatures.

In this case it is not the microfeatures themselves that is surprising, or the fact that we are able to act on perceived color and perceived shape. What is surprising, and difficult to assimilate within the conceptual framework of propositional attitude psychology, is that there seem to be perception–action links triggered by representations of microfeatures that are independent of representations of objects, or indeed of representations of other microfeatures.

The Ecological Approach to Perception and Action

J. J. Gibson's ecological approach to perception and action (Gibson 1966, 1979) is best known for the claim that the line between perception and cognition is far less sharply defined than it is standardly taken to be. We have ways of perceiving the world that have direct implications for action. Frequently what we perceive are the possibilities that the environment "affords" for action, so that we can act on how we perceive the world to be, without having to form or exploit beliefs and other propositional attitudes. An affordance is a resource or support that the environment offers a particular creature (the possibility of shelter, for example, or the availability of food). These affordances are objective features of the environment that are supposed to be directly perceived in the patterns of light in what Gibson terms the optic flow. Gibsonian psychologists describe organisms as "resonating to" or "directly sensitive to" the affordances in the distal environment.

To get from this basic claim about affordances to a direct challenge to the hegemony of the propositional attitudes, we need to consider the general account of the workings of perception that underlies Gibsonian claims about the direct perception of affordances. One of Gibson's major contributions to the study of vision is the proposal to reconstrue the visual field as a constantly moving and constantly reconfiguring set of illuminated surfaces and concomitant solid visual angles, rather than in terms of empty space containing bounded objects (figures on a ground). We do not, he thinks, ever see empty space surrounding discrete objects. What we see is a complex and gapless structure of surfaces. Some of these surfaces are surfaces of objects, while others are not (the various surfaces in the sky, for example). To each surface there corresponds a solid visual angle with its base at the face of the visible surface and its apex at the point of observation. We can, for simplicity's sake, think of these solid angles as cones, although of course their shape will vary with the visible outline of the surface in question. As the observer moves through the environment, the solid angles change, as one surface moves in front of another (relative to the perceiver) or as the observer approaches or moves away from the surface. This is the optic flow.

The ecological analysis of visual perception gives us an example of how representation in terms of microfeatures might work in practice. There is a fundamental mismatch between a characterization of the distal environment in terms of objects and properties (of the sort that might feature in specifications of propositional attitudes) and a characterization of the distal environment in terms of optic flow. Gibson's perspective on perception rests on the perception of microfeatures that resist assimilation to macrofeatures. These microfeatures include, for example:

• texture gradients (the decrease with distance of discriminable fineness of detail)
• the focus of expansion (the aiming point of locomotion that is also the vanishing point of optic flow)
• visual solid angles

Gibsonian accounts of perception attempt to show how behavior is controlled by perceptual sensitivity toward these microfeatures, which are properties of the global optic array, rather than of individual objects. Within its sphere of applicability, Gibsonian psychology certainly seems to provide an account of the "springs of action" that supports the narrow view of folk psychology by offering explanations of behavior that resist assimilation to the concepts and categories of propositional attitude psychology.

Dynamic Touch and Rotational Inertia

Perceptual psychologists working within a broadly Gibsonian tradition on the phenomenon of dynamic touch have provided good examples of behaviors that can be shown to involve responding to microfeatures of the environment that resist assimilation within the conceptual framework of commonsense psychology. It is well known that people can make accurate assessments of the spatial properties of objects by manipulating those objects. So, for example, people are remarkably accurate at detecting the length of objects by grasping those objects at a single point and moving the object around (without running their fingers over the whole object). One can get a feel for the phenomenon by picking up a pen, closing one's eyes, and rotating the pen with one's fingers—or taking a slightly larger object, such as a ruler, and rotating it around one's wrist.

Dynamic touch is a puzzling phenomenon, because the haptic system has no access to any direct perceptual information about the length of the pen or the ruler. The physiological underpinnings of dynamic touch are mechanoreceptors that provide information about the stretching, contraction, and twisting of muscles and tendons. Very little work is done by receptors on the surface of the skin, even at the point where contact is made with the object. Clearly there is some mechanical property (or properties) of objects that is reliably correlated with changes in the mechanoreceptors. The obvious candidates are weight and rotational force (torque), but neither of these can do the job. Perceived length is independent of both weight and torque, as can easily be appreciated by manipulating a pen and a pencil of the same length but different weights, and by manipulating both of them with different twisting forces. The key mechanical property must remain invariant through changes in torque and weight.

It turns out (Turvey 1996; Carello and Turvey 2004) that the relevant physical invariant is what is known as the inertia ellipsoid. The inertia ellipsoid is, roughly speaking, a way of characterizing an object that measures the object's resistance to being rotated. It is derived from the object's principal moments of inertia, where a principal moment of inertia quantifies an object's resistance to rotation around one of its axes of symmetry. An object's moment of inertia will vary according to the distribution of its mass, with higher concentrations of mass away from the object's center of gravity yielding a higher moment of inertia. So, for example, suppose we hang a weight from a metal rod. The further away the attachment point is from the rod's center of gravity, the greater the moment of inertia—and the more force will be required to rotate it. Once we know an object's axes of symmetry and its principal moments of inertia, we can characterize its overall resistance to being rotated in terms of an ellipse whose center is the intersection of the three axes of symmetry and whose surface is obtained from the reciprocal of the square roots of the principal moments of inertia.

It is a robust finding that an object's rotational inertia, as given by the inertia ellipsoid, is the invariant underlying perceived length. Nor is length the only quantity that can be detected by perceived touch. People can make reliable estimates of an object's weight from picking up the object. Amazeen and Turvey (1996) have established that perceived heaviness is also a function of rotational inertia, both when perceived heaviness accurately tracks and object's weight and when (as in the size-weight illusion) it leads to misleading estimates.[7]

This sensitivity to rotational inertia is a further example of the type of microfeatural sensitivity suggested by the Gibsonian approach to perception and action. We act on the world in virtue of our perceptual attunement to properties of objects and of the optic array that are fundamentally alien to the conceptual framework of commonsense psychology. The inertial ellipsoid is a mathematical object that stands to our commonsense thinking about objects and their dynamic and kinematic properties in something like the relation that the rules of transformational grammar stand to our everyday use of English. Subtle experimental work is required to identify rotational inertia as the relevant parameter in our haptic sensitivity to the spatial properties of objects.

The Influence of Situation in Social Psychology

The "springs of action" have been investigated by social psychologists as well as cognitive psychologists and neuroscientists. The research has been two pronged, investigating both why people behave the way they do and how we interpret that behavior. Two features of this research are particularly salient in the present context. The first has to do with the genesis of behavior. An overwhelming body of evidence highlights the importance of

7. The size-weight illusion is the illusion that larger objects of the same weight are perceived as heavier.

the situation in determining behavior. Situational changes that might seem at first sight to be insignificant have been shown to have a serious impact on behavior. The second feature is that subjects systematically underestimate the significance of the situation, making what has come to be known as the "fundamental attribution error" of overestimating the significance of character traits and personality in explaining and predicting behavior.

In one famous set of experiments (Darley and Batson 1973), groups of students at a Princeton theological seminary were sent from one building to another as part of an experiment putatively on religious education. Their task in the second building was to give a talk, with one group giving a talk on the Good Samaritan and another on jobs in seminaries. On the way over they passed an experimenter slumped in a doorway and moaning. Overall, 40 percent of the subjects stopped to offer some sort of assistance. What is striking, though, is the drastic difference between subjects who were told that they were running late (only 10 percent offered assistance) and subjects who were told that they had time to spare (where the figure was 63 percent). This discrepancy did not seem to be correlated with any other differences between the participants.

Other experiments have found what seem *prima facie* to be even more trivial situational factors having a large impact on behavior. Mathews and Canon (1975) explored the influence of ambient noise, showing that subjects are five times less likely to help an apparently injured man who has dropped some books when there is a power mower running nearby than when ambient noise is at normal levels. Isen and Levin (1972) found an another striking effect, discovering that people who had just found a dime were twenty-two times more likely to help a woman who had dropped some papers than people who had not found a dime. Experiments such as these have been carried out many times, and the powerful influence of situational factors has proved to be robust.

This experimental tradition poses numerous interesting philosophical problems, particularly with respect to the role that character plays in ethical theory (Doris 2002). For present purposes, what is interesting is the perspective that situationist social psychology casts on the genesis of behavior. It looks very much as if features of situations that do not in any sense count as commonsense psychological reasons for action can play a large role in determining how people behave. At least in the experimental paradigms it seems fundamentally inappropriate to seek explanations in terms of propositional attitudes that act as reasons for action. An important element in the springs of action seems to be relatively low-level features of the situation—what might, in fact, be termed situational microfeatures.

3   Computational Issues for the Broad Construal

Moving from the springs of action to social understanding and social coordination, let me begin with some very general computational reasons for skepticism about the idea that we can navigate the social world only through the conceptual framework of folk psychology.

The vast majority of our social interactions involve almost instantaneous adjustments to the behavior of others, whereas folk psychological explanation is a complicated and protracted business. It is no easy matter to attribute beliefs and desires and then to work either backward from those beliefs and desires to an explanation or forward to a prediction. According to the standard understanding of folk psychology as involving the application of a tacitly known theory of human behavior (the theory theory), to apply folk-psychological explanation is to subsume observable behavior and utterances under general principles linking observable behavior to mental states, mental states to other mental states, and mental states to behavior. As many authors have stressed, the application of these principles requires identifying, among a range of possible principles that might apply, the ones that are the most salient in a given situation. It requires identifying whether the appropriate background conditions hold, or whether there are countervailing factors in play. It requires thinking through the implications of the principles one does choose to apply in order to extrapolate their explanatory or predictive consequences. It would be an overreaction to suggest that the need to do all these things makes folk-psychological generalizations essentially useless. But it certainly makes them rather unwieldy. And it is no surprise that the paradigms of folk-psychological explanations given by theory theorists tend to be complicated inferences of the sort either found in the final chapters of detective novels (e.g., Lewis) or in dramatic and self-questioning soliloquies (e.g., Fodor). These are indeed striking cognitive achievements, but it seems odd to take them as paradigms of interpersonal cognition. Do our everyday cognitive interactions with people really involve deducing hypotheses from general principles, drawing out the deductive consequences (more accurately: the *relevant* deductive consequences) of those general principles, and then putting those hypotheses before the tribunal of experience?

The practical difficulties here are obscured by the narrow range of examples that tend to be considered. Folk-psychological explanation is usually considered by philosophers to be a one-on-one activity. This is exactly what one would expect given that the paradigms are the detective drawing together the strands of the case, or the puzzled lover trying to decode the behavior of her paramour. But social understanding is rarely as circumscribed as this. In many types of social interaction, a wide range of people is involved and the behavior of any one of them is inextricably linked with the behavior of the others. Suppose that the social understanding involved in such examples of social coordination is modeled folk psychologically. This would require each participant to make predictions about the likely behavior of other participants, based on an assessment of what those participants want to achieve and what they believe about their environment. For each participant, of course, the most relevant part of the environment will be the other participants. So, my prediction of what another participant will do depends on my beliefs about what he believes the other participants will do. The other participants' beliefs about what the other participants will do are in turn dependent on what they believe the other participants believe. And so on.

Plainly, there will be many layers in the ensuing regress, and the process of coming to a stable set of beliefs that will allow one to participate effectively in the coordinated activity will be lengthy and computationally demanding. Of course, none of this shows that there are any objections in principle to modeling coordinative social understanding in folk-psychological terms. Any such claim would be absurd, not least because we have a well-worked out mathematical theory that allows us to model social understanding in what are essentially folk-psychological terms (or at least a regimentation of them). Game theory is a theory of social coordination and strategic interaction using analogues of the folk psychological notions of belief and desires (in the guise of probability and utility assignments). What thinking about computational tractability should do, however, is at least to begin to cast doubt on whether this could be a correct account of the form of social understanding in the vast majority of situations.

The issue here should be distinguished from the debate between theory theorists and simulation theorists about how best to characterize folk psychology. Simulation theorists often appeal to considerations of computational tractability as evidence against the theory theory (Heal 1986). But computational problems arise equally for the simulation theory. Since a simulation simply involves using one's own mind as a model of the minds of the other participants in the interaction, a simulator would still need to plug into the decision-making processes an appropriate set of inputs for all the other participants and then run simultaneous simulations for all of them.

This is multiply problematic, however. There is, first of all, a straightforward question about how many simulations it is possible to run simultaneously. Since the practical details of how the process of simulation might work have not really been explored, there is little concrete to say about this. *Prima facie*, however, one might think that there will be some difficulties with the idea of multiple simultaneous simulations, given that a simulation is supposed to work by running one's own decision-making processes off-line and those processes are, presumably, designed to give an output for a single set of inputs. But there is an even more serious problem. The simultaneous simulations will not be independent of each other. Suppose that the interaction contains three participants, A, B, and C, in addition to me. To simulate B properly, I will need to have views about what A and C will do—without that information I will not have any sense of what initial beliefs it would be reasonable to attribute to B. But, by parity of reasoning, this information about what A and C will do will depend on each of them having information about what the other participants will do. It is very difficult to see how the notion of simulation can be stretched to accommodate not just simultaneous simulations, but simultaneous simulations that are interdependent. So, the simulation theory, no less than the theory theory, is bound to confront problems of computational tractability.

4   Social Understanding and Social Coordination without Propositional Attitudes?

The computational considerations just canvassed suggest that many aspects of social coordination and interaction might be accomplished by forms of social understanding that do not make use of the attribution of folk-psychological states—forms of social understanding that allow coordinated activity and social interaction without any metarepresentational interpretation of the other participants in the social transaction. But do we have any understanding of how this might take place? This section explores some areas of social coordination and interaction that it does seem to be possible to understand in non-folk-psychological terms.

Perception of emotion is a good place to start. The form and level of one's participation in social interactions is frequently a function of one's assessment of the emotional states of other participants. This is most clear when the interaction is a competitive one—a zero-sum game, for example (taking a game in the technical sense as a strategic interaction among players). It may be to my advantage, for example, to press ahead to take advantage of another participant's dilatoriness—or to retreat and retrench when I notice the aggressiveness of one of the competitors. But something similar holds for cooperative interactions. My own commitment to a shared project is likely to be at least partly determined by my sense of the extent to which my partners value the shared goal. And the exact form of my participation in the shared activity will be tailored to how I read my partners' varying and changing levels of enthusiasm. I need to be sensitive to whether and when my partners are bullish, bearish, frustrated, or enthusiastic. Without this we will not be able to work together effectively.

The various types of emotion perception implicated in social interactions have three important features. First, they are highly diachronic. Social interactions are extended processes in which the relevant affective valences are constantly changing. Successfully negotiating such interactions is not in any sense a matter of identifying relatively long-term dispositional states or character traits (the raw materials of propositional attitude psychology). The affective indices are in constant flux. Think, for example, of the emotional dynamics of a team game or a committee meeting. This makes folk-psychological attributions, whether derived through a process of simulation or through the application of a theory, particularly inapposite. The processes by which folk-psychological attributions are reached are too unwieldy to permit of rapid real-time monitoring and revision. Second, in many social interactions the actual content of the relevant affective and emotional states will be apparent from the context. Participants need to be sensitive not to what is represented but rather to the fine details of the attitudes taken to what can be presumed to be shared representational contents. The third point is the least obvious, but perhaps the most important. What matters in social interactions and coordinated activities is that the participants succeed in acting with due sensitivity to the affective and emotional states of other participants. There is no need for those affective and emotional states to be explicitly identified and attributed. These forms of social understanding do not require forming judgments about the emotional states of the other participants.

This last point needs to be emphasized. The simple claim that emotion perception is frequently subliminal and a matter of pattern recognition should be uncontroversial. It is clear that in many cases we directly perceive emotional states. This in itself does not count against the broad conception of folk psychology. Directly perceived emotional states can easily serve as inputs to the processes of simulation, or as the raw material to which the generalizations of theoretical folk psychology are applied. But my claim, rather, is that that we frequently act on the perception of emotional and affective states without explicitly identifying them. We regulate our own behavior as a function of our sensitivity to the emotional and affective states of those with whom we are interacting without at any point making explicit the identifications on which our behavior rests. Sensitivity to emotional states feeds directly into action without any attribution of emotional states. This is incompatible with the broad construal of the domain of folk psychology, for the essence of the broad construal is that social understanding requires categorizing the behavior of others in the concepts of folk psychology, in order to bring to bear either the mechanisms of simulation or the appropriate tacitly known theory.

Still, we have been considering types of social understanding that are all highly circumscribed. The issue is often not what other participants will do but how they will do it, since we may well know that other participants are constrained to act within narrowly prescribed limits. These are often not situations in which issues of explanation and prediction arise in the sort of ways for which one might think that folk-psychological forms of social understanding would be required. Moreover, the fact that many social interactions involve an element of "affect attunement" that is achieved without recourse to folk psychology hardly shows that no element of those interactions is controlled folk psychologically. Even someone sympathetic to the general line that many basic forms of social interaction fall outside the domain of folk psychology might pose the question of whether the type of deflationary account I have been offering really counts against the broad construal of the domain of folk psychology.

Let me start with the question of what happens in interpersonal situations that are *not* circumscribed by shared goals or a relatively small number of clearly defined possible outcomes. Those favoring the broad construal of the domain of folk psychology will suggest that, as soon as we move beyond highly circumscribed collaborative enterprises such as games or fixing an airplane, we enter a realm of interpersonal interaction that can be successfully negotiated only by fitting the behavior of other participants into the conceptual framework of folk psychology. In fact, however, it is far from clear that this is the case. The well-studied game-theoretical problem of how to behave in an indefinitely iterated prisoner's dilemma is a case in point, and one that has plausibly been argued to have wide application.

A prisoner's dilemma is any strategic interaction in which the dominant strategy for each player leads inevitably to a suboptimal outcome for all players. A dominant strategy for a given player is one that is more advantageous to that player than any other possible strategy, whatever the other players might do (it *dominates* any possible counterstrategy).[8] Although some authors have tried to argue otherwise, it is hard to see how it can be anything but rational to follow the dominant strategy in a *one-off* strategic interaction that obeys the logic of the prisoner's dilemma. But what about social interactions that have the same logic but are repeated?

Repeated interactions create the possibility of one player rewarding another for not having implicated him (or whatever the relevant noncooperative activity might be). Surely this will change what it is rational to do. In fact, however, it only does so in a limited range of situations. The well-known backward induction argument suggests that the rational course

8. In the standard example from which the problem derives its name, the two players are prisoners being separately interrogated by a police chief who is convinced of their guilt, but as yet lacks conclusive evidence. He proposes to each of them that they implicate the other, and explains the possible consequences. If each prisoner implicates the other then they will both end up with a sentence of five years in prison. If neither implicates the other, then they will each be convicted of a lesser offense and both end up with a sentence of two years in prison. If either prisoner implicates the other without being implicated himself, however, he will go free while the other receives ten years in prison. The dominant strategy for each player is to implicate the other. Since we are dealing with rational players who know each other to be rational, it follows that each will implicate the other, resulting in both spending five years in prison—even though had they both kept quiet they would have ended up with just two years apiece.

of action where one is certain in advance how many strategic interactions there will be will be to defect on the first play.[9] It is only when it is not known how many plays there will be that scope opens up for cooperative play. And this is where we rejoin the question of the domain of folk psychology. Suppose that we find ourselves, as we frequently do, in social situations that have the structure of an indefinitely repeated prisoner's dilemma. The issue may simply be how hard one pulls one's weight in the department.[10] It will be to my advantage to skip the examination meeting, provided that my colleagues do my work for me. But how will that affect their behavior when we next need to wine and dine a visiting speaker? Will I find myself dining tête-à-tête and footing the bill on my own?

It is natural to have two thoughts at this point. The first is that before I decide whether or not to skip the examination meeting I had better think about the potential consequences of future interactions. The second is that I can only do this by making a complex set of predictions about what my colleagues will do, based on my assessment of their preference orderings and their beliefs about the probability of each of us defecting as opposed to cooperating, and then factor in my own beliefs about how what will happen in future depends on whether or not I come to the examination meeting—and so on. This, of course, would be an application of the general explanatory framework of folk psychology (again on the simplification that utilities and probability assignments are regimentations of desires and beliefs). The broad construal of the domain of folk psychology is committed to saying that this is the way decision making proceeds in strategic situations of these kinds—simply because these strategic situations depend on social understanding and, according to the broad construal, all social understanding more complex than simple sensitivity to the emotional and effective states of others has to be a matter of folk-psychological explanation and prediction.

Even if we can make sense of the idea that strategic interaction involves these kinds of complicated multilayered predictions involving expectations

9. On the plausibility of the backward induction argument, see Bovens 1997 and Bermúdez 1999.

10. This is not, strictly speaking, a prisoner's dilemma, since it involves more than two players. The multiperson equivalent of the prisoner's dilemma is usually known as the tragedy of the commons.

about the expectations that other people are expected to have, one might wonder whether there is a simpler way of determining how to behave in that sort of situation. Game theorists have directed considerable attention to the idea that social interactions with the form of indefinitely repeated prisoner's dilemmas might best be modeled through simple heuristic strategies in which, to put it crudely, one bases one's plays not on how one expects others to behave but rather on how they have behaved in the past. The best known of these heuristic strategies is tit-for-tat, which is composed of the following two rules:

Always cooperate in the first round.
In any subsequent round do what your opponent did in the previous round.

The tit-for-tat strategy is very simple to apply, and does not involve any complicated folk-psychological attributions or explanations/predictions. All that is required is an understanding of the two basic options available to each player, and an ability to recognize which one of those strategies has been applied by other players in a given case. The very simplicity of the strategy explains why theorists have found it such a potentially powerful explanatory tool in explaining such phenomena as the evolutionary emergence of altruistic behavior (see Axelrod 1984 for an accessible introduction and Maynard Smith 1982 and Skyrms 1996 for more detailed discussion).

Of course, I am not suggesting that we should model extended social interactions in terms of tit-for-tat. Tit-for-tat has only a limited applicability to practical decision making, simply because, in a situation in which two players are each playing tit-for-tat, a single defection will rule out the possibility of any further cooperation. This is clearly undesirable, particularly given the possibility in any moderately complicated social interaction that what appears to be a defection is not really a defection (suppose, for example, that my colleague misses the examination meeting because his car broke down). So any plausible version of the tit-for-tat strategy will have to build in some mechanisms for following apparent defections with cooperation, in order both to identify where external factors have influenced the situation and to allow players the possibility of building bridges back toward cooperation even after genuine defection.

The important point is that strategies such as tit-for-tat do not involve any exploitation of the categories of folk psychology. They can be followed without the attribution of folk-psychological states to those with whom one is interacting. In fact, a stronger conclusion is warranted. Such strategies do not involve any processes of explanation or prediction at all. It is clear that no prediction is required, given that what I do in any particular situation is determined by how I interpret what the other player did in the previous encounter. It may seem that this introduction of the notion of interpretation allows folk-psychological notions of explanation to get a grip, but this would be a mistake. To apply tit-for-tat, or some descendant thereof, all I need to do is to work out whether the behavior of another player should best be characterized as a cooperation or a defection—and indeed to work out which previous behaviors are relevant to the ongoing situation. This will often be achievable without going into the details of why that player behaved as he or she did. Of course, sometimes it will be necessary to explore issues of motivation before an action can be characterized as a defection or a cooperation—and sometimes it will be very important to do this, given that identifying an action as a defection is no light matter. But much of the time, one might well get by perfectly well without going deeply at all into why another agent behaved as he or she did.

From a game-theoretical point of view, therefore, there is nothing mysterious about the idea that one can act effectively in complicated social interactions without bringing to bear the explanatory and predictive apparatus of folk psychology. Within game theory, construed as a normative theory of rational behavior, it can make perfectly good sense to adopt strategies that are, in an important sense, folk-psychologically "blind." The real question is the extent to which the normative theory applies descriptively. How frequently do we employ heuristically simple strategies in social interactions, taking our cue from very simple understandings of what other people have done—rather than from complicated attributions of folk-psychological states? The general considerations canvassed in the previous section seem to suggest that it's likely that we do. At the very least, this brief trip into game theory gives us a way of interpreting in non-folk-psychological terms a large class of social interactions that are *not* circumscribed by shared goals or a relatively small number of clearly defined possible outcomes.

To take stock, I have made a case for two claims:

(I) The form and level of one's participation in many social interactions is often a function of one's assessment of the emotional states of other participants in a way that feeds directly into action without any attribution of emotional states. This frequently occurs in social interactions circum-scribed by shared goals or a relatively small number of clearly defined pos-sible outcomes. Many such activities are controlled without anything that looks like a folk-psychological attribution at all.

(II)   We can participate effectively in social interactions that are not so circumscribed without making use of the predictive and explanatory appa-ratus of folk psychology.

But what about social interactions that do not fall under either (I) or (II)? *Ex hypothesi* these social interactions require explaining and predict-ing the behavior of others. Have we now arrived within the domain of folk psychology? As matters are generally understood by philosophers we must have arrived there, simply because it is pleonastic that explanation and prediction proceed in folk-psychological terms.

There is an important class of social interactions, however, in which it is true both that they involve predicting and/or explaining the actions of other participants and that the relevant predictions and explanations do not seem to proceed via the attribution of folk-psychological states. These are situations involving stereotypical routines and behavior patterns. Let us start with two very simple examples. Whenever one goes into a shop or a restaurant, for example, it is obvious that the situation can only be effectively negotiated if one has certain beliefs about why people are doing what they are doing and about how they will continue to behave. I can't effectively order dinner without interpreting the behavior of the person who approaches me with a pad in his hand, or buy some meat for dinner without interpreting the person standing behind the counter. But do I need to attribute folk-psychological states to these people in order to interpret them? Must these beliefs about what people are doing involve second-order beliefs about their psychological states? Surely not. Ordering meals in res-taurants and buying meat in butcher's shops are such routine situations that all one needs to do is to identify the person approaching the table as a waiter, or the person standing behind the counter as a butcher. That is all the interpretation required. These are both cases in which simply identify-ing social roles provides enough leverage on the situation to allow one to predict the behavior of other participants and to understand why they are behaving as they are. There is no need to make any folk-psychological attri-butions. There is no need to think about what the waiter might desire or the butcher believe—any more than they need to think about what I believe or desire. The point is not that the routine is cognitively transparent—that it is easy to work out what the other participants are thinking. Rather, it is that we don't need to have any thoughts about what is going on in their minds at all. The social interaction takes care of itself once the social roles have been identified (and I've decided what I want to eat).

The basic lesson to be drawn from highly stereotypical social interactions such as these is that explanation and prediction *need not* require the attribution of folk-psychological states. It would be too strong even to say that identifying someone as a waiter is identifying him as someone with a typical set of desires and beliefs about how best to achieve those desires. Identifying someone as a waiter is not a matter of understanding him in folk-psychological terms at all. It is understanding him as a person who typically behaves in certain ways within a network of social practices that typically unfold in certain ways. The point is that this is a case in which our understanding of individuals and their behavior is parasitic on our understanding of the social practices in which their behavior takes place. Nor, of course, is this understanding of social practices a matter of mastery of a primitive theory. We learn through experience that certain social cues are correlated with certain behavior patterns on the part of others and certain expectations from those same individuals as to how we ourselves should behave. Sometimes we have these correlations pointed out to us explicitly—more often we pick them up by monitoring the reactions of others when we fail to conform properly to the "script" for the situation.

This dimension of social understanding involves a type of reasoning clearly different from how folk-psychological reasoning is understood according to either the theory theory or the simulation theory. For proponents of the theory theory, social understanding involves what is essentially subsumptive reasoning. Folk psychology is a matter of subsuming patterns of behavior under generalizations and deducing the relevant consequences. For proponents of the simulation theory, in contrast, folk-psychological reasoning is a matter of running one's own decision-making processes off-line and feeding appropriate propositional attitude inputs into them for the person one is interpreting. For social understanding that involves exploiting one's knowledge of social routines and stereotypes, however, the principal modes of reasoning are similarity based and analogy based. Social understanding becomes a matter of matching perceived social situations to prototypical social situations and working by analogy from partial similarities. We do not store general principles about how social situations work, but rather have a general template for particular types of situation with parameters than can be adjusted to allow for differences in detail across the members of a particular social category. Researchers in artificial intelligence have called these social templates *frames*.[11]

The frame-based approach has obvious applicability to scenarios such as that in the restaurant. But is it natural to ask how much of our everyday social interaction can be modeled in this way? How much of our social understanding is a function of our mastery of social roles, frames and routines? The tentative hypothesis with which I would like to end is: rather more than we think. It would be odd, given the element of repetition in all our social lives, if we had to start *ab initio* each time we participate in a repeated social interaction—if we operated with general principles that need to be tailored to meet the demands of specific situations, with all the difficulties of relevance that such tailoring involves.

But what happens when we find ourselves in unfamiliar social situations? What happens when none of our frames can be brought to bear; when we have no obvious contextual cues that will allow us to get a handle on the likely behavior patterns of the other people with whom we are engaging; when the interaction is open ended and the potential payoffs and trade-offs too unclear for it to count as an instance of a type of prisoner's dilemma strategic interaction? Again, let me offer a tentative suggestion. Perhaps it is here that we arrive at the proper domain of folk psychology. The social world is often transparent, easily comprehensible in terms of frames, social roles, and social routines. Other agents can be predicted in terms of their participation in those routines and roles, while their emotional and affective states can simply be read off from their facial expression and the "tenor" of their behavior. When the social world is in this way "ready-to-hand," to borrow from Heidegger's characterization of the practical understanding of tools, we have no use for the reflective apparatus of folk psychology. We do not need to bring to bear the machinery of folk-psychological attribution to navigate through the social world, to accommodate ourselves to the needs and requirements of other people and to succeed in coordinated activities. But sometimes the social world becomes opaque. We find ourselves in social

11. The *locus classicus* is Minsky 1974/1997.

interactions where it is not obvious what is going on; which cannot easily be assimilated to prototypical social situations; where we cannot work out what to do simply on the basis of previous interactions with the other participants. And it is at this point that we find ourselves in need of the type of metarepresentational thinking characteristic of folk psychology—not as a mainstay of our social understanding, but rather as the last resort to which we turn when all the standard mechanisms of social understanding and interpersonal accommodation break down.

References

Aglioti, S., J. F. X. DeSouza, and M. A. Goodale. 1995. Size-contrast illusions deceive the eye but not the hand. *Current Biology* 5:679–685.

Amazeen, E. L., and M. T. Turvey. 1996. Weight perception and the haptic size-weight illusion are functions of the inertia tensor. *Journal of Experimental Psychology: Human Perception and Performance* 22:213–232.

Axelrod, R. 1984. *The Evolution of Cooperation*. Harmondsworth: Penguin.

Bermúdez, J. L. 1999. Rationality and the backwards induction argument. *Analysis* 59:243–248.

Bermúdez, J. L. 2003. The domain of folk psychology. In *Royal Institute of Philosophy Supplement*, ed. A. O'Hear. Cambridge: Cambridge University Press.

Bermúdez, J. L. 2005a. Arguing for eliminativism. In *Paul Churchland*, ed. B. L. Keeley. Cambridge: Cambridge University Press.

Bovens, L. 1997. The backward induction argument for the finite iterated prisoner's dilemma and the surprise exam paradox. *Analysis* 57:179–186.

Briscoe, R., and J. Schwenkler. 2015. Conscious vision in action. *Cognitive Science* 39:1435–1467.

Carello, C., and M. T. Turvey. 2004. Physics and psychology of the muscle sense. *Current Directions in Psychological Science* 13:25–28.

Carruthers, P., and P. K. Smith, eds. 1996. *Theories of Theory of Mind*. Cambridge: Cambridge University Press.

Churchland, P. M. 1981. Eliminative materialism and the propositional attitudes. *Journal of Philosophy* 78:67–90.

Churchland, P. M. 1989. Folk psychology and the explanation of human behavior'. *Philosophical Perspectives* 3:225–241.

Churchland, P. M. 1992. Activation vectors vs. propositional attitudes: How the brain represents reality. *Philosophy and Phenomenological Research* 52 (2): 419–424.

Churchland, P. M. 1998. Conceptual similarity across sensory and neural diversity: The Fodor/Lepore challenge answered. *Journal of Philosophy* 65:5–32.

Churchland, P. M., and P. S. Churchland. 1998. *On the Contrary: Critical Essays, 1987–1997*. Cambridge, MA: MIT Press.

Churchland, P. S., and T. J. Sejnowski. 1992. *The Computational Brain*. Cambridge, MA: MIT Press.

Clark, A. 2001. Visual experience and motor action: Are the bonds too tight? *Philosophical Review* 110:495–519.

Cohen, A., and U. Feintuch. 2002. The dimensional-action system: A distinct visual system. In *Common Mechanisms in Perception and Action: Attention and Performance XIX*, ed. W. Prinz and B. Hommel. Oxford: Oxford University Press.

Cohen, A., and R. Shoup. 1997. Perceptual dimensional constraints on response selection processes. *Cognitive Psychology* 32:128–181.

Currie, G., and I. Ravenscroft. 2002. *Recreative Minds: Imagination in Philosophy and Psychology*. Oxford: Oxford University Press.

Darley, J. M., and D. Batson. 1973. From Jerusalem to Jericho: A study of situational and dispositional variables in helping behavior. 1973. *Journal of Personality and Social Psychology* 27:100–108.

Davidson, D. 1963. Actions, reasons, and causes. *Journal of Philosophy* 60: 685–700.

Davies, M. K., and T. Stone, eds. 1995. *Folk Psychology: The Theory of Mind Debate*. Oxford: Blackwell.

Doris, J. 2002. *Lack of Character*. New York: Cambridge University Press.

Fodor, J. 1987. *Psychosemantics*. Cambridge MA: MIT Press.

Gibson, J. J. 1966. *The Senses Considered as Perceptual Systems*. Boston: Houghton Mifflin.

Gibson, J. J. 1979. *The Ecological Approach to Visual Perception*. Boston: Houghton Mifflin.

Gopnik, A., and A. Meltzoff. 1997. *Words, Thoughts, and Theories*. Cambridge, MA: MIT Press.

Gordon, R. 1986. Folk psychology as simulation. *Mind and Language* 1:158–171.

Heal, J. 1986. Replication and functionalism. In *Language, Mind, and Logic*, ed. J. Butterfield. Cambridge: Cambridge University Press.

Isen, A. M., and P. A. Levin. 1972. Effect of feeling good on helping: Cookies and kindness. *Journal of Personality and Social Psychology* 21:384–388.

Jacob, P., and M. Jeannerod. 2003. *Ways of Seeing: The Scope and Limits of Visual Cognition*. New York: Oxford University Press.

Lewis, D. 1994. Reduction of mind. In *Companion to the Philosophy of Mind*, ed. S. Guttenplan. Oxford: Blackwell.

Macdonald, C., and G. Macdonald. 1995. *Connectionism: Debates in Psychological Explanation*. Oxford: Blackwell.

Mathews, K. E., and L. K. Canon. 1975. Environmental noise level as a determinant of helping behavior. *Journal of Personality and Social Psychology* 32:571–577.

Maynard Smith, J. 1982. *Evolution and the Theory of Games*. Cambridge: Cambridge University Press.

Milner, A. D., and M. A. Goodale. 1995. *The Visual Brain in Action*. Oxford: Oxford University Press.

Minsky, M. 1974/1997. A framework for representing knowledge. In *Mind Design II*, ed. J. Haugeland. Cambridge, MA: MIT Press.

Perner, J. 1993. *Understanding the Representational Mind*. Cambridge, MA: MIT Press.

Prinz, W., and B. Hommel. 2001. *Common Mechanisms in Perception and Action: Attention and Performance*, vol. 19. Oxford: Oxford University Press.

Skyrms, B. 1996. *The Evolution of the Social Contract*. Cambridge: Cambridge University Press.

Treisman, A. 1996. The binding problem. *Current Opinion in Neurobiology* 6.

Turvey, M. T. 1996. Dynamic touch. *American Psychologist* 51:1134–1151.

Ungerleider, L. G., and M. Mishkin. 1982. Two cortical visual systems. In *Analysis of Visual Behavior*, ed. D. J. Ingle, M. A. Goodale and R. J. W. Mansfield. Cambridge, MA: MIT Press.

Von Eckardt, B. 1993. *What Is Cognitive Science?* Cambridge, MA: MIT Press.

Von Eckardt, B. 1994. Folk Psychology (1). In *A Companion to Philosophy of Mind*, ed. S. Guttenplan, 300–307. Oxford: Blackwell.

Afterword: Looking Ahead

My principal reason for revisiting and combining the essays in this volume was that they all converge on and develop a small number of basic themes. In the introduction, I try to bring those themes out and explain how the individual essays contribute to developing them. However, the process of editing the essays and thinking about how they connect together had a consequence that I probably should have foreseen. It made very clear where more work needs to be done. For that reason, I was very pleased when the referees for this volume suggested that I write an afterword identifying some of the challenges (and, hopefully, opportunities) that lie ahead in this area. I welcome being able at least to identify some of the gaps and problems that remain, even if I am not in a position at the moment to fill and solve them. But since this enterprise may seem a little self-indulgent, I will strive for brevity.

Several of the essays highlight the importance of a broadly Gibsonian approach to visual perception as revealing a form of nonconceptual self-consciousness in the structure of "ordinary," outward-directed perception. These are also the earliest published essays in this volume. The philosophical discussion still seems to me to be sound, but there are several areas where it is plain that more work is needed. Chapter 1 briefly touches on the relation between Gibson's ecological approach to visual perception and ongoing research in the neuroscience and neuropsychology of vision, particularly the "two visual systems" hypothesis. According to that hypothesis, most prominently developed by David Milner and Melvyn Goodale, vision is subserved by two systems that are both functionally and neuroanatomically distinct (Goodale and Milner 1996). Milner and Goodale distinguish between vision for perception (primarily concerned with object recognition and object identification) and vision for action (primarily concerned with how vision informs motor behavior).

Some aspects of Gibson's idea that vision is simultaneously coperception of the self and the environment seem to fit uneasily within this bifurcation of vision. The essence of Gibson's notion of an affordance, for example, is that we typically cannot separate out how we perceive and identify objects from our capacity to act on them. By the same token, self-specifying information in vision plays a structuring role in both identification and action. Moreover, as discussed in chapter 10 in the context of the Ebbinghaus illusion, Milner and Goodale suggest that vision for action can nonconsciously present information about objects that conflicts with how those objects are consciously perceived. If this is right, it has potential consequences for the idea that affordances and self-specifying information are part of the (conscious) content of visual perception. So, interesting and important questions remain at the interface between the neuroscience of vision, the ecological approach to visual perception, and the theory of content.

Answering these questions will hopefully shed light on another issue, which is that we need a clearer model of how self-specifying information features in the content of visual perception. It would be a fair criticism to make of my discussion of Gibson that I focus exclusively on making the case that the various types of self-specifying information are part of the content of perception, without providing a substantive account of what that content is in order to illustrate *how* they can feature in it. This is particularly important, given that the notion of nonconceptual content can be somewhat elusive. Certainly, Peacocke's theory of scenario content (Peacocke 1992), which is the best-developed account of the nonconceptual content of perception, focuses (as currently developed) primarily on the exteroceptive (outward-directed), rather than proprioceptive (self-directed), dimension of vision. And, of course, a fully satisfying account of the nonconceptual content of perception would be, at a minimum, multimodal, incorporating touch and hearing (and, to a lesser extent, smell and taste), as well as vision. It would also, ideally, be integrated with a comprehensive account of the nonconceptual content of bodily awareness, in order to explain the representational grounds of intentional action.

Having such a substantive account of the nonconceptual content available would no doubt make it easier to elucidate much more clearly the complex epistemic relations between nonconceptual self-consciousness and conceptual self-consciousness. Some progress is made on this in the discussion of the epistemology of "taking at face value" in chapter 3, but there is much more to be done in elucidating the justificatory relations that hold between (self-) perception and (self-conscious) belief. From a personal perspective, I would hope that progress in this area might be made by integrating the discussion here of nonconceptual forms of self-awareness with the model of self-conscious thought and self-reference I developed in *Understanding "I": Language and Thought* (Bermúdez 2017).

One of the principal themes of *Understanding "I"* is that the capacity for self-conscious thought (as manifested in, but not of course exhausted by, the ability to use the first-person pronoun "I" with understanding) depends on the ability to think of oneself as an object uniquely located in space and following a single path through space-time. Developing insights from Gareth Evans's *The Varieties of Reference* (Evans 1982), I suggest that this ability can be understood in terms of practical capacities for self-location—for superimposing an egocentric understanding of space upon a nonegocentric cognitive map of the spatial environment. There are plainly affinities between that way of thinking about what it is to be a full-fledged self-conscious subject and the notion of a nonconceptual point of view developed in chapter 2—and, correspondingly, questions about how the notions relate to each other, both from a developmental perspective and from an epistemic perspective.

A further interesting avenue of inquiry concerns autobiographical memory. In *Understanding "I,"* I offer an account of why autobiographical memory has the immunity property (the property of being immune to error through misidentification: IEM) that emphasizes the relation between judgments based on autobiographical memory and the experienced episodes from which those judgments are derived. The basic idea is that a judgment based on autobiographical memory has the immunity property exactly when it is derived from an earlier experienced episode that at that earlier time either gave rise to, or could have given rise to, a judgment with the immunity property.[1] In many cases, these experienced episodes will

---

1. I am thinking here of what one might think of as ordinary past-tense judgments based on autobiographical memory (such as "I went to the supermarket yesterday"), as opposed to *explicitly recollective* judgments (such as "I remember going to the supermarket yesterday"). The IEM status of this latter type of judgment is much easier to account for, since the immunity-generating grounds for the judgment are included in the content of the judgment.

have involved states (e.g., perceptual states) with nonconceptual content. This raises the question of how nonconceptual states can ground autobiographical memories. Does this grounding relation simply duplicate that between nonconceptual perceptual states and perceptual judgments, or does the memory context add new dimensions?

There is a related issue here. In *Understanding "I,"* I emphasize the close connections between autobiographical memory and the capacity to take a narrative perspective on one's one life. To have an autobiographical memory of an event is, in important part, to situate it within one's personal history. As ordinarily understood, being able to think about one's own personal history is a complex and sophisticated conceptual achievement—a paradigmatic form of linguistic self-consciousness. But, in line with the general approach of all the essays in this volume, we can ask whether this conceptual achievement emerges from, and/or is grounded in, a more primitive, nonconceptual way of experiencing oneself as existing over time. Is there, one might ask, a nonconceptual narrative self? And, if there is, what role does that nonconceptual narrative self play in underwriting and enabling our ability to conceptualize our personal history, to plan for the future, and to try to live up to the ideal of the person we want to be? Answering these questions will bring philosophical discussions of narrative and personal identity into dialogue with experimental studies of memory and the awareness of time in nonhuman animals and human infants.

The interface between philosophy and the cognitive sciences has been more systematically explored in the content of bodily awareness. But here too significant challenges remain. Several of the essays in this volume develop a model of the spatial content of bodily awareness—a model of how we experience the space of the body. This basic idea driving the model is that we experience the space of the bodily on a fundamentally non-Cartesian frame of reference. I am confident that this model will prove to be a powerful explanatory tool for understanding both normal and disordered bodily awareness, and the essays contain some programmatic suggestions in that direction. However, to make real progress, the model needs to be operationalized to bring it more clearly into contact with empirical studies of bodily awareness.

Chapter 8 takes initial steps toward fleshing out the model. It brings to bear an influential idea from kinesiology and robotics that the body can be modeled as rigid links connected by mechanical joints, and combines that idea with Marr and Nishara's suggestion that all objects (and the human body in particular) can be represented as generalized cones (Marr and Nishihara 1978). But kinesiologists and roboticists are not typically interested in the phenomenology of bodily awareness. And Marr and Nishihara's ideas about generalized cones were originally developed as part of a theory of vision, not of somatosensation. So plainly we still have considerable work to do in developing the model so that it can be brought to bear productively in experimental studies of how the body is experienced. Doing this will open up a range of experimental opportunities for exploring both normal bodily awareness and pathologies of bodily awareness in brain-damaged patients, as well as illusions of bodily awareness (such as the rubber hand illusion and the various whole body illusions).

The model developed here is a model of how the space of the body is experienced, which obviously falls short of a full account of the content of bodily awareness. It is one thing to say how we experience the location of a particular bodily event, and quite another to explain how that bodily event actually represents the ongoing state of the body. What sort of information about the body is carried within bodily awareness? How is it encoded? And how can it be integrated with information about the body derived from vision and the other exteroceptive sensory modalities?

Developing a full account of the content of bodily awareness that answers these questions will pay significant dividends in two different directions. In the first place, it will contribute to understanding both our capacities for planning intentional actions and our abilities to execute complex movements. (I mention these separately because it seems that they involve different types of bodily information—coarse-grained for action-planning and much finer-granted for motor control.) Second, it will help explain the source of our sense of ourselves as embodied creatures—as a special kind of physical object distinctive in ways brought out vividly by Merleau-Ponty, as discussed in chapter 5. Our experience of the body *qua for-itself* (to borrow Merleau-Ponty's phrase) has multiple sources, but surely somatosensation, proprioception, kinesthesis, and the other forms of bodily awareness are among the most important elements.

Another important element in our experience of ourselves as physical objects of a highly distinctive kind must surely be our awareness of our own agency. This raises another set of important problems directly related to issues discussed in this volume. It has become common for philosophers and cognitive scientists to refer to a "sense of agency." In one way, this can be perfectly harmless terminology—if the expression "sense of agency" is simply a shorthand for our awareness of our own agency. But it is sometimes interpreted as if there were some kind of qualitative marker of agency, a specific feeling that marks one out as the author of one's actions.

The potential equivocation here closely matches that between different ways of understanding the putative "sense of ownership" discussed in chapters 6 through 9. In those essays, I outline and defend a deflationary account of the sense of ownership, accepting that there is a positive phenomenology of ownership but offering a reductive account of that phenomenology, as opposed to postulating a specific "feeling of mineness." It seems likely that a similarly deflationary approach will prove profitable for understanding the sense of agency. Chapter 9 provides support for that thesis, particularly in the suggestion that agency provides a common thread between our sense of ownership for our own bodies and body parts (what I called φ-ownership) and our sense of ownership for our thoughts (ψ-ownership).

Turning from our awareness of our own agency to analyzing what that agency consists in, chapter 10 explores the relation between intentional action and commonsense psychology. It points to a range of phenomena suggesting, first, that there are ways of thinking about the springs of intentional action that do not involve the propositional attitudes, and, second, that we can navigate the social world and coordinate with other agents without engaging the explanatory framework of commonsense psychology. The obvious challenge here is to investigate how far these suggestions about the etiology and explanation of action can be scaled up, so that we have an accurate picture of the scope of commonsense psychology. There is a broad spectrum of possibilities. At one end lies the view, widespread in philosophy and in some currents of thinking in cognitive psychology (particularly the computational theory of mind as developed by Jerry Fodor) that "intentional action" is more or less synonymous with "action resulting from, and explicable in terms of, beliefs, desires, and other propositional attitudes." At the other end lies eliminative materialism and the view that the explanatory framework of propositional attitude psychology is an otiose fiction. But there are many possible ways of steering between the two extremes.

At least three vibrant research programs in cognitive science are relevant to those projects of charting the scope and limits of commonsense psychology. One, already briefly considered above, is the "two visual systems" hypothesis, which has built into it the idea that the springs of action deploy two different systems, both functionally and neuroanatomically. The second explores social understanding in prelinguistic and nonlinguistic creatures. There has been extensive investigation of how well (if at all) nonlinguistic animals and young children understand psychological concepts, including propositional attitudes. Work on implicit false belief tasks (as proposed, e.g., in Onishi and Baillargeon 2005) has been taken to suggest that even young infants are capable of understanding basic psychological concepts such as belief. Likewise, experiments into the "theory of mind" of primates (and a range of other mammals) have been taken to suggest comparable metarepresentational abilities in nonhuman animals. As I have suggested elsewhere, however, these two research paradigms may be better interpreted as helping us to conceptualize alternative modes of social understanding that bypass the propositional attitudes (Bermúdez 2003, 2009a). Finally, it seems likely that the *predictive brain* research program, which treats the brain as a Bayesian hypothesis-testing machine (Hohwy 2013; Clark 2015), will yield powerful insights into how we can predictively model and navigate social interactions without deploying the cumbersome machinery of propositional attitude psychology.

This discussion raises a further challenge. The narrower the domain of commonsense psychology turns out to be, the more important it is to develop a model of rationality that can apply to action that is not driven by the propositional attitudes. Whether we are thinking about rational action and rational choice informally (through some version of the belief-desire law that rationality typically requires acting so as to best satisfy one's desires in the light of available information) or more formally (through some version of expected utility theory, which is the touchstone theory of rationality in the social and cognitive sciences), the conceptual framework is provided by propositional attitude psychology. This is obvious for the belief-desire law, and follows in the case of expected utility theory if we think of utilities and probabilities as regimentations of desires and beliefs respectively (Bermúdez 2009b). So, if we whittle away at the connection between intentional action and propositional attitude psychology, and if we want to retain the idea that intentional action can be assessed for rationality, then we need either a new theoretical framework, or a new way of applying the old framework.

So, quite plainly, we have a more than plentiful supply of problems to solve and questions to answer. The bodily self is a rich topic, where progress will require cutting across many of the standard divisions of academic life. That is why it is so difficult. But this is also why it is so exciting. I plan to continue working on these problems and questions, and I hope others will too.

References

Bermúdez, J. L. 2003. *Thinking without Words*. New York: Oxford University Press.

Bermúdez, J. L. 2009a. *Decision Theory and Rationality*. Oxford: Oxford University Press.

Bermúdez. 2009b. Mindreading in the animal kingdom. In *The Philosophy of Animal Minds*, ed. R. W. Lurz. Cambridge: Cambridge University Press.

Bermúdez, J. L. 2017. *Understanding "I": Language and Thought*. Oxford: Oxford University Press.

Clark, A. 2015. *Surfing Uncertainty: Prediction, Action, and the Embodied Mind*. Oxford: Oxford University Press.

Evans, G. 1982. *The Varieties of Reference*. Oxford: Oxford University Press.

Goodale, A. D., and M. A. Milner. 1996. *The Visual Brain in Action*. Oxford: Oxford University Press.

Hohwy, J. 2013. *The Predictive Mind*. Oxford: Oxford University Press.

Marr, D., and H. K. Nishihara. 1978. Representation and recognition of the spatial organization of three-dimensional shapes. *Proceedings of the Royal Society of London* 200:269–294.

Onishi, K. H., and R. Baillargeon. 2005. Do 15-month-old infants understand false beliefs? *Science* 308:255–258.

Peacocke, C. 1992. *A Study of Concepts*. Cambridge, MA: MIT Press.

Index

www.ingramcontent.com/pod-product-compliance
Lightning Source LLC
Chambersburg PA
CBHW032344280326
41935CB00008B/443